# BASIC Second Edition

*

# BASIC Second Edition

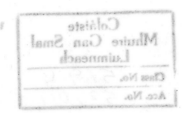

**Michel Boillot**
**L. Wayne Horn**

*Pensacola Junior College*

WEST PUBLISHING CO.

St. Paul / New York
Los Angeles / San Francisco

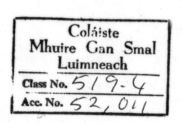
COPYRIGHT © 1976 By WEST PUBLISHING CO.
COPYRIGHT © 1979 By WEST PUBLISHING CO.
50 West Kellogg Boulevard
P.O. Box 3526
St. Paul, Minnesota 55165

Printed in the United States of America.

Library of Congress Cataloging in Publication Data

Boillot, Michel H.
    BASIC.

    Includes index
    1. Basic (Computer program language)  I. Horn, Lister
Wayne, joint author.  II. Title.
QA76.73.B3B64    1979        001.6'424        78–23757

ISBN 0–8299–0190–6

3rd Reprint—1980

# PREFACE To The Second Edition

This text presents concepts of BASIC programming interwoven with logical problem solving and selected computer concepts and is suitable for use in any course whose objectives include computer usage with BASIC and whose appeal is to students with a broad range of abilities and interests. We have used an outline type of presentation to reduce the possible reading difficulties and have attempted throughout to minimize verbiage and present all concepts in a clear, concise fashion. Our illustrations and exercises have been chosen to illustrate the application of the computer to a variety of disciplines.

Each topic is presented in essentially the same fashion. The first experience the reader has with a topic takes the form of a BASIC program or other illustration using the concepts to be learned. The purpose of these sections of each chapter is to give the reader an overall view of how the topic is to be used and how it relates to what he already knows.

Following the overall view is a section devoted to a detailed presentation of the topic supplemented by appropriate examples. Everything necessary to the understanding of the material is presented here.

A third section answers for the reader such typical questions as, "Can I do this?" or "If I do that, what happens?" Included in these sections is a discussion of error messages and debugging aids.

Finally, presentation for each topic is supplemented by a section containing sample programs (or other illustrations) relating to the topic. Both scientific and business-related problems are presented to give the reader a better overall understanding of the BASIC language and how it can be used.

Additionally, each chapter contains a section devoted to selected computer concepts and specifics of BASIC that are important for a thorough understanding of the computer and its application but which may be considered as optional for those interested only in obtaining a general idea of programming concepts.

The last section of each chapter contains a set of exercises and programming problems divided into three subsections. The first subsection, entitled "Self Test," contains short-answer, objective questions and short coding exercises to enable the reader to test his comprehension of the material in that chapter. Answers to the self test exercises are included at the end of the chapter. The second subsection contains programming exercises covering such topics as business problems, mathematical/logical problems, and physical science/engineering problems. The third subsection, entitled "Projects," contains programming assignments of a more substantial nature, many of which use the case study approach. Also included in this section are exercises dealing with games and random processes.

v

The authors found it difficult to choose specific features of BASIC to present because of the lack of standardization among implementations of the language. The so-called Dartmouth BASIC developed by Kemeny comes the closest to being a standard as any system. We have tried to select a subset of the most common features for presentation in the beginning of each chapter, reserving other less common (or less useful) features for the optional sections. The description of procedures for using computer terminals presented another serious problem, and we have tried to discuss procedures that might be used on a teletype but at the same time indicate to the students that they must consult local reference material for specifics. Finally, describing an operating system to beginning students is an almost impossible task, since specifics vary so greatly among computing systems. We have tried to indicate features that may be present, but again the reader is cautioned to check local sources for specific information. A text of this nature can serve only as a general guide to using the computer with BASIC, not as a detailed reference manual for a specific implementation of BASIC or any other computing system. Therefore, it must be supplemented by locally supplied materials which are impossible to reproduce in textbook form.

Because of its unique method of presentation, its unusual organization of subject matter, and its broad range of illustrations and exercises, BASIC should prove useful to students and teachers in a wide variety of academic institutions. We sincerely hope that our efforts in producing this book prove beneficial to those attempting to learn to use the BASIC language. We wish to thank users of the first edition for their suggestions, many of which have been incorporated into this second edition. Any errors that may appear are, of course, the responsibility of the authors, who will very much appreciate having them brought to their attention.

M. Boillot
L.W. Horn

## NOTATION

The general form for BASIC statements and commands should be interpreted according to the following notational conventions:

1. Words in small letters are supplied by the programmer.
2. Words in capital letters are key words which should be included as shown.
3. Any special characters, such as equal signs, commas, quotation marks, and number signs, must be included as shown.
4. An optional part of a statement is included in brackets ([ ]).
5. One and only one of the words enclosed in braces ($\{$ $\}$) must be chosen.
6. Ellipsis points ($\cdot$ $\cdot$ $\cdot$) are used to indicate that one or more elements of the preceding form may be present.

# CONTENTS

†

# COMPUTERS
# AND COMPUTING

## 1-1   The Electronic Brain

*News Item:* When the *Apollo 13* flight was jeopardized by unforeseen events, new flight plans produced by computers were available in just 84 minutes. One person working on the problem could have performed the task in 1,040,256 years. With a desk calculator, the time could have been cut to 60,480 years.

*News Item:* Mathematical Application Group, Inc., has announced a commercially available animation technique called Synthavision that uses the computer to construct visuals that when photographed resemble conventionally produced cartoons.

*News Item:* In New Haven, Connecticut, a computer has been installed to control parking at the new Veteran's Memorial Coliseum.

*News Item:* At Bell Laboratories in Murray Hill, New Jersey, a computer has been programmed to produce synthetic human speech. No prerecorded voice is utilized: The computer "reads" sentences and commands a voice synthesizer to produce the proper sounds.

The computers mentioned in these news items are the high-speed, internally programmed, electronic computers that have become the unseen "brain" behind most of the business transactions of everyday life. Computers have also had an incalculable influence on government, science, and the arts in the years since the first fledgling computer was invented in the mid-1940s.

Today computers are being applied to every conceivable problem. One has only to pick up any popular magazine to read about newer and larger problems being solved by computers. The computer has become an indispensable tool in all scientific and commercial endeavors.

# 1-2    Computers—What Are They?

Computers are automatic electronic machines that can accept data, store vast amounts of information, and perform arithmetic at high speeds to solve complex problems. Without human intervention, computers can process long sequences of instructions (called a *program* and discussed in later sections of this book) to solve a variety of problems ranging from business problems, such as payrolls, to scientific problems, such as the calculation of satellite trajectories.

## 1-2-1    Organization of a Computer

The computer may be thought of as a system composed of five components or subsystems, as shown in Figure 1-1. These components and their functions are as follows:

1.  The *input* unit feeds information from the outside world to the computer. This information includes both data and instructions (program[1]). Input units are capable of reading information recorded on such different mediums as punched cards or magnetic tape, or from terminals. The information read from these devices is placed into appropriate memory locations.

2.  The *memory* unit stores information. It holds the sequence of instructions (or program) necessary to solve a particular problem and any additional data required. The memory is divided into locations that each have an address (are *addressable*). Instructions and data are stored in these cells.

3.  The *control* unit fetches the instructions and data from memory and executes the instructions one at a time with the help of either the input/output or arithmetic/logical unit. All of the other components operate as directed by the control unit.

4.  The *arithmetic/logical* unit consists of the electronic circuitry that performs arithmetic operations such as addition, multiplication, subtraction, and division, and logical operations such as comparison of numbers.

5.  The *output* unit can transfer or copy the contents of certain memory locations onto some external medium such as punched cards, punched paper tape, magnetic tape, a printed page produced by a teletype or line printer, or a cathode ray tube (CRT) screen for visual display.

It is quite common to refer to the memory, control, and arithmetic/logical units collectively as the *central processing unit (CPU)*. The CPU may be thought of as the seat of intelligence of the entire computer system. The input and output functions may be performed by devices located at some distance (a few feet or many miles) from the CPU.

---

[1]Data is the information (raw facts) to be processed by a program. For example, if a program were designed to sort names into alphabetical order, then the names to be sorted would be the data for that program.

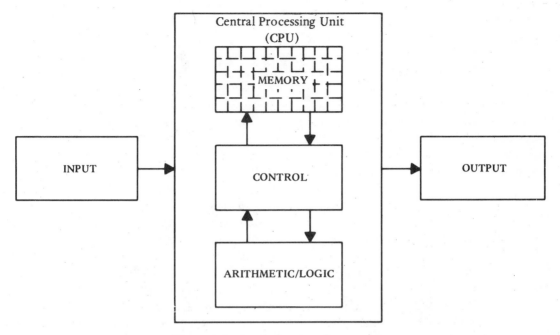

**Figure 1-1**    Logical units of a computer.

## 1-2-2    Why Use a Computer

A computer is a problem-solving machine. However, it cannot be said that the computer is suitable for solving all problems. It is sometimes more economical to solve relatively simple problems and problems that occur infrequently by mechanical methods. If, on the other hand, a problem requires the processing of a large volume of input or output, is repetitive in nature, or requires great processing speeds and accuracy, it may be worthwhile and necessary to use a computer. There are, of course, problems that cannot be solved without computers. For example, in a spacecraft-launching operation data relayed to the ground by a spacecraft must be analyzed instantaneously to allow controllers to make on-the-spot decisions; only a computer can record and analyze the mass of data fast enough for such decisions to be practical.

## 1-2-3    Computer Programs

An electronic computer may be called an electronic "brain," but its function and problem-solving ability depends on the intelligence of a human being who directs and controls the machine. This person is called a *programmer* and is responsible for giving the computer a set of instructions consisting of the necessary steps required to derive a solution to a given problem. The set of instructions that controls the computer is called a *program.*

A program can be executed by the computer only when it is stored in the computer's memory and is in machine language code. Machine language is the only language the computer can understand. It is a language in which arithmetic/logical operations are represented by machine-recognizable numeric codes and in which memory locations containing data and program instructions are represented by numeric addresses. Machine language programs are very detailed and hence difficult to write. Machine languages will vary from one computer manufacturer to another; such languages are machine-dependent, reflecting the design of the particular computer. Other types of languages (called *high-level languages*) have been developed to allow the user to formulate problems in a much more convenient and efficient manner. Such languages are problem-oriented rather than machine-oriented. High-level languages are machine-independent; programs written in such languages can be processed on any type of computer. High-level languages must ultimately be translated into machine language before they can be executed by the computer. Special programs called *language translators* or *compilers* have, therefore, been developed to provide this translation service. BASIC (*Beginner's All-purpose Symbolic Instruction Code*) is an example of a high-level language.

The following example will help you understand how a language such as BASIC, instead of the machine language of the computer, is used by the programmer.

Each memory location has an "address." Suppose we wanted to add the data contained in memory locations 065 and 932 and to store the result in location 752. The machine instruction for this might be "43065932752." The first two numbers are called the *operation code*. The operation code is used by the control unit to determine what action (add, multiply, etc.) is to be performed on the data in the specified memory locations. Following the identification of the operation, the operands are given. Operands represent the addresses of the data to be used. The data we wish to add occurs in memory locations 065 and 932. We are going to store our result in location 752. The machine language instruction is broken down as follows:

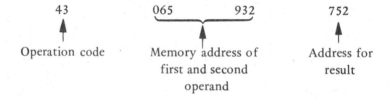

In the computer, this instruction would be represented in binary (0's and 1's).

In BASIC programs, arithmetic operations are indicated by the symbols + (addition), − (subtraction), ∗ (multiplication), / (division), and ↑ or ∗∗ (exponentiation). Each memory location is assigned a symbolic name. Let us agree to call location 065 by the symbolic name $P$, location 932 by $X$ and location 752 by $A$. Then the BASIC instruction equivalent to the machine instruction "43065932752" would be

$$\text{LET } A = P \cdot X$$

In practice, the high-level language programmer never needs to worry about machine addresses or operation codes. The BASIC programming system takes care of all such details, allowing the programmer to focus attention on the logic of the problem.

## 1-2-4   Conversational Computing

The very first computers required the user to prepare a program in some suitable form (usually punched cards) and submit it to the computer for processing. The computer executed each program one at a time. The user received his results, generally in printed form, at some later time. This mode of operation (known as *batch processing*) has several limitations, particularly in an educational environment. The user must wait some period of time between submitting his program and receiving his results. This is particularly annoying when a student is learning a new computer language and is apt to make mistakes. It may require many submissions of his program to receive an error-free output.

An alternative to batch processing is found in *conversational computing,* in which the user communicates directly with the computing system via a communication terminal (hard copy, Teletype, visual screens, etc.). The user enters his program one statement at a time. The computing system can evaluate the statement and inform the user immediately if it is not correct, allowing him to make any necessary changes before proceeding.[2] When a complete program has been entered, the system can then execute (*run*) the program, providing the solution almost immediately. Moreover, the user may design programs that engage in a dialogue with any number of persons entering data into the system.

The communication link between the terminal and the computer takes many forms. Telephone links are quite commonly used. To initiate communications via the telephone, the user must dial the number of the computer and place the telephone receiver in a special device (called a *modem*) that is attached to the communications terminal.

In all but the smallest systems, the user must establish his identity to the computer before he can make use of the computing facility. This is done to enable the system to account for the time used, to bill users accordingly, and to establish what resources are available to individual users. Before a person can make use of a conversational system, it is generally necessary to have an assigned account number and perhaps also a special password. After establishing the communications link, the user enters his account number and password. If these match a list kept by the computing system, the user is allowed to proceed; if not, the user may not have access to the computing facility. These steps, called a *sign-on procedure,* are quite specific to a particular computing system. An equally important operation is the *sign-off procedure,* which is followed when the user is finished. Almost all systems have a command such as "GOOD BYE" or "BYE" that terminates the user's communications with the system and releases the terminal for another user. It is important that the sign-off procedure be followed after each session at a terminal. If a user does not sign off, the next person may continue without signing-on, and the time used by both persons will be charged to the first user's account.

To familiarize himself with the computing system, the reader should consult a user's manual normally available at his computing installation. Before attempting to write a BASIC program on a given system, the user should learn the sign-on/sign-off procedures and other idiosyncracies of his particular computing system. A co-worker or fellow student who has just made a run on the system may also be helpful in this regard.

# 1-3   You Might Want To Know

1. Just how fast do computers operate?

   *Answer:* The latest model computers operate at speeds measured in nanoseconds (1 nanosecond = 1 billionth of a second). For example, the ILLIAC IV is capable of executing 100 to 200 million instructions per second.

---

[2]On some systems using batch BASIC, the user must type all program statements before getting any feedback. The program is then compiled and all errors are identified to the user.

2. I can't conceive of how fast a nanosecond is. Can you help me?

*Answer:* Yes. One nanosecond is to one second what one second is to 32 years. One nanosecond is the approximate time required for light to travel one foot.

3. Is there any limit to the internal speed of a computer?

*Answer:* Electrical signals are propagated at speeds approaching the speed of light (1 foot/nanosecond). Integrated circuits packing many thousands of transistors per square inch have been designed to minimize the length of the interconnections through which electrical signals are propagated; this reduces the time it takes a signal to travel from one transistor to another in the circuit. Figures 1-2 and 1-3 illustrate the size and density of an integrated single chip microprocessor.

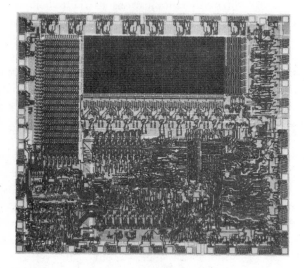

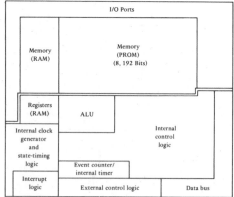

**Figure 1-2** Magnified view of the Intel 8748 single chip microcomputer (courtesy Intel Corporation).

**Figure 1-3** Functional map of the 8748 microcomputer (actual size: 5.6 X 6.6 millimeters).

4. Computers may be very fast and powerful devices, but aren't there problems that even the most powerful computer cannot handle?

*Answer:* Yes. If a computer one billion times faster than the fastest available today were to analyze all possible outcomes of the first move in a chess game, it would require on the order of $10^{100}$ hours (many hundreds of billions of years).

5. What computer languages are there besides machine language and BASIC?

*Answer:* One survey reported over 600 computer languages in more or less widespread use. Many of these were special-purpose languages oriented to a single application. Some of the better-known languages include:

| | |
|---|---|
| FORTRAN | (*FOR*mula *TRAN*slation) |
| COBOL | (*CO*mmon *B*usiness *O*riented *L*anguage) |
| RPG | (*R*eport *P*rogram *G*enerator) |

|  |  |
|--|--|
| PL/I | (*Programming Language I*) |
| ALGOL | (*ALGOrithmic Language*) |
| APL | (*A Programming Language*) |

6.  How many versions of BASIC are there?

*Answer:* Every computer manufacturer implements a BASIC system that is somewhat different from the others. Most BASIC systems are measured against the "standard" system developed at Dartmouth College by Kemeny; however, there will probably be minor differences between Dartmouth BASIC and the BASIC system the reader has for his use. The manufacturer's user's guide written specifically for the BASIC at the reader's computer system is a worthwhile investment and may save hours of frustration and inconvenience. The serious student should consult a BASIC user's guide as he or she studies this text.

# 1-4   A Model Computer

Let us consider a very simple model computer that operates conceptually in much the same manner as its larger real-life counterparts (see Figure 1-4). The input medium is a terminal where numbers have been entered (typed). The memory unit consists of a group of sequentially numbered "pigeonholes." Each "hole" or location in the memory can hold one instruction or one number. Locations can be referred to either by name or by address. The arithmetic/logical unit is represented by a desk calculator capable of performing arithmetic and logical operations. The role of the control unit is played by a human operator who can fetch instructions from memory one at a time and execute them; he can also fetch data from or store data into various memory locations. The types of instructions he is capable of executing include:

1.  *Input.* Read a value from the input medium and store that value in a specified memory location. For example, the instruction

READ H

will cause one value on the input medium to be read and stored in a memory location called *H*.

2.  *Conditional branching.* Perform a comparison test between two values using the logical unit and branch to a specified memory location if the test condition is met. If the condition is not met, no transfer occurs, and the following instruction is taken from the next memory location. For example, the instruction

IF H < 40 GO TO 11

causes the control unit to first fetch the value *H* from memory and then request the logical unit to compare that value with 40. If the logical unit reports that the value of *H* is less than 40, the control unit fetches the next instruction from location 11. If the value of *H* is greater than or equal to 40, the next instruction is taken from the next sequentially numbered location. Hence a conditional transfer allows a program to process a particular instruction(s) if a certain condition is met or process another different instruction(s) if that condition is not met.

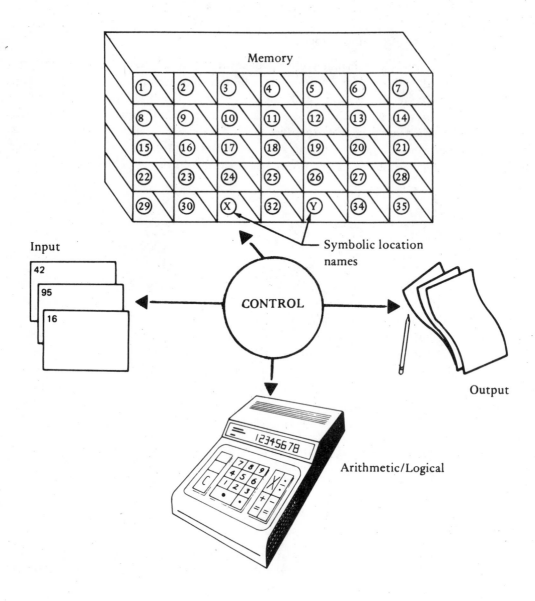

**Figure 1-4**   A model computer.

3. *Calculations.* Perform calculations using the arithmetic unit and place results in desired memory locations. For example, the instruction

$$\text{LET P} = 2 * \text{H}$$

will cause the control unit to fetch the value contained in memory location $H$ and activate the arithmetic unit to multiply that value by 2. The final result is then stored in memory location $P$.

4.  *Unconditional branching.* Take the next instruction from a specified memory location. For example, the instruction

GO TO 5

causes the control unit to fetch the next instruction from location 5 rather than from the next sequentially numbered location. Unconditional branching, then, simply means transfer directly to a particular instruction in memory.

5.  *Output.* Copy a value from a memory location onto the output medium. For example, the instruction

PRINT H, P

will cause the contents of $H$ and $P$ to be written out on the output pad.

6   *Termination.* Cease execution of instructions for this program and wait for a new program to be loaded into memory. For example, the instruction

END

causes the program to terminate. No more instructions in this program are executed.

To illustrate the concepts just discussed, let us write a short program to calculate and write out an amount of pay owed an employee who is paid $2 an hour with time and a half for all hours in excess of 40. The complete instructions to solve this problem might be as follows:

| | |
|---|---|
| 1  INPUT H | Determine number of hours worked from time card. |
| 2  IF H > 40 GO TO 5 | Check if number of hours is greater than 40. |
| 3  LET P = 2 * H | If not, compute regular pay, |
| 4  GO TO 6 | and go to print pay. |
| 5  LET P = 80 + 3 * (H − 40) | If hours are greater than 40, compute regular pay, which is $80, plus overtime at rate of $3 per hour. |
| 6  PRINT P, H | Print pay and number of hours. |
| 7  END | Stop. |

Now, suppose this program has been loaded in memory as shown in Figure 1-5. (This loading function can be performed by manually keying in the program at the terminal.) After execution of the instruction at 1, the value read from the input unit (38 in this example) is placed in location $H$. The computer system will have automatically reserved a location for $H$. In the second instruction, the logic unit will determine that the contents of location $H$ are not greater than 40; hence, the next instruction to be executed comes from location 3. After the instruction at 3 is executed, the contents of location $P$ become 2 * 38 = 76. The instruction at

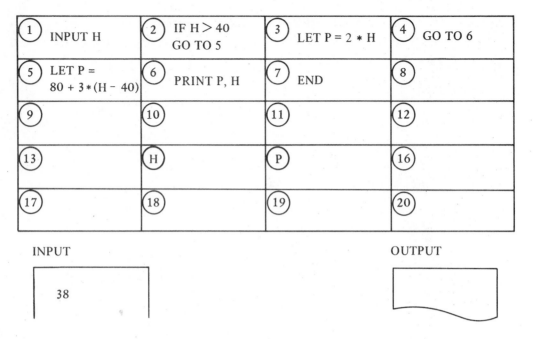

**Figure 1-5**  Payroll program with sample input.

location 4 causes the control unit to take its next instruction from location 6. The instruction at location 6 will cause the contents of locations *H* and *P* to be copied onto the output medium. The instruction at location 7 causes the control unit to stop and wait for the next program. The status of the model computer after execution of this program will be as shown in Figure 1-6.

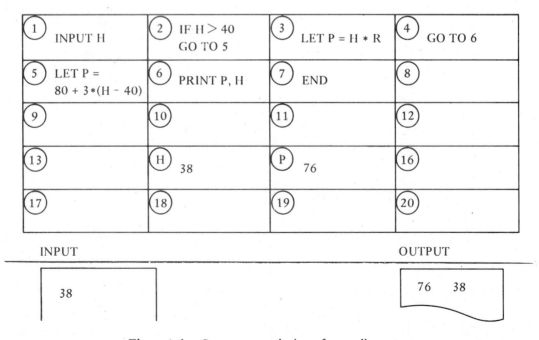

**Figure 1-6**  Status at conclusion of payroll program.

# 1-5    Computers—What Makes Them Tick

## 1-5-1    Computer Hardware

The physical configuration (the *hardware* or machinery) used for the logical components illustrated in Figure 1-1 varies greatly from one computing system to another. Typically the memory, control, and arithmetic/logical units are grouped together and referred to as the *central processing unit (CPU)*. The CPU varies in size from a small box in a typical minicomputer (see Figure 1-7) to a fairly large unit in a typical medium-scale computer (see Figure 1-8). The internal construction of the CPU, the technology used for the memory unit, and the speed at which instructions are executed vary greatly from one computer to another. Modern systems tend to make great use of microminiaturized integrated circuits, making possible significant reduction in sizes and increase in processing speeds (see Figure 1-2).

The hardware used for input and output devices also varies greatly from one system to another. Some devices, such as the line printer, the card punch, and the graph plotter (see Figure 1-9), can be used as output devices only. Other devices, such as the punched card reader, can be used only as an input device. Some devices can be used for both input and output purposes, although generally not simultaneously. Such devices include the hard copy terminal (see Figure 1-10), the punched paper tape reader/punch (which is usually attached to the Teletype), the CRT (cathode ray tube) console (see Figure 1-11), the magnetic disk drive, and the magnetic tape drive. The latter two devices are sometimes referred to as *mass storage* devices because they are capable of storing large quantities of data and can be accessed by the CPU very rapidly.

The input/output devices for a particular system may be located physically close to the CPU or at some distance—in an adjacent room or miles away. In the latter case, data may be transmitted to the CPU via telephone lines. This technique is called *telecommunication*. The user may dial up the computer's number to initiate communication, identify himself, transmit a program and/or data, and receive results at his terminal. When the user is finished, he can release the telephone line for another user.

A typical computing system will generally include a great variety of input/output devices. Most of these devices are electromechanical and thus operate at far slower speeds than CPU internal processing speeds, where processing is wholly electronic. Therefore, if the CPU were required to wait for such devices to perform a complete operation (a data transmission from a Teletype, for example), the advantage of the tremendous internal speeds of the CPU would be greatly reduced. In most computer installations, the CPU is equipped with one or more channels. A *channel* is a special-purpose device that controls input/output operations (I/O); it relieves the CPU of the task of communicating directly with input/output devices. The CPU, for example, will instruct a channel to perform an output operation (e.g., write out results on a printer), and while the channel is busy servicing this output request, the CPU can continue processing instructions. In this way, CPU computations are carried out concurrently with input/output operations, which greatly increases the efficiency of the computer system.

Computers can be used in many different types of operating environments, each reflecting different organizational needs, hardware configurations, and economic bases. Of special interest are multiprogramming and time-sharing environments. In a multiprogramming setting, several programs are present in memory at one time. While a channel is servicing an I/O request for a

**Figure 1-7** Hewlett-Packard 2108A central processing unit (courtesy Hewlett-Packard Company).

**Figure 1-8** Hewlett-Packard 3000 central processing unit (courtesy Hewlett-Packard Company).

**Figure 1-9** A plotter (courtesy Hewlett-Packard Company, Data Systems Division).

**Figure 1-10** A hard copy terminal (courtesy Hewlett-Packard Company).

**Figure 1-11** A CRT console (courtesy Digital Equipment Corporation).

particular program, the CPU can start processing a new program or resume processing a program temporarily interrupted by a previous I/O request; or each program may be interrupted periodically to allow execution of other programs in memory. In a time-sharing environment, numerous terminals (Teletypes, CRT's, etc.) are attached to the CPU by ground cables or telephone lines. These terminals allow users to communicate directly (*on-line*) with the computer. Users enter their programs directly into the system via terminal stations. To the user at the terminal, it appears that he has the computer all to himself and that only his program is being executed by the CPU. In reality, the CPU may be servicing several other users concurrently. This is accomplished by allowing each user a small slice of time and by processing each user's program in turn. Thus while one user is typing BASIC instructions on a teletype, the CPU may be processing another user's program. The most significant advantage of time sharing is that the user has immediate access to the computer; feedback is instantaneous. In addition, computer utilization costs can be significantly lowered by multiuser participation.

## 1-5-2   Software

The term *software* is generally used to describe the set of programs (written by the programmer) which causes the computer or hardware to come to life, that is, to function. There are three basic software categories:

1.   Translation programs.

2.   Operating system programs.

3.   User-processing programs.

Translation programs (compilers) are programs used by the computer system to translate high-level languages or problem-oriented languages into machine language. These translation programs are generally supplied by the hardware manufacturer.

Operating system programs are usually supplied by the computer manufacturer to assist in the overall operation of the computer system. They are used to regulate and supervise the sequence of activities going on at any time in the system. These programs minimize operator intervention in the actual operation of the computer and ensure a smooth, fast, and efficient transition among the varied tasks performed by the system. Other operating system programs aid the programmer in his own work; examples of such programs are utility and library programs. Following is a list of functions performed by some of the more important operating system programs:

1.   Load programs into memory from mass storage.

2.   Print messages for the operator and the programmer regarding the status of the program.

3.   Perform job accounting by keeping track of who uses the computer and for how long.

4.   Handle requests for input/output from executing programs.

5.   Handle the collection of data from telecommunication lines (in a time-sharing system).

6.   Schedule the slice of time to be allocated each user's program (in a time-sharing system or multiprogramming system).

7. Perform some routine processing of data such as sorting and copying the contents of one data set onto a specified device.

8. Maintain the store of programs on the mass storage device—adding programs to the store, deleting those no longer needed, and so forth.

9. Attempt to recover from and/or correct errors that may occur in any segment of the computing system.

10. Interpret the job set up and job control instructions specified by the programmer.

At the heart of most operating systems is a program variously called the *supervisor*, the *executive*, or the *monitor*. This program is usually resident in memory at all times and performs many essential tasks, such as program loading and error checking. This resident portion of the operating system loads other, less often used routines as they are required.

User processing programs, sometimes called *applications programs*, are those programs written by individual users to solve particular problems. They may be written in a generalized fashion and modified as needed to fit the peculiar requirements of a particular system, or they may be constructed exactly to satisfy specific needs. For example, a company may construct its own payroll system, or it may purchase (or rent) a general set of payroll programs and modify them if necessary. Companies guard their processing programs as a very important company asset. Extensive security measures are taken to avoid the loss or theft of programs. A considerable store of programs is usually available to a computer user; in fact, the usefulness of a computer may well depend more on the variety and efficiency of the available software than on any single aspect of the hardware.

It is of interest to note that over the last decade or so computer hardware has undergone dramatic cost reductions that have not been accompanied by corresponding reductions in computer software costs. On the contrary, software development costs have soared to the point where now in a typical computer operation approximately 85 percent of the total computer system budget is earmarked for software costs, as opposed to only 5 percent in 1950.

# 1-6 Assignments

## 1-6-1 Self Test

1. List the five components of a computer system and explain the function of each.

2. Define the following:

   | | | |
   |---|---|---|
   | a. CPU | e. Nanosecond | i. Batch environment |
   | b. CRT | f. Machine language | j. Conversational computing |
   | c. Program | g. Unconditional branch | k. Compiler |
   | d. Data | h. Conditional branch | l. Software |

3. What values will be written by the program in Figure 1-5 if the input value is 47.5 instead of 38?

4. Determine which of the following statements are true and which are false:

   a. A compiler is a program that translates machine code into a high-level language.

   b. The part of a machine language instruction that tells the computer what to do is called an *operation code*.

   c. Each memory location has a corresponding address.

   d. Computer hardware consists of all the physical components that make up a computer system.

   e. High-level languages are machine-independent.

   f. The term *software* refers to such material as punched cards, paper/magnetic tape, etc.

   g. In a batch-processing environment, the user receives an almost instantaneous response to his program.

   h. Time sharing is made possible by the use of time slices.

   i. Multiprogramming means that instructions from two or more programs can be processed at the same time by the CPU.

5. Modify the program in Section 1-4 to read both the number of hours worked and the rate of pay from one input card. The output line should contain the pay, hours worked, and the rate. What could you do to your program to read more than one input card?

## 1-6-2  Projects

1. If you are working in a conversational computing environment, determine the sign-on, sign-off, and other procedures necessary to run a BASIC program. If your system uses batch BASIC, determine the operating system instructions and the exact makeup of the job deck to compile and run a BASIC program.

2. Make a list of tasks to which computers have been applied. Pool your list with the others in your class to get a feeling for the important role the computer plays in our society.

3. List some problems that would not be suitable for solution by means of a computer. Are there any conditions that would change your assessment of the feasibility of a computer solution?

## 1-6-3  Answers to Self Test

1. Input: Device which reads information from some medium.
   Output: Device which writes information onto some medium.
   Memory: Stores program instructions and data.
   Arithmetic/logical: Circuitry which performs arithmetic and decisions on the data.
   Control: Executes program instructions.

2. a. CPU: Central processing unit—Memory, arithmetic/logical, and control units.

b.    CRT: Cathode ray tube—Input/output visual display device.

c.    Program: Instructions to solve a problem.

d.    Data: Information to be processed by a program (numbers, lists of names, etc.).

e.    Nanosecond: One billionth of a second.

f.    Machine language: Numerical language inherent in the design of the particular computer.

g.    Unconditional branch: GO TO—branch or transfer to same location each time the instruction is executed.

h.    Conditional branch: IF—branch based on whether a condition is true or false.

i.    Batch environment: Computing system in which programs and data are processed some period of time after submission of programs.

j.    Conversational computing: Computing system in which user's instructions and data are analyzed and processed immediately.

k.    Compiler: A program which translates a high-level language such as BASIC into machine language.

l.    Software: A set of programs which causes the computer to function.

3.    102.5; 47.5

4.    a. F    b. T    c. T    d. T    e. T    f. F    g. F    h. T    i. F

5.    Program to process one card:

```
10  INPUT H,R
20  IF H > 40 GO TO 50
30  LET P = R * H
40  GO TO 60
50  LET P = 40 * R + 1.5 * R * (H – 40)
60  PRINT H,R,P
70  END
```

Program to process more than one card:
Substitute GO TO 10 for statement 70 in the above program.

# FLOWCHARTING

## 2-1    Algorithms, Programs, and Flowcharts

As a problem solver, the computer can function only if it is given instructions as to how to proceed. A set of instructions for solving a problem is called an *algorithm*. Algorithms of one type or another are used daily by people to solve such routine problems as baking a cake, operating an electrical appliance, or solving a quadratic equation. Algorithms may be expressed in verbal or in symbolic form. A useful algorithm must be expressed in a way that can be understood and executed by the person (or machine) for which it is intended. A computer *program* is a specific example of an algorithm intended for a machine. It is expressed in a symbolic language that the computer can readily understand and execute.

Because of the logical organization and sequencing of program instructions and because of requirements of specific computer languages, it is usually difficult to write a computer program without first expressing the algorithm in some preliminary form. For a simple problem, a verbal outline of the steps required may suffice; for more complex problems, however, a widely used tool is the program flowchart. A *flowchart* is a pictorial representation of the logic (method) used to solve a particular problem. It is a diagram illustrating the sequence of steps (instructions) that a person or machine must execute to derive the solution to a problem. A flowchart is particularly useful for visualizing paths through the logic of an algorithm. For example, the algorithm of Figure 1-5 (computing pay given the number of hours worked) could be expressed in flowchart form as shown in Figure 2-1. Note that there are two paths through the algorithm; the path taken depends on the particular value of $H$ supplied at execution time. Since there is generally more than one correct method to solve a problem, one should expect that there might be any number of flowcharts to describe various methods for solving a given problem.

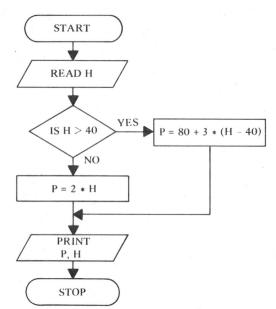

Find the number of hours (H) punched on a card or typed on a terminal.

Is the number of hours greater than 40? If so, compute total pay, which includes overtime ([H − 40] times time and a half rate) and go and write pay and hours. Otherwise, compute regular pay, meaning hours is less than 40. The asterisk * means multiplication.

Write out the value of P and H and stop.

**Figure 2-1** . Flowchart for the algorithm of Figure 1-5.

# 2-2   Flowchart Symbols

In program flowcharts, the symbols shown in Figure 2-2 are generally used. Each symbol or *block* represents a different type of operation. Written within the blocks are instructions to indicate (in general terms) what operation is to be performed. It is not necessary to express the instructions used in a flowchart block in any particular computer language; it is sufficient that the instructions used reflect the general functional operations used in the computing system. From the flowchart, it will be possible to write computer programs in a number of different languages. The emphasis in the flowchart is on the logic required for solving a problem rather than on the mechanics or specifics of a programming language.

### 2-2-1   The Terminal Block

An oval-shaped symbol⬭ is used to mark the point at which execution of instructions is to begin and end. The instruction START may be used to mark the beginning point; the instruction END or STOP may be used to mark the ending point. A flowchart may have only one starting point (entry point) but may have many ending points.

### 2-2-2   The Input/Output Block

A parallelogram-shaped symbol ▱ is used for input and output instructions. For an input operation, the instruction (command) READ or INPUT, followed by a list of names

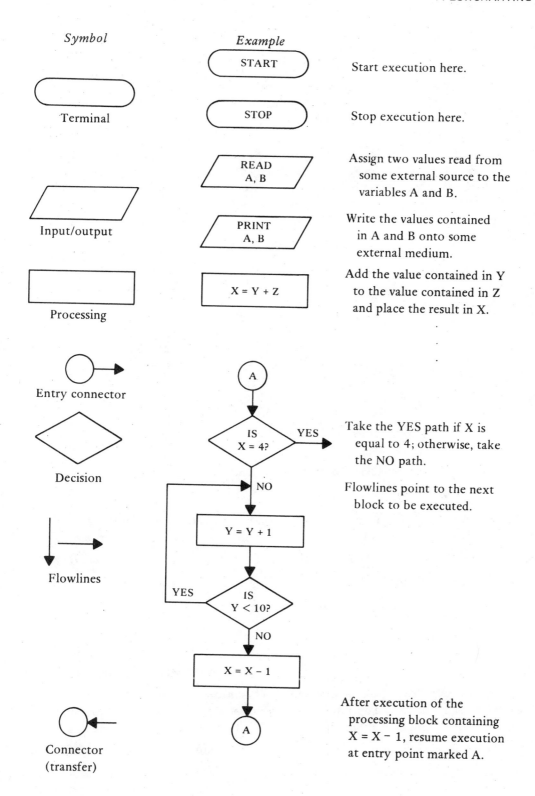

| *Symbol* | *Example* | |
|---|---|---|
| **Terminal** | START | Start execution here. |
| | STOP | Stop execution here. |
| **Input/output** | READ A, B | Assign two values read from some external source to the variables A and B. |
| | PRINT A, B | Write the values contained in A and B onto some external medium. |
| **Processing** | X = Y + Z | Add the value contained in Y to the value contained in Z and place the result in X. |
| **Entry connector** | A | |
| **Decision** | IS X = 4? → YES | Take the YES path if X is equal to 4; otherwise, take the NO path. |
| **Flowlines** | NO → Y = Y + 1 | Flowlines point to the next block to be executed. |
| | YES ← IS Y < 10? | |
| | NO → X = X – 1 | |
| **Connector (transfer)** | A | After execution of the processing block containing X = X – 1, resume execution at entry point marked A. |

**Figure 2-2** Program flowchart symbols.

(variables) separated by commas, is used. These names or variables can be thought of as symbolic names given to memory locations into which the data read is to be stored. Rather than give each memory location a numerical address—which would be hard to remember and not very meaningful—symbolic names are used to represent the data; i.e., each item read is given a name. The computer, not the programmer, determines which exact memory cell is to be used to store the particular data.

Variable names should be chosen to convey the nature of the data to be processed. For example, the segment flowchart in Figure 2-3 shows that two numbers are to be entered from a terminal and stored in two memory locations called $H$ (hours) and $R$ (rate). Other names, such as $X$ and $Y$, could just as well have been used instead. Here again, judicious selection of names $H$ and $R$ serves to better identify and document the nature of the transaction under consideration.

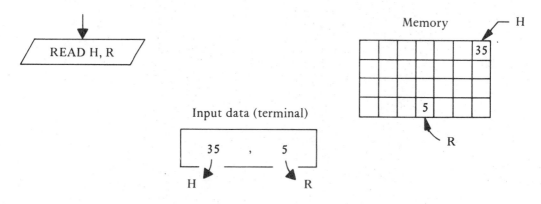

Figure 2-3    Meaning of the READ block.

For an output operation, the instruction PRINT, followed by a list of memory locations (variables), is used. The contents (value) of each location is to be printed onto some output device. For example, the block /PRINT P, H/ indicates that values in locations $P$ and $H$ are to be displayed (written) onto some device.

## 2-2-3    The Processing Block

A rectangular-shaped symbol ☐ is used for processing instructions. The most common form for expressing these instructions is the *replacement statement*. A replacement statement specifies the arithmetic operations to be performed on constants and/or variables and the location (variable) into which the value computed is to be placed. For example, the block P = 2 * H specifies that the contents (value) of $H$ is to be multiplied by 2 and the result is to be placed into $P$. Any sequence of operations can be performed, but there must be a single variable specified as the destination for the value calculated (only one variable on the left-hand side of the equal sign).

## 2-2-4    The Decision Block

A diamond-shaped symbol ⬦ is used to denote decisions. A common means of expressing a decision is in terms of a question that can be answered yes or no. The question must involve only mathematical relations such as equality ($=$), less than ($<$), greater than ($>$), less than or equal to ($\leq$), greater than or equal to ($\geq$), or not equal to ($\neq$). The decision block is the only block from which two different logical paths may be selected. Flowlines indicate the path to be taken depending on the decision made. For example, consider the decision block

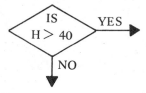

If the value of $H$ is greater than 40, the path marked YES is taken; otherwise the NO path is taken.

## 2-2-5    Flowlines

The sequence of instructions to be executed in a flowcharted algorithm is denoted by straight lines with an arrowhead such as ⟶ or ↓ . The direction of flow is always in the direction pointed out by the arrowhead.

## 2-2-6    Connector Blocks

When it is inconvenient to draw flowlines to connect one area of the flowchart to another, connectors are often used. Connectors serve two purposes:

1.    To identify a block by a label for reference purposes.

2.    To indicate transfer to another labeled block.

The symbol used for a connector is a small circle ◯ . A label is placed in the connector block. When the flowline points away from the connector, such as ◯⟶ , the connector is being used to denote any entry point, that is, a block to which transfer will be made from some point in the flowchart. When the flowline points toward the connector, as in ⟶◯ , the connector is being used to indicate a transfer; that is, execution should resume at an entry point with the same symbol as used in the connector at the transfer point. For example, consider the following flowchart segment:

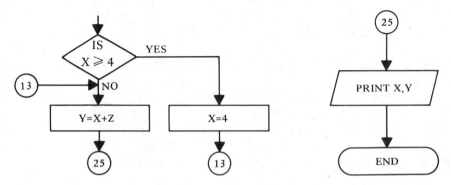

If the value of $X$ is greater than or equal to 4, the block $X = 4$ is executed and a transfer is made to the entry point labeled "13." If $X$ is not greater than or equal to 4 (i.e., $X$ is less than 4), the block $Y = X + Z$ is executed and transfer is made to the entry point marked "25," which contains the PRINT instruction. This flowchart is equivalent to

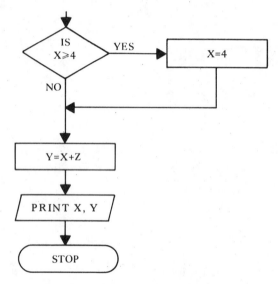

Note that in a flowchart it is possible to have many transfer connectors such as ────▶(48). However, only one entry connector, such as (48)────▶, may be designated in the same flowchart.

# 2-3    You Might Want To Know

1.    Are program flowcharts of any use once a program has been written?

*Answer:* Yes, program flowcharts serve as documentation of the logic used in the program. Any changes that need to be made to a program may be visualized more easily by referring to the flowchart rather than the actual program.

2.  How does one learn to draw flowcharts?

*Answer:* Flowcharting involves not only understanding the way in which computing systems work but also (as in any problem-solving environment) the ability to think logically. A systematic approach is necessary: One must analyze what is known and what is wanted and generate a sequence of instructions required to proceed from what is known to obtain the desired output. With experience, one will find the language of flowcharts a very useful aid in making a problem analysis complete and logically correct.

3.  What kinds of flowcharts other than program flowcharts are there?

*Answer:* In relation to computers, other kinds of flowcharts are system flowcharts, which show the relationship among various programs in a system. In other technological fields, flowcharts may be used as an aid in visualizing relationships among entities of various systems or processes.

4.  Are the program flowchart symbols standard?

*Answer:* There is a fair degree of standardization in the use of flowchart symbols in materials with recent publication dates. Older books may use a set of symbols that are somewhat different. For example, the input/output block may be represented by the symbol $\diagdown\phantom{xx}\diagup$ . In some texts, the symbol $\bigcirc\phantom{xx}$ is used for input and the symbol $\square$ is used for output.

5.  Often computer output consists of alphabetic as well as numeric characters. How can this be indicated on a flowchart?

*Answer:* A common means of indicating alphabetic or *literal* data to be written onto an output device is to use quotations around the desired characters in an output block. For example, the block $\diagup$ "PAY =", P $\diagup$ would indicate that the characters "PAY =" are to be printed, followed by the value in location P.

# 2-4  Examples

## 2-4-1  A Compound Interest Problem

Suppose we wanted to compute the interest on $100 at 5 percent compounded yearly for four years and to print out the principal and interest for each year, and we didn't know the formula to compute the interest. A flowchart could be constructed as shown in Figure 2-4. This flowchart illustrates a sequence of instructions that are processed repeatedly (*loop*).

The variable $P$ (principal) is initially set (*initialized*) to 100. At the end of the first year, when the interest $I$ has been computed, the new principal $P$ is equal to the old principal $P$ plus the interest $I$. This is accomplished through the statement $P = P + I$ (the first time through the loop the new $P$ = old $P + I = 100 + 5 = 105$). The next time through the loop, the interest is computed on this new principal. The values that are assumed by the variables are shown

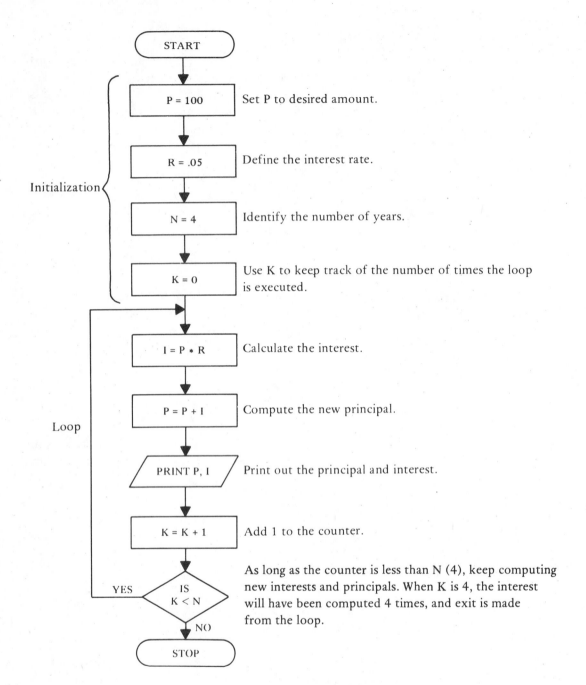

**Figure 2-4** Compound interest flowchart.

(*tabulated*) in Figure 2-5. Each time a new value is computed for a variable, the new value replaces (destroys) whatever value was previously assigned to the variable.

Note how the variable $K$ is used as a counting variable to count the years. $K$ is initially set to 0. Each time the interest and principal have been computed for one year, $K$ is incremented by one (1 is added to $K$). In that way, $K$ keeps track of the number of times the principal and interest are computed. When $K$ reaches the value $N$ (4 in this example), an exit is made out of

| P | R | N | K | I | COMMENTS |
|---|---|---|---|---|----------|
| 100 | .05 | 4 | 0 |  | Initial values. |
| 105 |  |  | 1 | 5 | First time through the loop. |
| 110.25 |  |  | 2 | 5.25 | Second time through the loop. |
| 115.76 |  |  | 3 | 5.51 | Third time through the loop. |
| 121.55 |  |  | 4 | 5.79 | Fourth time through the loop. K is equal to N, therefore processing is terminated. |

**Figure 2-5**    Tabulation of the values assumed by variables in Figure 2-4.

the loop, since the principal and interest will have been computed $N$ (4) times. Note that in the flowchart of Figure 2-4 the block $\boxed{N = 4}$ could have been omitted. The decision block would then become $\langle$ IS $K < 4 \rangle$.

## 2-4-2  Computation of an Average

Six grades are entered one at a time on a terminal as instructed by the computer. We wish to compute the grade average and write it out. The flowchart for this problem is shown in Figure 2-6. Note that the sum is initially set to 0, as it should be when no grades have yet been read. Each time a grade $G$ is entered (read), it is added to $S$, thereby reflecting the sum of the grades entered so far. Note also the use of the counter $I$ to keep track of how many values are read. When $I$ has a value of 6, six grades have been read, and the average is computed and printed. See the tabulation in Figure 2-6.

## 2-4-3  Search for Largest Grade

Each record of a set of records contains a grade (0–100). It is not known how many records there are in the set. We want to draw a flowchart to print the highest grade. Since we don't know how many records there are, we could add to the set of records a last record with a negative grade on it, so that every time we read a record we can ask the question "Is the grade read negative?" If it is, it means the end of the set has been reached; otherwise more records need to be read.

To determine the largest grade requires that we compare successively a new grade with the highest grade found so far (Max); if the new grade read is larger than Max, we replace Max by the new grade; otherwise we keep on reading grades until we find one that is larger than Max (if there is one). At the end of the program, Max is the highest grade. To start the comparisons, we can set Max equal to the first grade (after all, if there were only one grade Max would be the highest score!). A flowchart with accompanying tabulation is shown in Figure 2-7.

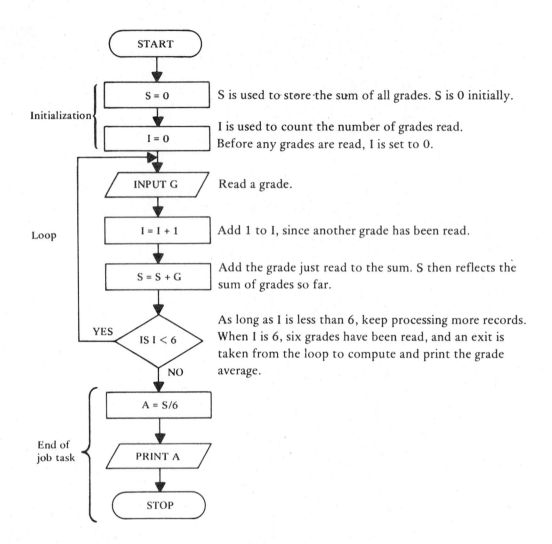

S is used to store the sum of all grades. S is 0 initially.

I is used to count the number of grades read. Before any grades are read, I is set to 0.

Read a grade.

Add 1 to I, since another grade has been read.

Add the grade just read to the sum. S then reflects the sum of grades so far.

As long as I is less than 6, keep processing more records. When I is 6, six grades have been read, and an exit is taken from the loop to compute and print the grade average.

Grades read

| 10 |
| 50 |
| 60 |
| 90 |
| 80 |
| 70 |

Tabulation of Values of Variables

| S | G | I | A |
|---|---|---|---|
| 0̶ | | | |
| 1̶0̶ (10 + 0) | 1̶0̶ | 1̶ | |
| 6̶0̶ (10 + 50) | 5̶0̶ | 2̶ | |
| 1̶2̶0̶ (10 + 50 + 60) | 6̶0̶ | 3̶ | |
| 2̶1̶0̶ (10 + 50 + 60 + 90) | 9̶0̶ | 4̶ | |
| 2̶9̶0̶ (10 + 50 + 60 + 90 + 80) | 8̶0̶ | 5̶ | |
| 360 (10 + 50 + 60 + 90 + 80 + 70) | 70 | 6 | 60 |

**Figure 2-6**   Computation of an average grade.

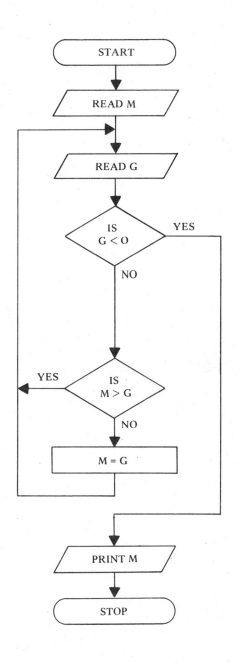

Set Max equal to first grade.

Read another grade.

Are there any more grades?

No; is Max still largest grade?
Yes; read more grades.

No; replace Max by grade
and read more grades.

Yes; print Max and stop.

Grades read

| |
| --- |
| 38 |
| 47 |
| 23 |
| 14 |
| 59 |
| −2 |

Tabulation of values
of variables

| M | G |
| --- | --- |
| 38 | 47 |
| 47 | 23 |
|  | 14 |
| 59 | 59 |
|  | −2 |

Figure 2-7    Search for highest grade.

## 2-5  Assignments

### 2-5-1  Self Test

1.  Determine the output produced by each of the following flowcharts:

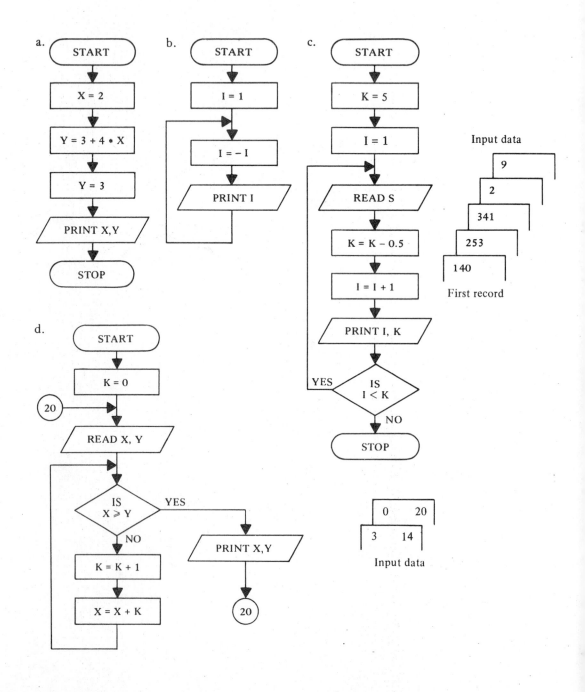

**2.** Determine the number of records read by each of the following flowcharts.

a.

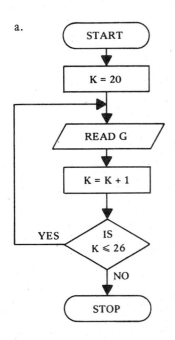

b.

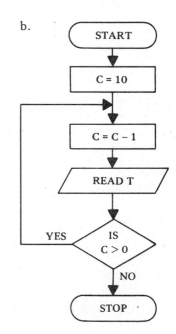

c.

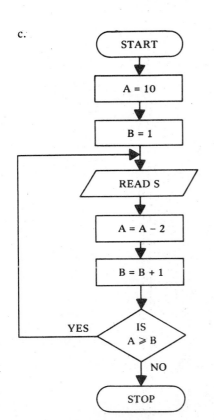

d.

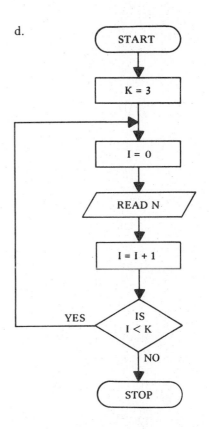

3. Write down any six positive numbers, one per record, and determine the action of the following flowcharts on the six numbers (each READ reads one number per record).

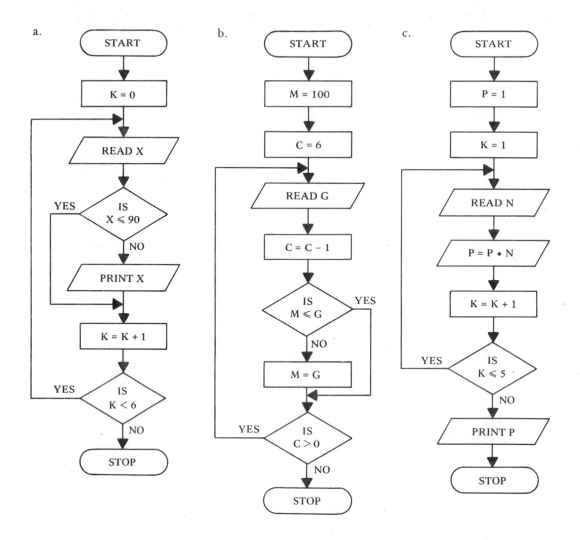

a.

b.

c.

4. How could the flowchart of Figure 2-4 be modified to compute the interest compounded twice a year? monthly? daily?

5. Modify the flowchart of Figure 2-4 to accept the principal, rate, and number of years as input.

6. How would one modify the flowchart of Figure 2-6 to compute the average of 20 grades?

7. How would you modify the flowchart to Figure 2-7 to find the smallest grade?

## 2-5-2 Exercises

1. Draw a flowchart to input two numbers and print the largest. Do the same for three numbers accepted from input.

2. Draw a flowchart to calculate and write out the area of a rectangle for values of length and width accepted from input.

3. A salesman is assigned a commission on the following basis:

| SALES | COMMISSION |
|---|---|
| $00–$500 | 2% |
| over $500 | 5% |

Draw a flowchart to input an amount of sale and compute and print out the salesman's commission.

4. Draw a flowchart to print the numbers 2, 4, 6, 8, $\cdots$ 200.

5. Draw a flowchart to solve quadratic equations of the form $ax^2 + bx + c = 0$ for values of $a$, $b$, and $c$ accepted from input. Recall that $x = \dfrac{-b \pm \sqrt{b^2 - 4ac}}{2a}$. (Don't forget that the discriminant may be negative!)

6. Draw a flowchart to compute N! = $1 \cdot 2 \cdot 3 \cdot 4 \cdots$ N. For example, 4! = $1 \cdot 2 \cdot 3 \cdot 4$ = 24.

## 2-5-3 Projects

1. Look up your favorite recipe in a cookbook and express it as a flowchart. Do you need decision blocks?

2. Draw a flowchart for a typical school day and contrast it with a flowchart for your Saturday activities. Start both flowcharts at your time of awakening.

## 2-5-4 Answers to Self Test

1. a. 2  3    b. −1  1   −1  1  etc.    c. 2  4.5;  3  4;  4  3.5    d. 18  14;  21  20

2. a. 7    b. 10    c. 4    d. infinite

3. a. Prints values for X which are greater than 90.
   b. M will store the smallest value of G.
   c. Value of P will be the product of the values of N.

4. To compound interest twice a year change the value of N to 4 * 2 = 8 and the interest rate R to .05/2 = .025. For monthly interest, N = 4 * 12 and R = .05/12. For daily interest, N = 4 * 365 and R = .05/365.

5.    Replace the first 3 replacement statements with

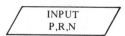

6.    Change the decision block to

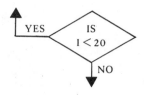

7.    Change the second decision block to

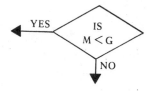

# BASIC STATEMENTS: LET, PRINT, TERMINATION, SYSTEM COMMANDS

## 3-1    Problem Example

Mr. Sunshine wants to deposite $1,500 at a savings institution. He considers a local bank and a credit union. The credit union requires a nonrefundable membership fee of $15. Deposits earn 6.25 percent at the credit union and 6 percent at the bank; interest is compounded once yearly. Mr. Sunshine will need the money in two and a half years. Which institution should Mr. Sunshine consider? The formula to compute the value of the investment $T$ is

$$T = P(1 + I)^N$$

where $I$ is the interest rate, $N$ is the number of years, and $P$ is the principal. A program to print investments at both institutions is shown in Figure 3-1.

Analyze carefully the program in Figure 3-1 and the results produced by the BASIC program. Note the three types of BASIC statements:

1.  The replacement statement with key word LET.

2.  The output statement with key word PRINT.

3.  The termination statements with key words STOP and END.

Note also the system command RUN, which is an instruction to the BASIC operating system to tell it to execute or process the program.

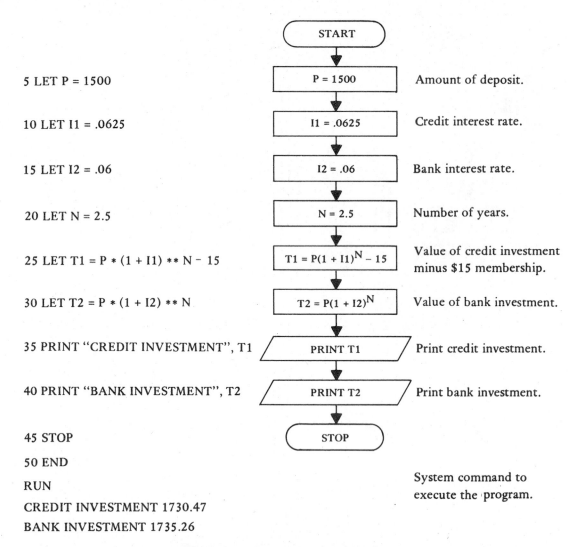

5 LET P = 1500 — Amount of deposit.

10 LET I1 = .0625 — Credit interest rate.

15 LET I2 = .06 — Bank interest rate.

20 LET N = 2.5 — Number of years.

25 LET T1 = P * (1 + I1) ** N − 15 — Value of credit investment minus \$15 membership.

30 LET T2 = P * (1 + I2) ** N — Value of bank investment.

35 PRINT "CREDIT INVESTMENT", T1 — Print credit investment.

40 PRINT "BANK INVESTMENT", T2 — Print bank investment.

45 STOP

50 END

RUN — System command to execute the program.

CREDIT INVESTMENT 1730.47

BANK INVESTMENT 1735.26

**Figure 3-1**  Investment computation.

# 3-2  Elements of the BASIC Language

### 3-2-1  Character Set

The characters used in BASIC are grouped into three standard classes:

1. *Alphabetic.* The alphabetic characters are ABCDEFGHIJKLMNOPQRSTUVWXYZ.

2. *Numeric.* The numeric characters are 0123456789.

3. *Special.* The special characters are . , ; " + − * / = ( ) $<>\uparrow$ \$ and the character "blank," which is equivalent to "space" on the keyboard.

Figure 3-2 illustrates the Teletype keyboard commonly used in BASIC.

**Figure 3-2**    Teletype keyboard (courtesy of Teletype Corporation).

## 3-2-2   Constants

A constant is a quantity whose numerical value is fixed and explicitly stated; in other words, it is a number that may be preceded by a sign (+ or −). Decimal points may be used.

**Examples of valid constants**

$$300 \qquad -2.31 \qquad 62504. \qquad +0.3 \qquad -14$$

Imbedded blanks (blanks between first and last digit) do not affect the value of the constant: 6    32 = 632 = 6    3    2

**Examples of invalid constants**

| | |
|---|---|
| 634,123 | No commas are allowed. |
| 23.24. | Only one decimal point is allowed. |
| $30.40 | Character $ is invalid. |
| 111−222−333 | Character − is invalid. |

The allowable size (magnitude) of numbers and their representation using exponents is discussed in Section 3-6-1.

## 3-2-3   Variables

Unlike a constant, a variable may assume different values. Variable names are limited to a single letter or a letter followed by a single digit. One can think of a variable as a name given to a memory location into which certain data is to be stored. Variable names are automatically assigned memory locations by BASIC.

**Example of valid variable names**

$$X, W1, Z0 \ (0 = zero)$$

**Example of invalid variable names**

| | |
|---|---|
| 1A | Does not start with letter. |
| HRS | Too many characters. |
| A% | Invalid character %. |
| −B | Invalid first character −. |

## 3-2-4   Expressions

An expression may be a constant or a variable or any combination (mixture) of constants and/or variables linked by arithmetic operation symbols. Parentheses may be included to denote the order of computations. The allowable arithmetic operation symbols are

| | | | | |
|---|---|---|---|---|
| + | Addition | | − | Subtraction |
| * | Multiplication | | / | Division |
| ** | Exponentiation | or | ↑ | Exponentiation (check your system) |

**Example of valid expressions**

| BASIC EXPRESSION | ALGEBRAIC EXPRESSION |
|---|---|
| A | $a$ |
| 14 | 14 |
| (A/B) * C | $\frac{a}{b} \cdot c$ |
| A * B − 30 | $ab - 30$ |
| −C | $-c$ |
| (A * B) ** 2 | $(ab)^2$ |
| (−C + 1.4) * D | $(-c + 1.4)\, d$ |
| −3.7 | $-3.7$ |
| X ** .5 | $\sqrt{x}$ |
| ((A − B) ** 3) ** .25 | $\sqrt[4]{(a - b)^3}$ |

**Example of invalid expressions**

| | |
|---|---|
| 3(A + B) | Should be  3 * (A + B). |
| A − (B + C * (K) | Should be  A − (B + C * (K)). |
| X * −3 | Should be  X * (−3). |

When parentheses are present in an expression, the operation within the parentheses is performed first; if parentheses are nested, the innermost set of parentheses is performed first.

When no parentheses are present, operations are performed according to the following rules of precedence:

| OPERATION | PRECEDENCE |
|-----------|------------|
| ** | High |
| * or / | Intermediate |
| + or − | Low |

Operations with higher precedence are performed before operations with lower precedence. The operations addition/subtraction, multiplication/division are performed in order from left to right according to the rules of precedence. Exponentiations are performed in order from right to left. If the operations have equal priority, they are evaluated left to right.

**Examples**

1.  A − B + C      B is subtracted from A, and the result is added to C.
    3 − 2 + 5      $(3 − 2) + 5 = 1 + 5 = 6$

2.  A + B * C      Since multiplication has priority, B * C is computed; the result is then added to A, giving A + (B * C).
    3 + 2 * 3      $3 + (2 * 3) = 3 + 6 = 9$

3.  A/B * C        Since multiplication and division have same priority B is first divided into A (A/B), and the result of the division is multiplied by C. This is different from A/(B * C).
    9./4. * 2.     $(9./4.) * 2. = 2.25 * 2. = 4.50$

4.  A/B/C          First A/B is performed, and the result is then divided by C; you will get the same answer if you calculate A/(B * C).
    8/4/2          $\frac{8}{4} \div 2 = 2 \div 2 = 1$

5.  (A + B)/C * D  The parentheses indicate that the sum of A + B is to be performed first. The sum is then divided by C, and the result is multiplied by D, giving
    $$\frac{A + B}{C} * D \text{ not } \frac{A + B}{C * D}$$
    (3. + 6)/3. * 6.    $\frac{9.}{3.} * 6 = 3. * 6. = 18.$

6.  A + B * C ** 2  Since exponentiation has highest priority, $C^2$ is computed. This result is then multiplied by B, since multiplication has the next highest priority. Finally, this result is added to A, giving A + (B * (C ** 2)).
    3 + 3 * 2 ** 2   $3 + (3 * 2^2) = 3 + (3 * 4) = 3 + 12 = 15$

7.  A ** B ** C     Exponentiations are evaluated from right to left; therefore B is first raised to the power C, and this result is then used as the power of A, giving A ** (B ** C) not (A ** B) ** C

$$3 ** 2 ** 3 \qquad 3 ** (2 ** 3) = 3 ** 8 = 6561$$
$$\text{not}$$
$$(3 ** 2) ** 3 = 9 ** 3 = 729$$

### 3-2-5  Character Strings

All data processed so far has been numerical in nature. However, often it may be convenient or necessary to process alphabetic or alphameric information; to create lists of names, addresses, and so forth; to generate labels and headings of reports; or to print messages reflecting a particular outcome of a program. Alphanumeric data is defined as a sequence of letters, digits, and special characters (such as . , = *). For example "1201 NORTH 11 AVE" is a string of seventeen characters consisting of six digits, three blanks, and eight letters; it is commonly referred to as a *character string* or a *literal string* or a *literal constant.* Zip code numbers, telephone numbers, and Social Security numbers are other examples of character strings. Character strings are not processed numerically (they do not participate in additions, subtractions, etc.); however, they may be used in relational expressions in IF statements.

Character string constants or literals are always enclosed in quotes. The maximum number of characters allowed in a literal string will vary from system to system. Note that the quote (") is a single key stroke that is not the apostrophe symbol (').

The following are examples of character strings:

"SAM"

"X+Y="

"8061 ACACIA DR"

"34"

A string variable is a variable that will assume the value of a string constant. It is formed by appending a $ to any variable name. For example, A$ and Z$ are valid character string variable names. A1$ and B9$ are permissible in some systems; in other systems, only a single letter followed by a $ may be used for a character string variable. On some systems a single quote may be used to enclose the literal string.

# 3-3    BASIC Statements

### 3-3-1  The Replacement Statement LET

A replacement statement specifies arithmetic operations to be performed and the location (variable) into which the value computed is to be placed. The general form of the replacement statement is

*statement-number* LET *variable = expression*

The value of the *expression* is first computed, and the result is placed (stored) in the *variable* (left-hand part of the statement). The equal sign used in the replacement statement must be understood as a replacement sign rather than as a mathematical equality. Accordingly, the statement LET $X = X + 1$ is quite legitimate, since it means "Add 1 to whatever is currently in memory location $X$ and store the result back into $X$ (destroying whatever value was there before)."

**Examples of valid replacement statements**

| | |
|---|---|
| 5    LET X = 3.123 | Define X to be 3.123 (place 3.123 into location X); whatever was in X before is destroyed. |
| 4    LET C1 = (A + B)/C | Compute A + B, divide by C and call result C1. |
| 10  LET B$ = "GROSS PROFIT" | The string GROSS PROFIT is stored in B$. |

**Examples of invalid replacement statements**

| | |
|---|---|
| 5    LET 3.16 = X | A variable, not a constant, must be on the left-hand side of the equal sign. How can you store the value in X in 3.16? |
| 10  Y = 2 * X + 1 | Missing key word LET. On some systems it is valid. |
| 15  LET X + Y = 1 | An expression cannot occur on the left-hand side of the equal sign. How could 1 be stored in the sum of two memory locations? |
| 20  LET A1 = "PROFIT" | A1 is not a valid variable name for a string constant. |
| 25  LET A = "3" + 2 | You cannot mix string constants and arithmetic constants. |

On most BASIC systems, the user can use the *multiple arithmetic statement.* This statement allows the initialization of more than one variable at a time.

**Example**

> 5    LET X = Y = Z = 1    Set X, Y, and Z to 1.
>
> 10   LET A$ = "ACCOUNT RECEIVABLE"
>
> 15   LET B$ = C$ = A$    B$ and C$ contain the string in A$.

## 3-3-2   Statement Numbers

Each BASIC statement must be numbered. Statement numbers must be unsigned integers not exceeding five digits. In most systems, statements may be entered in any desired order; the system will sort the statements in order when the program is listed or executed. Statements will be processed by the computer in ascending order unless a decision statement (IF) or unconditional transfer (GO TO) is encountered. These statements are discussed in Chapter 4. In general, it is a good idea to number the statements in increments of 5, 10, or more. This practice makes it easier to insert statements between two statements for editing purposes.

**Example**

If you typed in the following statements in the order indicated:

$$10 \quad LET \ X = 3$$
$$20 \quad PRINT \ X,Y$$
$$15 \quad LET \ Y = X ** 3$$

BASIC would rearrange these statements in the following order:

$$10 \quad LET \ X = 3$$
$$15 \quad LET \ Y = X ** 3$$
$$20 \quad PRINT \ X,Y$$

### 3-3-3   The PRINT Statement

The general form of the PRINT statement is

*statement number* PRINT *expression-list*

where the *expression-list* can be, alternatively,

| | |
|---|---|
| a variable | PRINT X |
| an expression | PRINT (H − 40)*R*1.5+H*R |
| a character string | PRINT "PAY HOURS RATE" |
| a combination of the above separated by commas or semicolons | PRINT "PAY=";P, "HOURS=", H |

An output line on a typical terminal consists of 75 print positions. The line is generally divided into five zones (15 characters each). A comma between items in the expression list provides for wide spacing between items on the output line (each item is printed in a separate zone), whereas a semicolon provides for compact spacing between items (one or two blanks between numeric fields and none between character strings). A more complete discussion of output control is provided in Section 3-6-2. Figure 3-3 illustrates a variety of PRINT statements with commas and semicolons. The reader is advised to look at each statement carefully.

### 3-3-4   The Termination Statements STOP and END

The last BASIC statement in a BASIC program should always be the END statement. For that reason, the END statement should always be the highest-numbered statement in your program. The END denotes the physical end of all BASIC statements. If you type BASIC statements after the END statement, these will not be processed by BASIC.

The STOP statement tells BASIC where in your program you want to stop processing instructions. It identifies the logical end of your program at run time (during execution). There may be more than one STOP statement in any one BASIC program. The general forms of the termination statements are

*statement-number* STOP

*statement-number* END

```
10   LET  X=0.2  ⎫
15   LET  Y=15   ⎬  Initialization of constants
20   LET  Z=-3.9 ⎭
25   PRINT"00000000011111111112222222222233333333";  ⎫
30   PRINT"33444444444455555555555666666666777777"   ⎬  To provide easy column
35   PRINT"12345678901234567890123456789012345678";  ⎬  identification on output
40   PRINT"89012345678901234567890123456789012345"   ⎭
45   PRINT
50   PRINT X,Y,Z                              Zone spacing: numeric        : commas
55   PRINT X;Y;Z                              Compact spacing: numeric     : semicolons
60   PRINT"HOURS","RATE","PAY"                Zone spacing: string data    : commas
65   PRINT"HOURS";"RATE";"PAY"                Compact spacing: string data : semicolons
70   PRINT "HOURS",Y                          Zone spacing: numeric + string data
75   PRINT "HOURS";Y                          Compact spacing: numeric + string data
80   PRINT "X=",X,"Y=",Y        ⎫
85   PRINT "X=";X,"Y=";Y        ⎬  Combination commas and semicolons
90   PRINT "TOTAL=";X+Y+Z       ⎭
95   PRINT 2.34*X/Y-Z**2           Expression numeric
96   STOP
99   END
```

Column identifiers

```
RUN

0000000001111111111222222222233333333334444444444555555555566666666667777777
1234567890123456789012345678901234567890123456789012345678901234567890123456789012345

 0.2           15            -3.9
 0.2   15  -3.9
HOURS          RATE          PAY
HOURSRATEPAY
HOURS          15
HOURS 15
X=             0.2           Y=            15
X= 0.2         Y= 15
TOTAL= 11.3
-15.1788
```

**Figure 3-3**    Examples of PRINT statements.

# 3-4    You Might Want To Know

1. Does it matter where I start typing my BASIC statements?

   *Answer:*  No, it does not matter. Imbedded blanks are also allowed in statements.

   *Example:*  The following statements are equivalent:

   $$10 \text{ LET} \quad X \quad = \quad C1 \quad +4$$

   $$10LETX = C1 + 4$$

2. When I have typed a BASIC statement, how do I transmit the line?

   *Answer:*  **Press the RETURN key, or Control-C on certain systems (see Figure 3-2).**

3. How can I force BASIC to print a blank line on the output?

   *Answer:*  Use the PRINT statement with no expression-list (PRINT all by itself). A blank line will be printed if the last variable in the preceding PRINT list did not specify a comma (,) or a semicolon (;).

4. I make an error in typing a statement and I want to correct it. What do I do?

   *Answer:*  Errors can be corrected in the following ways:

   a. Erase the last character(s) typed. The method for doing this depends on the particular system being used. (Some systems allow for backspacing and retyping.)

   b. Erase the entire line. Generally this can be done by pressing the ESCape key, but this too depends on the system in use. Refer to the operating manual for your system.

   c. Press RETURN key and ignore any response or error messages from the system. Type the corrected BASIC statement, including the same statement number. This new statement will replace the old statement.

   *Example:*

   | | |
   |---|---|
   | If you want to type | $10 \text{ LET } X = (3 + Z/4)\uparrow2$ |
   | and you typed | $10 \text{ LET } X = (3 - Z/4)\uparrow2$ |

   *Action:*

   | | |
   |---|---|
   | Hit RETURN and retype | $10 \text{ LET } X = (3 + Z/4)\uparrow2$ |

5. I have typed a BASIC statement and hit the RETURN key. The system stops and on a new line prints an error message.

   *Action:*  An error has been made in the preceding statement. Consult the manufacturer's BASIC reference manual to determine the error type. Correct the statement and retype entire BASIC statement; then press RETURN.

6.  My complete BASIC program has been typed and is executing; that is, RUN has been typed. The computer stops and prints

ERR XX AT YYYY

*Meaning:* This is an execution or run time error at statement number YYYY. Consult reference manual to determine the nature of the error (XX) and change the logic of the program appropriately.

*Example:*

```
10  LET X = 0
15  LET Y = 5/X
20  PRINT Y

RUN

ERR  16  AT  0015       The error code and/or message may
                          differ from system to system.
```

*Meaning:* The code 16 is an error code to denote an arithmetic error (division by 0). The code number 15 is the statement at which the error has been made.

*Action:* At this point, if the user meant X to be 10, he can replace statement 10 by a new statement by typing

```
10  LET  X = 10        The user presses RETURN and types RUN

RUN

.5                      .5 would be printed.
```

7.  Suppose I have corrected all errors in my program, which now executes (runs) correctly, and I want to obtain a clean listing of the entire program without the statements in error and the corrections. How do I do so?

*Answer:* Most systems will allow the user to list his program by typing the command LIST followed by pressing the RETURN key.

8.  The other day I typed my program and listed it. Curiously enough, statements that were not mine made their appearance in my listing and caused run time errors. How can I avoid this situation?

*Answer:* To clear memory of any leftover code, type the command NEW. To start a new program, it is always recommended to first type NEW. The system command NEW will erase all existing program statements at your terminal. See your own system specifications for details.

9.    How do I obtain a paper tape of the program?

*Answer:* Many systems with slow speed paper tape punchers will allow the user to generate a paper tape copy by typing the command LIST, then depressing the punch ON key on the paper tape punch unit, and finally hitting the RETURN key. To read paper tape into memory, insert paper tape in reader and press the START switch. For other systems, consult the BASIC operational procedures. Many systems will allow storing of the program into special files that may be recalled by the user for subsequent use. The command SAVE is often used with the command GET to retrieve the program.

10.    If I forget to initialize a variable to a particular value, and I use that variable in a calculation, what will BASIC do?

*Answer:* Most BASIC systems will initialize variables to 0, but to be certain you should initialize your own variables.

11.    I can't fit the entire expression-list of the PRINT statement on one line because there is not enough room on that line for the list of variables. What should I do?

*Answer:* Break down the PRINT statement into two or more consecutive separately numbered PRINT statements.

12.    Can BASIC renumber or resequence the statements of my program?

*Answer:* Yes. Most systems will use one of the following commands (commas are sometimes required):

| | |
|---|---|
| RENUM $\Big\}$ n1 inc<br>RESEQUENCE<br>RENUMBER n1 STEP inc | In all cases, this means "Renumber the first statement n1 with increments of inc for the following statements. If inc is omitted, an increment of 10 is automatically provided. |
| RESEQ n1—n2 base inc | Resequence n1 through n2 starting at base with increment inc. |

*Example:* To renumber an entire program in such a way that the first BASIC statement is numbered 5 and each following statement is incremented by 10, the following command might be used:

RENUM 5 10

All references to old statement numbers in the program are updated to reflect the new numbering system.

13.    Is it permissible to perform exponentiation on negative numbers?

*Answer:* One should exercise care in writing expressions such as $(-4)\uparrow 2$, since exponentiation may involve logarithmic computations where the log of negative numbers is not defined. Instead, use $(-4)*(-4)$ or if the expression is too lengthy, use $(ABS(-4))\uparrow 2$. (ABS means absolute value.) Note that negative exponents are perfectly valid; $4\uparrow(-2)$ has value 1/16.

# 3-5    Programming Examples

### 3-5-1    Income Calculation

Mr. X. is a widower with three children aged 12, 16, and 19. His monthly salary is $1,023.36. His monthly contribution to a retirement plan is 4.5 percent of his first nine months' salary; retirement deductions are spread over a 12-month period. For each child under 18, he receives $119.25 in child support from Social Security. His monthly Social Security deduction is 5.85 percent of his monthly income, and his federal income tax is 13.6 percent of his yearly gross (deducted on a monthly basis). Monthly payments for life insurance equal 9.6 percent of his monthly salary after Social Security and federal tax deductions. Write a program to compute his monthly spendable income after taxes, deductions, and supplemental support income. A program to solve this problem is shown in Figure 3-4.

| | |
|---|---|
| 10 LET C = 119.25 | Support per child. |
| 15 LET I = 1023.36 | Monthly salary. |
| 20 LET R = (9 * I * .045)/12 | Monthly retirement plan deduction. |
| 25 LET S = .0585 * I | Monthly Social Security deduction. |
| 30 LET F = .136 * I | Monthly federal income tax. |
| 35 LET T = I - (R + S + F) | Net after deductions. |
| 40 LET L = .096 * (I - F - S) | Monthly life insurance payments. |
| 45 LET T1 = T - L | Net minus life insurance payments. |
| 50 LET T1 = T1 + 2 * C | Plus child support. |
| 55 PRINT "SPENDABLE INCOME IS"; T1 | |
| 60 END | |

RUN

SPENDABLE INCOME IS 949.144

**Figure 3-4**    Income tax calculation.

### 3-5-2    Finite and Infinite Sums

Consider the sum of the following 1,000 terms

$$SUM = \frac{1}{2^0} + \frac{1}{2^1} + \frac{1}{2^2} + \frac{1}{2^3} + \cdots + \frac{1}{2^{999}} = 1 + \frac{1}{2} + \frac{1}{4} + \frac{1}{8} + \cdots + \frac{1}{2^{999}}$$

This is a geometric progression, and its sum can be computed as follows:

$$SUM = \frac{a(1 - r^n)}{1 - r}$$

where:   $a$ is the first term of the progression ($a = 1$)
$r$ is the ratio of any two consecutive terms ($r = 1/2$)
$n$ is the number of terms to be added ($n = 1,000$)

The infinite sum

$$1 + \frac{1}{2} + \frac{1}{2^2} + \frac{1}{2^3} + \cdots + \frac{1}{2^{999}} + \cdots \text{ and so forth can be}$$

computed as SUM = $\dfrac{a}{1-r}$

Let us write a program to compute the sum of the first 1,000 terms, the infinite sum, and the difference between these two sums. See Figure 3-5.

```
05  LET N = 1000
10  LET A = 1
15  LET R = .5
20  LET S1 = A*(1−R**N)/(1−R)
25  LET S2 = A/(1−R)
30  PRINT
35  PRINT "THE FINITE SUM IS";S1
40  PRINT "THE INFINITE SUM IS";S2
45  PRINT "THE DIFFERENCE IS";S1−S2
50  END

RUN

THE FINITE SUM IS 2
THE INFINITE SUM IS 2
THE DIFFERENCE IS 0
```

Figure 3-5    Calculation of the sum of a geometric progression.

# 3-6    Discussion

## 3-6-1    Number Representation

The specifics of number representation may vary from one computer to another depending on the computer manufacturer. (See the computer manufacturer's reference manuals for more details.) Arithmetic operations are carried out in floating-point mode. The range of floating-point numbers is approximately $10^{-76}$ to $10^{76}$. The range depends on the computer system. The number of significant digits may vary from 6 to 15 digits depending on the system.

Constants in BASIC can be expressed in two different notations:

1.    Decimal notation, with or without decimal points.

*Examples:*   45.67, −12.3, 11240, −48216.

2.  Exponent notation where the character E is used to represent the decimal base 10, followed by a two digit number (with or without sign) to represent the exponent (power).

*Examples:*

LET X = 3.456 E + 2   where   3.456 E + 2 = 3.456 × $10^2$ = 345.6.

LET Y = –3.E–3        where   –3.E–3 = –3 × $10^{-3}$ = –.003.

LET Z = 1.23E0        where   1.23E0 = 1.23 × $10^0$ = 1.23.

On output, in many systems any constant that can be represented as six digits and a decimal point is printed in decimal notation. All other constants are printed in exponent notation (see Figure 3-6).

```
10 LET X = 123456
20 LET Y = 123456789012345        Note loss of significant digits on
30 LET T = .0003245               output. Number is rounded off.
35 LET Z = 22.1E3
40 PRINT X; Y; T; Z
50 END

RUN

123456    1.2345679E + 14    3.245E − 4    22100
```

**Figure 3-6**   Different forms of numeric output.

BASIC uses the binary base for number representation, and hence most fractional decimal numbers cannot be represented exactly on the computer. For example, .1 has an infinite binary representation, and therefore the internal representation for .1 is a close approximation to 1/10. Also, there are many rational numbers that cannot be represented exactly in decimal notation. For example, 10/3 = 3.3333. . . . In such cases, only the first six or seven significant digits (depending on systems) are retained; the last digit is rounded.

**Examples**

2.5645288. . . would be rounded to 2.56453
2.33333. . .   would be rounded to 2.33333
2.55555. . .   would be rounded to 2.55556

## 3-6-2 Output Spacing

Both the comma and semicolon can be used to control printer spacing. Note that examples 1 and 2 produce the same output.

**Example 1**

```
00100 LET X = 3
00110 LET Y = 4
00120 PRINT "THE VALUE OF X IS"; X, "THE VALUE OF Y IS"; Y
00130 END

RUN

THE VALUE OF X IS 3     THE VALUE OF Y IS 4
```

**Example 2**

```
00100 LET X = 3
00110 LET Y = 4
00120 PRINT "THE VALUE OF X IS"; X,        Note the comma (,) after X.
00130 PRINT "THE VALUE OF Y IS"; Y
00140 END

RUN

THE VALUE OF X IS 3     THE VALUE OF Y IS 4
```

Note the two PRINT statements in example 2 for one line of output. The output produced is the same as in example 1. The terminal comma (,) of the PRINT statement numbered 120 means that the data that is to be printed next will be printed on the same line but at the next zone on that line.

**Example 3**

```
00100 LET X = 3
00110 LET Y = 4
00120 PRINT "THE VALUE OF X IS"; X       Note a blank (no comma) after X.
00130 PRINT "THE VALUE OF Y IS"; Y
00140 END

RUN

THE VALUE OF X IS 3
THE VALUE OF Y IS 4
```

Note the use of two print statements for two lines of output. In this case the absence of a comma (,) or or a semicolon (;) after the variable X at statement 120 causes the next PRINT statement to resume printing on a new line.

**Example 4**

```
00100 LET X = 3
00110 LET Y = 4
00120 PRINT "THE VALUE OF X IS"; X;      Note the semicolon (;) after X.
00130 PRINT "THE VALUE OF Y IS"; Y
00140 END


RUN


THE VALUE OF X IS 3 THE VALUE OF Y IS 4
```

Note the use of two PRINT statements for one line of output. The end semicolon at statement 120 forces the next print operation to resume on the same line one blank from the previous datum. If the two output fields are literals, no blanks separate these fields as shown in line 65 Figure 3-3.

# 3-7    Assignments

## 3-7-1   Self Test

1.  Determine whether the following statements are valid or invalid. Give reason if invalid. (Statement numbers have been purposely omitted.)

|  |  |
|---|---|
| a.  LET X = −X | h.  LET 3X = Z |
| b.  LET A + B = C | i.  PRINT X = 4 |
| c.  LET A$ = THE CAT | j.  LET Y1 = Z(Z + 1) |
| d.  LET Z19 = A + B | k.  LET G = A/−A1 |
| e.  LET X = X + 1 | l.  LET B2 = D • Y − 7.93 |
| f.  LET I = $\frac{C}{D}$ | m.  LET A1 = −(A1) + M5 − 3M |
| g.  LET B$ = "111'" + "222" | n.  PRINT A, B, 3.2 |

2.  Evaluate each of the following expressions for A = 3, B = −2, J = 0, and I = 4.

    a.  A ↑ 2 + B          e.  A/B∗B          i.  J/I

    b.  I + 2/3            f.  A/B ∗ 3 + A    j.  I/J

    c.  A ∗∗ B            g.  A/B/2          k.  A ∗∗ 2 ∗∗ 3

    d.  A ∗ 3. + B ∗ 4    h.  A/B + 2        l.  J ↑ B

3.  Translate the following algebraic expressions into BASIC.

    a.  $x(y + z)$                    d.  $\dfrac{a}{xy}$              g.  $y + a^x$

    b.  $\dfrac{a}{b} \cdot c$        e.  $y^{1/3}$                   h.  $p(1 + i/n)^{ny}$

    c.  $ax^2 + bx + c$               f.  $-x^2$                      i.  $n(t/p)^{1/n} \cdot y - n$

4.  Write a program to convert −139.65° Fahrenheit into centigrade. The formula is

$$C = \frac{5}{9}(F - 32)$$

5.  Write a program to compute and print the length of the hypotenuse of a right triangle, given its two legs .0056 and 135.77.

6.  Write a program to interchange the values contained in memory locations S and T.


## 3-7-2   Exercises

1.  Write a program to approximate the Julian date (introduced by Julius Caesar in 46 B.C.) equivalent to the calendar date given in the form month, day. The Julian date is the day of the year. January 1 has Julian date 1, February 2 has Julian date 33, December 31 has Julian date 365, etc. A formula for approximating the Julian date is (month − 1) ∗ 30 + day. Determine the Julian dates for November 7, May 25, and March 21.

2.  Write a program to print out your initials by magnifying them; for example

```
    MMM          MMM        BBBBBBB
    MMMM        MMMM        BBB    B
    MMMMM     MMMMM         BBBBBBB
    MMM MMMM MMM            BBB    B
    MMM   MM   MMM          BBBBBBB
```

3.  Write the program in Section 3-5-2 in more compact form.

4.  Mr. X. is a bricklayer. Last year his gross pay was $23,564.99. After deducting 5.85 percent for Social Security and 23.5 percent for income tax from his gross pay, was his net income greater than Mr. Y.'s net income? Mr. Y. is a teacher who grossed $19,874 but had $850.45 deducted for his income retirement plan and 16.03 percent of his gross income for income tax purposes. Print Mr. X. and Mr. Y.'s salaries.

5.  With an interest rate $I$ of 6 percent and a principal $P$ of $1,956.45 deposited for an 11-year period in a savings account, write a program to compute a total principal $T$, given the formula

$$T = P(1 + I)^N$$

where $N$ is the number of years.

6.  Suppose the principal of $P$ of exercise 5 is compounded daily for the same period of 11 years. Write a program to compute

   a.  The total principal given by the formula

$$T = P\left(1 + \frac{I}{J}\right)^{J \cdot N}$$

   where $J$ is the number of times the interest is compounded per year.

   b.  The difference between total amounts when the principal is compounded once and 360 times a year.

   c.  What would the principal be after 11 years and 7 months? (*Hint:* Express $N$ as total months divided by 12.)

7.  A wholesaler accepts a $5,000 promissory note at 7 percent in lieu of cash payment for delivered goods. Write a program to compute the maturity value of the note for a 30-, 60-, and 90-day short-term loan. The formula to compute the maturity value $S$ is $S = P(1 + I \cdot N)$, where $P$ is the principal, $I$ is the interest rate, and $N$ is the number of years. If days rather than years are required, express $N$ as number of days divided by 360.

8.  Write a program to evaluate each of the formulas for the indicated values (use $\pi = 3.1415$) and print the answers with appropriate literal headings.

   a.  Simple interest      $i = Prt$          for $r = .04$      $t = 3$      $p = 100$

   b.  Volume of a cube    $v = c^3$          for $c = 3.167219$

   c.  Area of a circle     $A = \pi r^2$        for $r = 6.2$

   d.  Volume of a cone    $v = \frac{1}{3} \pi r^2 h$      for $r = 9.1$      $h = 4.932747$

9.  Write a program to compute and print the area and the length (perimeter) of each of the following:

   a.                          b.                          c.

5.3
4.1

5.05
13.73

.08

10. Write a program to verify that for $x = 1.3$ and $y = .7$ the following formulas are correct:

    a.   $\sin(2x) = 2 \sin(x) \cos(x)$

    b.   $\cos(x + y) = \sin(x) \cos(y) - \sin(y) \cos(x)$
        Use the BASIC functions SIN (expression) and COS (expression).

11. Fifteen seconds after dropping a stone into a well, the stone hits the surface of the water. Determine the height of the well given the formula $d = 1/2gt^2$, where $d$ is the distance, $g$ is the force of gravity (9.81 meter/s), and $t$ is the time in seconds.

12. Write a program to compute the infinite sum of the following geometric progressions whenever possible:

    a.   $1 + 2 + 4 + 8 + 16 + \cdots$

    b.   $3 - 9 + 27 - 81 + \cdots$

    c.   $4 + 2 + 1 + 1/2 + 1/4 + \cdots$

    d.   $9/10 + 9/100 + 9/1000 + \cdots$

13. For four resistors $R_1$, $R_2$, $R_3$, and $R_4$ in parallel, the overall resistance $R$ is given by

$$\frac{1}{R} = \frac{1}{R_1} + \frac{1}{R_2} + \frac{1}{R_3} + \frac{1}{R_4}$$

where $R_1$, $R_2$, $R_3$, and $R_4$ are respectively 1.5, 3, 4.5, and 6 ohms. Write a program to compute $R$.

14. Write a program to determine whether $x = 1.3$ is a root of the polynomial

$$\frac{17}{3} x^{17} + 4x^8 - .76x^2 - 686$$

## 3-7-3   Projects

1. The Sullivans would like to take a summer trip abroad in a year and a half. They figure their expenses will be just over $3,500. Mr. Sullivan saves regularly at a credit union where interest paid is 6.5 percent on deposits. What should the Sullivans' minimum monthly deposit be to afford the vacation abroad? What would their deposits have to be if employment conditions forced them to deposit four times per year? (Assume deposits are equal.) The formula to calculate the regular deposit $R$ is

$$R = P \left( \frac{i/n}{(1 + i/n)^{n \cdot y} - 1} \right)$$

where     $P$ = amount to be saved (future value)

           $i$ = interest rate

           $n$ = deposits/year

           $y$ = number of years

2.  Mary Soule and her husband would very much like to buy the Pitts' house. The Pitts are asking $46,000 conventional with $4,000 down or $51,000 for VA with nothing down. In either case, a 30-year mortgage is sought. Financing charges are at 8 percent for VA and 8.25 percent for conventional. (Equal monthly payments are to be made.) The Soules have another option: Mary's father is willing to give them free $4,900 for a down payment, on the condition that they assume with him a 9.5 percent interest mortgage for the next 22 years and 8 months on the remainder of the conventional price, with equal payments four times a year. In terms of today's dollar value, what is the Soules' best financial arrangement? Identify in each case the total costs involved as well as the interest paid. The formula to compute the regular payment $R$ (monthly, quarterly, etc.) is

$$R = \frac{\dfrac{\text{interest} \cdot \text{principal}}{\text{no. payments per year}}}{1 - \left(\dfrac{\text{interest}}{\text{no payments per year}} + 1\right)^{(\text{no. payments per year}) \cdot \text{years}}}$$

If the number of years to pay is expressed in terms of years and months, convert to months and divide by 12.

3.  The date for any Easter Sunday can be computed as follows. (Let X be the year for which it is desired to compute Easter Sunday.)

Let A be the remainder of the division of X by 19.
Let B be the remainder of the division of X by 4.
Let C be the remainder of the division of X by 7.
Let D by the remainder of the division of (19A + 24) by 30.
Let E be the remainder of the division of (2B + 4C + 6D + 5) by 7.

The date for Easter Sunday is then March (22 + D + E). Note that this can give a date in April. To compute the remainder R of the division of I by J use the BASIC statement LET R = I – J * INT (I/J). INT is called the integer function; INT(X) finds the greatest integer not larger than X (for example, INT (9.78) = 9). Write a program to assign a year for the variable X and compute the date for Easter Sunday for that year using the formula 22 + D + E.

## 3-7-4   Answers to Self Test

1.  a.  Valid.
    b.  Invalid; expression is on the left side of the "=".
    c.  Invalid; the character string must be enclosed in quotes.
    d.  Invalid; Z19 is an invalid variable name.
    e.  Valid.
    f.  Invalid; division is expressed using the "/".
    g.  Invalid; addition is an arithmetic operation not used on character strings.
    h.  Invalid; 3X is an invalid variable name.
    i.  Invalid; the "=" is not used in the PRINT statement.
    j.  Invalid; there must be a multiplication sign between Z and (Z + 1).

    k.   Invalid; the expression −A1 must be enclosed in parentheses.

    l.    Invalid; D·Y is an invalid variable name.

    m.  Invalid; 3M is an invalid variable name.

    n.   Valid.

2.   a.   7    b.  4.66667    c.  .1111    d.  1    e.  3    f.  −1.5    g.  −.75

      h.   .5    i.  0    j.  Invalid; division by zero.    k.  6561    l.  Division by 0.

3.   a.   X ∗ (Y + Z)    b.  A / B ∗ C    c.  A ∗ X ∗∗ 2 + B ∗ X + C

      d.   A / (X ∗ Y)    e.  Y ∗∗ (1 / 3)    f.  −(X∗∗2)

      g.   Y + A ∗∗ X    h.  P ∗ (1 + I/N) ∗∗ (N ∗ Y)

      i.   N ∗ (T / P) ∗∗ (1 / N ∗ Y) − N

4.   10  LET F = −139.65

     20  LET C = 5/9∗(F − 32)

     30  PRINT C

     40  END

5.   10  LET A = .0056

     20  LET B = 135.77

     30  LET H = (A∗∗2 + B∗∗2) ∗∗ .5

     40  PRINT H

     50  END

6.   10  LET X = S

     20  LET S = T

     30  LET T = X

# BASIC STATEMENTS:
# GO TO, IF/THEN, INPUT,
# TAB, REM, ON/GO TO

## 4-1    Problem Example

Employees of Charlie's Eatery are paid at the hourly rate of $6.50 for the first 40 hours. The overtime rate for hours in excess of 40 is 1.5 times the regular rate. Write a BASIC program to read an employee's name and number of hours worked and compute and print the employee's total pay and number of overtime hours (if any).

An example of a program to solve this problem is shown in Figure 4-1. Analyze the program carefully and note the new BASIC statements introduced in this chapter:

1.    The input statement INPUT to enter data into the computer.

2.    The decision statement IF/THEN to branch to a nonsequential instruction.

3.    The transfer statement GO TO, which transfers control to another statement.

4.    The annotation statement REM used to document the program.

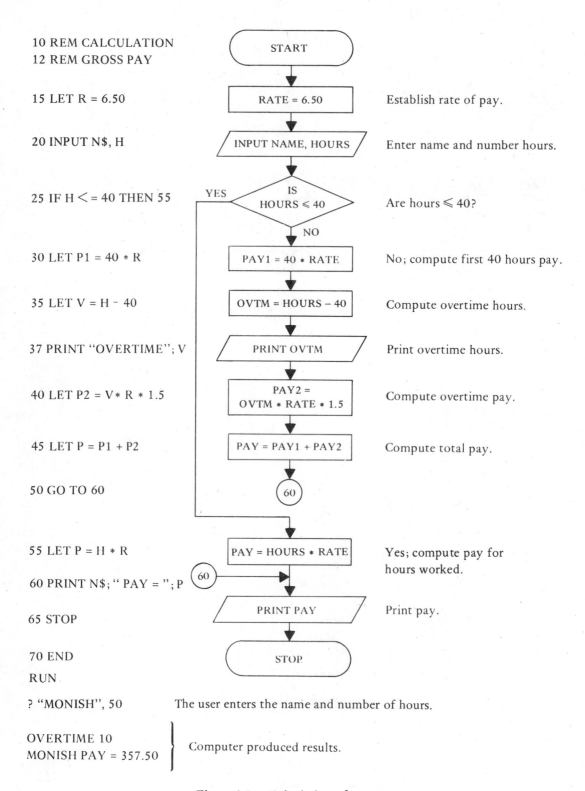

10 REM CALCULATION
12 REM GROSS PAY

15 LET R = 6.50      RATE = 6.50      Establish rate of pay.

20 INPUT N$, H      INPUT NAME, HOURS      Enter name and number hours.

25 IF H < = 40 THEN 55     YES     IS HOURS ≤ 40     Are hours ≤ 40?

NO

30 LET P1 = 40 * R      PAY1 = 40 * RATE      No; compute first 40 hours pay.

35 LET V = H - 40      OVTM = HOURS – 40      Compute overtime hours.

37 PRINT "OVERTIME"; V      PRINT OVTM      Print overtime hours.

40 LET P2 = V * R * 1.5      PAY2 = OVTM * RATE * 1.5      Compute overtime pay.

45 LET P = P1 + P2      PAY = PAY1 + PAY2      Compute total pay.

50 GO TO 60      60

55 LET P = H * R      PAY = HOURS * RATE      Yes; compute pay for hours worked.

60 PRINT N$; " PAY = "; P      60

     PRINT PAY      Print pay.

65 STOP

70 END
RUN

? "MONISH", 50      The user enters the name and number of hours.

OVERTIME 10
MONISH PAY = 357.50      Computer produced results.

**Figure 4-1**    Calculation of gross pay.

# 4-2    BASIC Statements

## 4-2-1    INPUT Statement

So far, the only way we have defined variables (assigned them a value) is by means of the replacement statement. For example, in the program of Section 4-1 we defined the rate as RATE = 6.50. The drawback to defining variables this way is that the program is written too specifically; it computes a pay only for a fixed rate of $6.50. If we wanted to use the same program for different values of RATE, we would have to reset RATE each time to different values.

Another way to assign any value to a variable is to use the INPUT statement. The general form of the INPUT statement is

*statement-number* INPUT *variable-list*

where *variable-list* is a list of variables separated by commas.

The INPUT statement allows the program to accept data during the execution of the program. When the program is in execution and the INPUT instruction is encountered, the BASIC system types a question mark (?) at the terminal. The user can always use some of the following methods to enter the desired list of values into the system:

1.  He can type a list of values corresponding in number and order to the items specified in the variable list of the INPUT statement. Each value must then be separated from one another by a comma. The list of variables is terminated by a carriage return. For example:

        10  PRINT "ENTER HOURS, RATE, AND BONUS IN THAT ORDER"
        15  INPUT H, R, B
        20  PRINT "TOTAL PAY =";H * R + B
        RUN
        ENTER HOURS, RATE, AND BONUS IN THAT ORDER
        ?  20, 5, 50  ◄──────────────── User supplied values.
        TOTAL PAY = 150 ◄──────────── Computer printout.

2.  The user types one value at a time, each value followed by a carriage return. The system then replies by a question mark (?) or other message as many times as needed to satisfy the variable list of the INPUT statement.

        5  INPUT X, Y, Z1
        7  PRINT X, Y, Z1
        8  END


        RUN

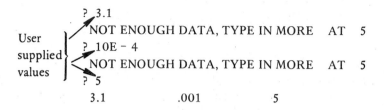

                3.1               .001            5

3.   On some systems, unlike the preceding example, BASIC will not ask you to type more data but will ask you to enter all data items on one line, as follows:

```
 5  INPUT H,R,B
10  PRINT "PAY"; H * R + B
99  END
RUN
? 20  ERROR AT 5—RETYPE
? 20,5,50        Three items separated by commas must be entered all together.
PAY 150
```

If more values are entered than there are variables in the INPUT statement, an error will occur and the user will need to retype the exact number of values.

When entering character strings (number of allowable characters in the string will vary among systems) via the INPUT statement, the strings should be entered with quotation marks.\* Commas must separate input data items.

```
10  PRINT "NAME, BIRTHDATE, AGE, ADDRESS"
15  INPUT N$, B$, A, L$
20  PRINT N$; " "; L$
25  PRINT A; B$
30  END
RUN
? "HORN", "11/07/41", 37, "18 N 17TH ST."
HORN  18 N 17TH ST.
37  11/07/41
```

In BASIC programs that contain numerous INPUT statements, it may become desirable to precede each INPUT statement in the program with a PRINT message reminding the user of the nature and order of the variables to be entered at execution time; otherwise the user may no longer recall what values are supposed to be entered and in what order when the system replies ? and requests a value(s). For example:

---

\*On some systems the user may enter literal data without any quotation marks.

```
10  PRINT "ENTER SOCIAL SECURITY, AGE, AND SEX (1 = M, 2 = F)"
20  INPUT S,A,S1
99  END
RUN
ENTER SOCIAL SECURITY, AGE, AND SEX (1 = M, 2 = F)
?  111222333, 36, 2
```

## 4-2-2    The Unconditional Transfer Statement GO TO

The general form of the GO TO statement is

*statement-number* GO TO *transfer-statement-number*

A BASIC program consists of a sequence of BASIC statements. BASIC will process these statements one after another in sequential order. When BASIC encounters a GO TO statement, it will transfer control to the statement specified, that is, processing will continue at the *transfer-statement-number*. This allows the programmer to bypass certain instructions in his program. It also allows the program to branch back to repeat (reprocess) certain instructions or certain procedures; this is called *looping*. (If in the program of Figure 4-1 we replaced statement 65 by the statement GO TO 20, BASIC would process the entire program more times with a new value for N$ and H each time.)

**Example 1**

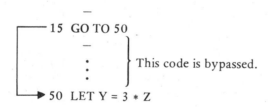

**Example 2**

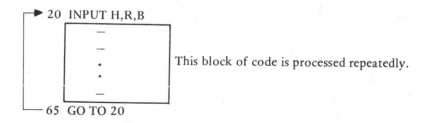

## 4-2-3    The Decision Statement IF/THEN

Recall that the central processing unit (CPU) has a unit to carry out logical operations. This hardware enables the computer to make comparisons and decisions based on the result of the comparison. The IF statement allows the computer to transfer to a nonsequential instruction in a program, depending on whether or not certain conditions are met. In this way, a program can contain several alternate paths that are data-dependent. Certain blocks of code may be bypassed as a result of transferring to a nonsequential instruction.

In Figure 4-1, if $H \leqslant 40$, the block of statements 30 through 50 are bypassed and processing resumes at 55. If H is not $\leqslant 40$, i.e., it is greater than 40, the next statement (30) is executed.

The general form of the IF statement is

$$\textit{statement-number} \text{ IF } \textit{relational-expression} \quad \begin{Bmatrix} \text{GO TO} \\ \text{THEN} \end{Bmatrix} \quad \textit{transfer-statement-number}$$

where the *relational-expression* consists of two arithmetic expressions or character string variables linked together by one of the relational operators shown in Figure 4-2. The reader may think of a relational-expression as a proposition, i.e., a statement that is either true or false. For example, the statements "P = 100" or "H $\leqslant$ 40" are either true or false. The *statement-number* is the statement transferred to if the *relational-expression* is true, that is, the condition specified in the decision statement is met. If the condition is not met (*relational-expression* is false), control is passed to the statement immediately following the IF statement. Note that character strings should not be compared to numeric expressions.

| RELATIONAL (COMMON) | OPERATORS (OCCASIONAL) | MATHEMATICAL SYMBOLS | MEANING |
|---|---|---|---|
| = | .EQ. | $=$ | Equal to |
| < | .LT. | $<$ | Less than |
| <= | .LE. | $\leqslant$ | Less than or equal to |
| > | .GT. | $>$ | Greater than |
| >= | .GE. | $\geqslant$ | Greater than or equal to |
| <> | .NE. | $\neq$ | Not equal to |

**Figure 4-2**     BASIC relational operators.

The IF statement can be flowcharted as follows:

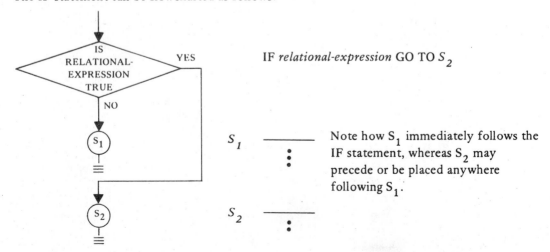

IF *relational-expression* GO TO $S_2$

$S_1$ _____
    ⋮

$S_2$ _____
    ⋮

Note how $S_1$ immediately follows the IF statement, whereas $S_2$ may precede or be placed anywhere following $S_1$.

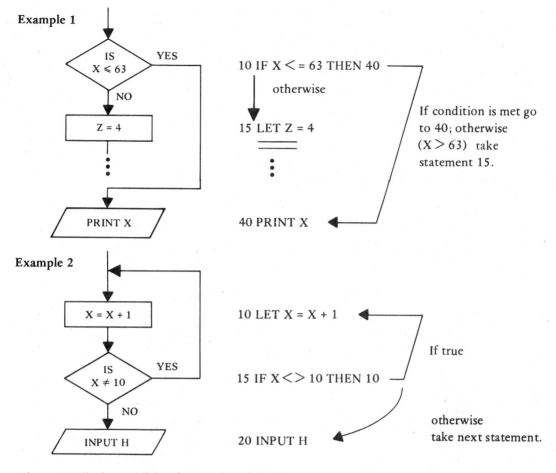

Figure 4-3 displays additional examples of decision statements.

a.   1 IF X = 0 THEN 5          If X = 0 transfer to statement 5; otherwise process the
     3 LET A = 4                next statement (3) (meaning X is not equal to 0).

b.   4 IF (X − Y)↑2 < Z THEN 40     If $(X − Y)^2 < Z$ process statement 40; otherwise
     8 IF Z > 2 THEN 60             $((X − Y)^2 \geqslant Z)$ fall through and execute statement 8.

c.   5 IF X ** .5 > = 2 THEN 50     If $\sqrt{X} \geqslant 2$, go to 50; if $\sqrt{X} < 2$, print X.
     7 PRINT X

d.   2 IF X + Y <> J − K THEN 70     If $X + Y \neq J − K$, go to 70; otherwise input A.
     6 INPUT A

e.   5 IF R$ = A$ THEN 30         If the two strings are equal, go to 30;
     7 LET R$ = "DOG"            otherwise store the characters DOG in R$.

f.   6 IF N$ = "YES" THEN 60       If the variable N$ contains the string "YES",
     7 PRINT N$                   transfer to 60; otherwise print N$.

To better understand the IF statement and its interaction with other BASIC statements, consider the following examples:

**Example 1**

Input a temperature $T$ and write a program to identify the temperature as follows:

> IF $T > 32$ Print the message "COOL TO HOT".
> IF $T = 32$ Print the message "FREEZING".
> IF $T < 32$ Print the message "BITING COLD".

The flowchart and program are shown in Figure 4-4. The reader is asked to carefully analyze the program in Figure 4-4 and understand why statements 40 and 70 are needed. If the temperature $T$ were 32 and both GO TO statements were omitted, the program would print the following messages in succession:

> FREEZING
> BITING COLD
> COOL TO HOT

Note, however, that there is no need for a statement GO TO 90 right after statement 80, since the STOP statement immediately follows.

    There are, of course, many other ways to code the program of Figure 4-4. An alternative is shown in Figure 4-5, which illustrates the placement of the STOP statement other than at the physical end of the program.

    Note again the position of the END statement as the very last statement in the program. The STOP, on the other hand, tells BASIC when to stop executing instructions at run time (after RUN has been typed). The STOP denotes the logical conclusion of the program.

**Example 2**

Enter three values and print largest value. (If all three are equal, print that one value.) The flowchart and program to solve this problem are shown in Figure 4-6.

    Note that in the case of statement 45 the IF statement transfers control directly to statement 35 whenever N1 < N3. This is perfectly legal, even though the beginning programmer may sometimes be tempted to code the following, which, though not incorrect, is awkward:

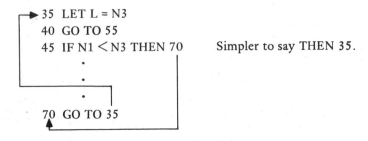

```
   35  LET L = N3
   40  GO TO 55
   45  IF N1 < N3 THEN 70          Simpler to say THEN 35.
               .
               .
               .
   70  GO TO 35
```

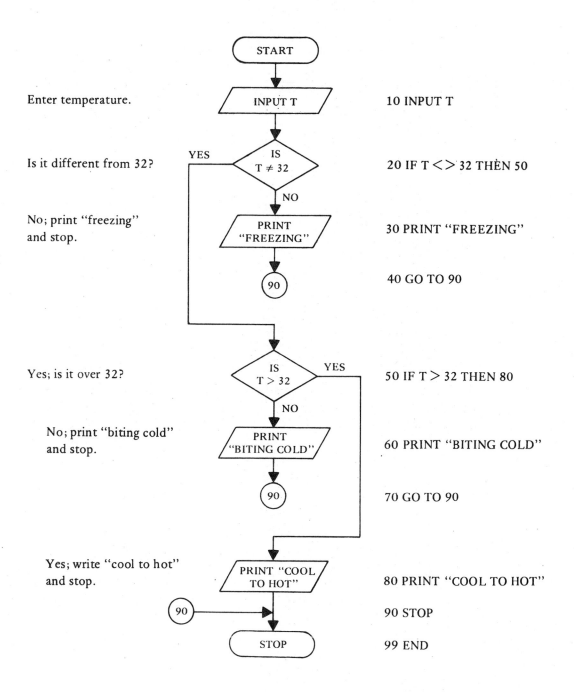

**Figure 4-4**    A three-way decision.

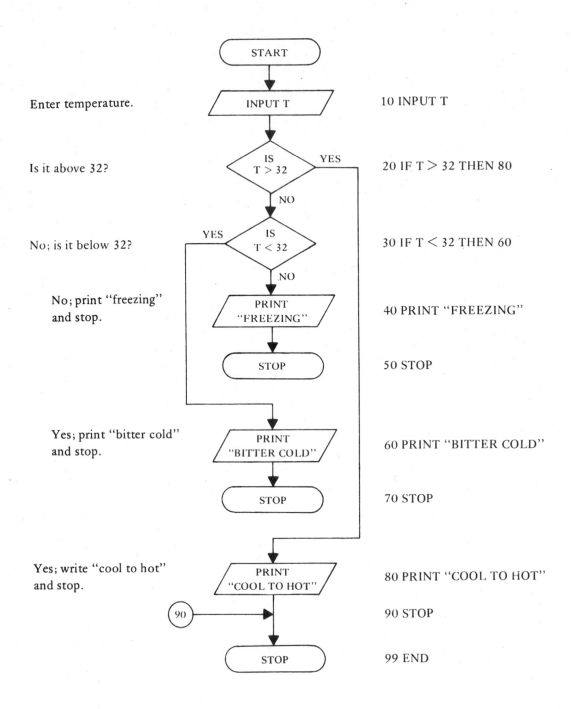

Enter temperature.                                    10 INPUT T

Is it above 32?                                       20 IF T > 32 THEN 80

No; is it below 32?                                   30 IF T < 32 THEN 60

No; print "freezing"                                  40 PRINT "FREEZING"
and stop.

                                                      50 STOP

Yes; print "bitter cold"                              60 PRINT "BITTER COLD"
and stop.

                                                      70 STOP

Yes; write "cool to hot"                              80 PRINT "COOL TO HOT"
and stop.

                                                      90 STOP

                                                      99 END

Figure 4-5    Various positions of the STOP statements.

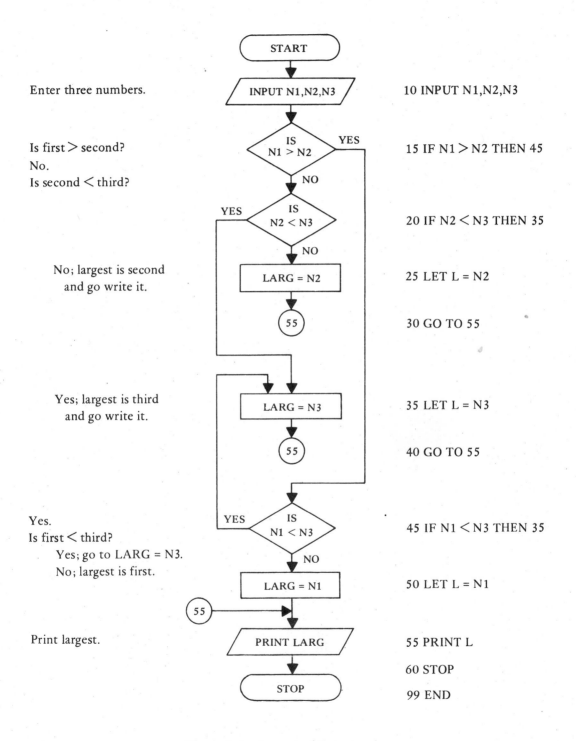

**Figure 4-6**    Largest of three numbers.

### 4-2-4   The REM Statement

The general form of the REM statement is

*statement-number* REM *literal-characters*

REM (remark) is a key word, and the *literal-characters* are supplied by the programmer. Although the REM statement requires a *statement-number*, it is not an executable statement. Hence, when a REM statement is encountered in the program, control passes automatically to the next executable statement. Figure 4-7 illustrates the use of the REM.

```
10 REM   SOMETIMES WHEN A PROGRAM IS LENGTHY THE PROGRAMMER MAY
20 REM   FIND IT HELPFUL TO EXPLAIN WITHIN THE PROGRAM THE PURPOSE OF
30 REM   ONE OR MORE BASIC STATEMENTS, THE USE OF A PARTICULAR
40 REM   VARIABLE OR THE FUNCTION OF SPECIFIC PROGRAM SEGMENTS. THE
50 REM   PRACTICE OF INTERSPERSING REM STATEMENTS THROUGHOUT THE
60 REM   PROGRAM CAN BE VERY HELPFUL WHEN THE PROGRAMMER AT A LATER
70 REM   DATE DECIDES TO REVIEW OR MAKE REVISIONS TO PARTS OF HIS
80 REM   PROGRAM. FOR ANOTHER USER WHO WISHES TO USE THE PROGRAM, REM
90 REM   STATEMENTS HELP UNDERSTAND THE OVERALL PROGRAM STRUCTURE.
99 END
```

**Figure 4-7**   REM statements.

# 4-3   You Might Want To Know

1.  What can I do to stop the system when my program is caught in a loop?

    *Example:*
    ```
    5  INPUT N
    10  PRINT N
    15  PRINT "OH AM I IN TROUBLE"
    20  GO TO 5
    ```

    *Answer:* In many systems, you can press the ESC (escape) key and then change the logic of your program. In some other systems, somewhat elaborate instructions are needed; therefore you should consult ahead of time with your computer center to determine the correct procedures.

2.  Suppose that while I am entering a value into the system as a result of an INPUT statement I key in a wrong value and I realize my error before pressing the RETURN key. What do I do?

    *Answer:* Press either the CTRL and X keys at same time to erase the entire line and retype the entire line or press CTRL and A keys to erase the character(s) desired and retype character(s) needed. Some systems will allow you to backspace over the mistyped characters.

3.  Suppose that while I am entering a numeric value into the system as a result of an INPUT statement I type an illegal value — for example, special characters or alphabetic data — and then press RETURN. What do I do?

    *Answer:* The system will detect an error and type "\?" or some other message. Consult your reference manual for more details.

    *Action:* The programmer then types in the corrected value and proceeds as usual.

```
05  INPUT N
10  PRINT N * N
15  END
RUN
?   I
    ILLEGAL INPUT, RETYPE INPUT AT 5
?   12
    144
```

    If an incorrect numerical value has been entered, there is no way to alter that value other than to RUN the program again!

4.  In this chapter, all IF statements in the flowcharts are illustrated with the YES branch extending horizontally and the NO branch vertically. Can I draw my flowcharts as follows?

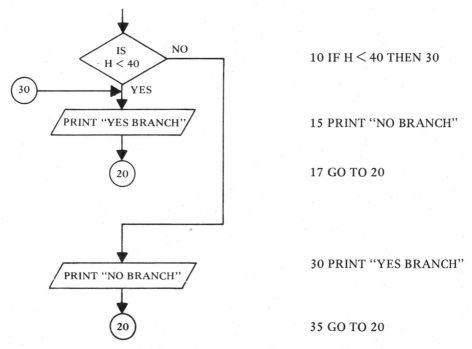

10 IF H < 40 THEN 30

15 PRINT "NO BRANCH"

17 GO TO 20

30 PRINT "YES BRANCH"

35 GO TO 20

    *Answer:* Certainly. For the beginning student, it may be easier to have the YES branch sticking out horizontally; otherwise there is no one-to-one match between the flowchart blocks and BASIC statements. In any event, many students may not wish to draw their flowcharts in vertical fashion as shown in this text but may wish to spread out all over right and left — and that's all right!

5.   Is the following the best way to code the given flowchart?

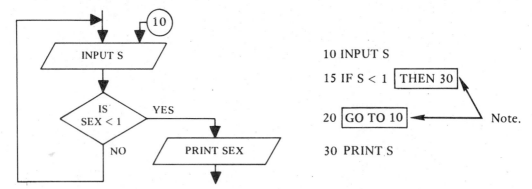

*Answer:* The code is correct; however, in most cases there is *no* need for a GO TO statement to follow the IF statement. The decision block could be rewritten more elegantly in this manner:

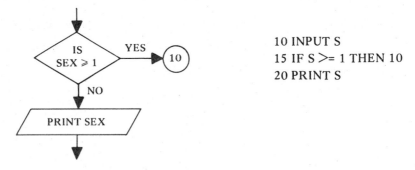

# 4-4   Programming Examples

### 4-4-1   Conversation between User and Terminal

The following coding segment illustrates a conversation between a third grader and a computer terminal. The computer is used as an adjunct teacher to test the student's general knowledge. For example, the following conversation might take place:

MY NAME IS JOE. WHAT IS YOUR NAME
?   "MICHAEL"
MICHAEL HOW OLD ARE YOU
?   8
WHAT IS 2*8 MICHAEL
?   15
SORRY. TRY AGAIN
?   16
GOOD. NAME FIRST AMERICAN PRESIDENT
?   "WASHINGTON"
VERY GOOD MICHAEL. THAT WILL BE ALL

The program to generate the above dialogue is shown in Figure 4-8.

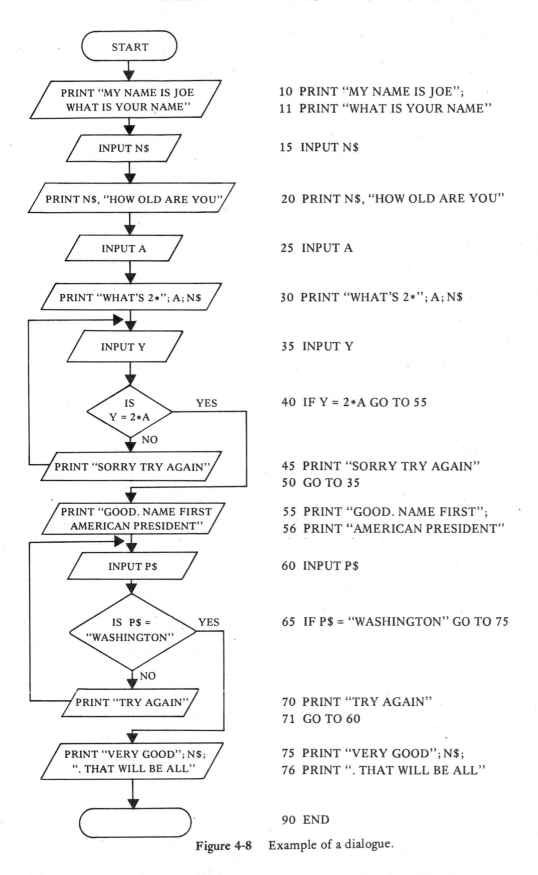

| Flowchart | BASIC code |
|---|---|
| START | |
| PRINT "MY NAME IS JOE WHAT IS YOUR NAME" | 10 PRINT "MY NAME IS JOE";<br>11 PRINT "WHAT IS YOUR NAME" |
| INPUT N$ | 15 INPUT N$ |
| PRINT N$, "HOW OLD ARE YOU" | 20 PRINT N$, "HOW OLD ARE YOU" |
| INPUT A | 25 INPUT A |
| PRINT "WHAT'S 2*"; A; N$ | 30 PRINT "WHAT'S 2*"; A; N$ |
| INPUT Y | 35 INPUT Y |
| IS Y = 2*A    YES | 40 IF Y = 2*A GO TO 55 |
| NO | |
| PRINT "SORRY TRY AGAIN" | 45 PRINT "SORRY TRY AGAIN"<br>50 GO TO 35 |
| PRINT "GOOD. NAME FIRST AMERICAN PRESIDENT" | 55 PRINT "GOOD. NAME FIRST";<br>56 PRINT "AMERICAN PRESIDENT" |
| INPUT P$ | 60 INPUT P$ |
| IS P$ = "WASHINGTON"   YES | 65 IF P$ = "WASHINGTON" GO TO 75 |
| NO | |
| PRINT "TRY AGAIN" | 70 PRINT "TRY AGAIN"<br>71 GO TO 60 |
| PRINT "VERY GOOD"; N$; ". THAT WILL BE ALL" | 75 PRINT "VERY GOOD"; N$;<br>76 PRINT ". THAT WILL BE ALL" |
| | 90 END |

**Figure 4-8**   Example of a dialogue.

### 4-4-2    Solution of a Quadratic Equation

Let us write a program to determine the roots of the quadratic equation $ax^2 + bx + c = 0$. The three constants $a$, $b$, and $c$ are entered at execution.

If there are no real roots, print the message "NO REAL ROOTS".

If the roots are equal, print the message "EQUAL ROOTS = XX".

If the roots are unequal, print the message "ROOT1 = XX    ROOT2 = XX".

Recall that the formula to compute the roots of a quadratic equation is:

$$x_1 = \frac{-b + \sqrt{b^2 - 4ac}}{2a} \qquad \text{and} \qquad x_2 = \frac{-b - \sqrt{b^2 - 4ac}}{2a}$$

If $b^2 - 4ac < 0$,  roots are imaginary.

If $b^2 - 4ac = 0$,  roots are equal.

A program to solve this problem is shown in Figure 4-9.

### 4-4-3    FHA Mortgage Insurance

The Federal Housing Authority (FHA) insures home mortgages up to $45,000. The down payment schedule is as follows:

3% of the amount up to $25,000
10% of the next $10,000
20% of the remainder

Input a mortgage amount and compute the down payment required. Reject any application over $45,000. A flowchart and program is shown in Figure 4-10.

# 4-5    Features

### 4-5-1    The TAB Function

The general form of the TAB function is

TAB (*expression*)

where *expression* is evaluated to an integer value that tells the terminal where the next character is to be printed on the output line.

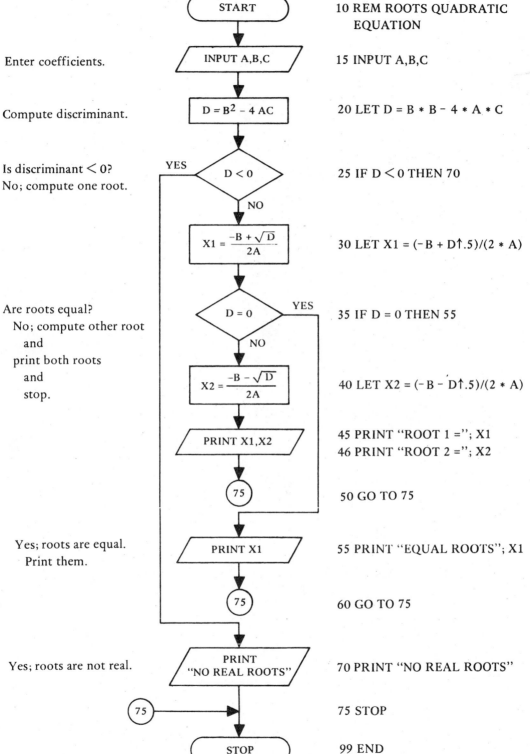

Enter coefficients.

Compute discriminant.

Is discriminant $< 0$?
No; compute one root.

Are roots equal?
  No; compute other root
    and
  print both roots
    and
     stop.

Yes; roots are equal.
  Print them.

Yes; roots are not real.

10 REM ROOTS QUADRATIC
    EQUATION

15 INPUT A,B,C

20 LET D = B * B - 4 * A * C

25 IF D $<$ 0 THEN 70

30 LET X1 = (- B + D↑.5)/(2 * A)

35 IF D = 0 THEN 55

40 LET X2 = (- B - D↑.5)/(2 * A)

45 PRINT "ROOT 1 ="; X1
46 PRINT "ROOT 2 ="; X2

50 GO TO 75

55 PRINT "EQUAL ROOTS"; X1

60 GO TO 75

70 PRINT "NO REAL ROOTS"

75 STOP

99 END

**Figure 4-9**   Solution of a quadratic equation.

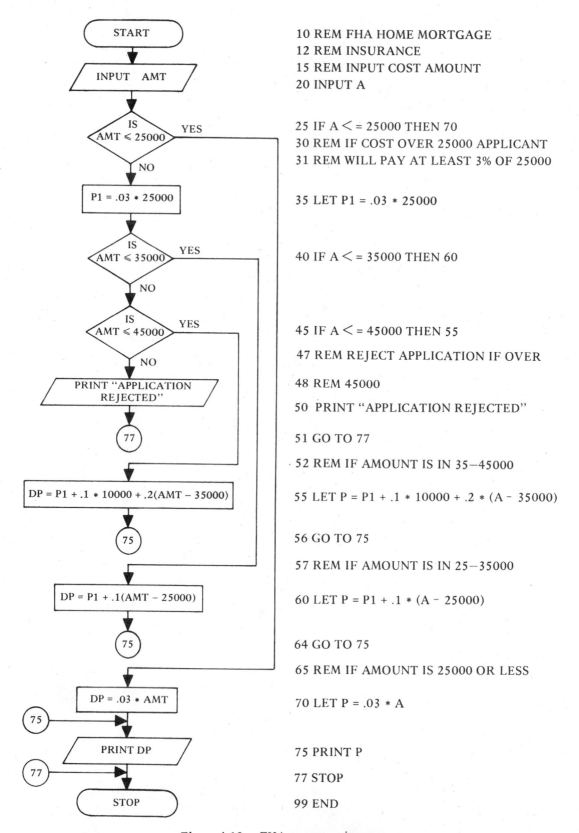

10 REM FHA HOME MORTGAGE
12 REM INSURANCE
15 REM INPUT COST AMOUNT
20 INPUT A

25 IF A < = 25000 THEN 70
30 REM IF COST OVER 25000 APPLICANT
31 REM WILL PAY AT LEAST 3% OF 25000

35 LET P1 = .03 * 25000

40 IF A < = 35000 THEN 60

45 IF A < = 45000 THEN 55
47 REM REJECT APPLICATION IF OVER
48 REM 45000
50 PRINT "APPLICATION REJECTED"
51 GO TO 77
52 REM IF AMOUNT IS IN 35−45000
55 LET P = P1 + .1 * 10000 + .2 * (A − 35000)
56 GO TO 75
57 REM IF AMOUNT IS IN 25−35000
60 LET P = P1 + .1 * (A − 25000)
64 GO TO 75
65 REM IF AMOUNT IS 25000 OR LESS
70 LET P = .03 * A
75 PRINT P
77 STOP
99 END

**Figure 4-10**   FHA mortgage insurance.

One problem with output in BASIC is that the comma and the semicolon, due to their predefined numeric fields, may be unsatisfactory in creating an attractive printout.

The TAB function is a BASIC language formatting feature, available in many versions of BASIC, which allows more exact spacing of print fields. For example, in the following illustration

10 PRINT A$; TAB (15); "COST"

the value assigned to the string variable (field) A$ will be printed; the terminal will then space to the print position specified within the set of parentheses immediately following the key word TAB (print position 15) and print the word COST. The number within the parentheses is the number of the column in which the first letter of the string COST will be printed.

In this illustration, the variable A$ is followed by a semicolon. If it had been followed by a comma, the terminal would have spaced to the next zone before detecting the TAB(15) request. The TAB function is ignored when the terminal has passed the specified print position. Therefore, it is best to use the semicolon rather than the comma in those PRINT statements where the TAB function is used.

The TAB function can be put to great advantage to "dress up" an output as shown in Figure 4-11.

```
10    PRINT"00000000011111111112222222222233333333";
20    PRINT"334444444444555555555566666666666777777"
30    PRINT"12345678901234567890123456789012334567";
40    PRINT"89012345678901234567890123456789012345"
45    PRINT
50    PRINT TAB(23);"COMMUNITY TELEVISIONS"
60    PRINT TAB(27);"BALANCE SHEET"
65    PRINT TAB(27);"AUGUST 31,1979"
75    PRINT TAB(15);"ASSETS";TAB(47);"LIABILITIES AND EQUITY"
99    END

RUN

00000000011111111112222222222233333333334444444444555555555566666666666777777
12345678901234567890123456789012345678901234567890123456789012345678901234545

                      COMMUNITY TELEVISIONS
                         BALANCE SHEET
                         AUGUST 31,1979
            ASSETS                        LIABILITIES AND EQUITY
```

**Figure 4-11**    Output using the TAB function.

## 4-5-2    ON/GO TO Statement

The ON/GO TO feature may not be a BASIC standard feature. See if your system supports it. It is a useful and convenient statement that allows transfer to many different points in a program. In essence, it is a multiple IF statement. The general form of the statement is

*statement-no.* ON *expression* GO TO *statement-no.-1, statement-no.-2, . . . statement-no.-n*

where the *expression* will be evaluated to an integer value and *statement-no.-1*, etc., are statement numbers defined in the program. The mechanics of the ON/GO TO is as follows:

>   If the value of the *expression* is 1, control is transferred to *statement-no.-1*
>   If the value of the *expression* is 2, control is transferred to *statement-no.-2*
>
>                         .
>                         .
>                         .
>
>   If the value of the *expression* is *n*, control is transferred to *statement-no.-n*

**Examples**

| | |
|---|---|
| 20  ON N GO TO 3,57,100,4 | If N = 3 control is transferred to 100. |
| 15  ON J – 2 * K GO TO 30,10 | If J – 2 * K = 1, go to statement 30. |
| | If J – 2 * K = 2, go to statement 10. |
| 30  ON Y↑I GO TO 10,20,60 | If Y↑I = 1,2,3 go to 10,20, and 60, respectively. |

It should be noted that if the expression does not evaluate to an integer, it is truncated to the lower integer value. Also if the expression evaluates to an integer that is greater than the number of statements present in the list of statements or evaluates to an integer that is zero or negative, the ON statement is ignored and control is passed to the next statement.

A complete program may help the reader better understand how to use the ON/GO TO.

**Problem**

Input a college classification code and print its equivalent as a word. The meanings of the codes are as follows:

| CLASS CODE | INTERPRETATION |
|:---:|:---:|
| 1 | Freshman |
| 2 | Sophomore |
| 3 | Junior |
| 4 | Senior |

The program to solve this problem is shown in Figure 4-12.

```
10 REM INPUT NUMERIC CLASS CODE
15 INPUT K
20 ON K GO TO 45,55,65,75
25 REM IF K IS NEITHER 1,2,3, OR 4 PRINT ERROR MESSAGE
30 PRINT "INVALID CODE, RETYPE"
35 REM ASK USER TO REENTER CODE
40 GO TO 15
45 PRINT "FRESHMAN"
50 GO TO 80
55 PRINT "SOPHOMORE"
60 GO TO 80
65 PRINT "JUNIOR"
70 GO TO 80
75 PRINT "SENIOR"
80 STOP
99 END
```

**Figure 4-12**    Use of the ON/GO TO statement.

# 4-6    Assignments

## 4-6-1    Self Test

In the decision symbol

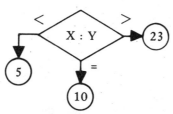

the colon is to be interpreted as "compared to." The decision symbol means if $x < y$ go to 5; if $x = y$ go to 10; if $x > y$ go to 23. In BASIC, such a symbol must be broken down into two IF statements.

1.    Write the BASIC IF statements for each of the following cases:

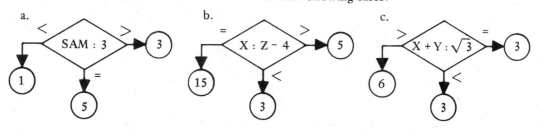

2. Write the BASIC code for the following flowcharts:

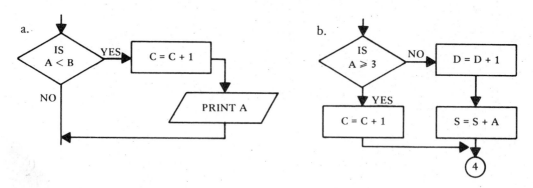

3. Write flowcharts and BASIC statements for each of the following:

a. If B is larger than or equal to 60, increase C by 1, then go to statement 1; otherwise go directly to statement 1.

b. If X is larger than M, assign this value to M; otherwise continue.

c. If H is greater than 40, compute the wage as 1.5*H*R;
   if H is equal to 40, compute wage as 1.02*H*R;
   if H is less than 40, compute wage as H*R.

d. If X is greater than 0 but less than 3*A, go to 7.

e. If both A and B lie between 1 and 8 inclusive, go to 8; otherwise go to 4.

f. If X exceeds 4 while Y is less than 5, or if X is less than 5 while Y is greater than 4, go to 10; otherwise stop.

## 4-6-2 Exercises

1. Final grades in a course are determined by adding scores obtained on three tests T1, T2, and T3. Students get a PASS grade if the sum of the three scores is above 186 and a FAIL otherwise. Write a program to enter three scores, and determine the grade. Print the input scores, the average, and the final letter grade.

2. Enter a name, a rate of pay, and a number of hours worked, and write a program to produce the following output:

> NAME
> OVERTIME HOURS IS XXX
> OVERTIME PAY IS XXX
> TOTAL PAY IS XXX

If the number of hours is less than 40, the two overtime entries in the output should not be included.

3.  Write a program to enter two numbers and print the larger of the two. Can you do this with only one PRINT statement?

4.  Change the program of Figure 4-6 to print a message if all three numbers are equal.

5.  An income tax agent is checking wage earners in the income bracket $20,000 to $30,000. Enter federal taxes paid and gross earnings. If taxes paid are below 27.5 percent of gross earnings, compute amount due and print a stern message to the wage earner specifying the amount due. (Taxes are 27.5 percent of gross earnings in the interval $20,000 to $30,000.) If the amount due is over $5,000, add on a penalty charge of 1.5 percent of amount due. Reject entries with income outside the range $20,000–$30,000.

6.  A salesman receives a commission of 10 percent on all sales if he has sold at least $10,000 worth of merchandise in a pay period, but only 8.5 percent if his sales are below $10,000. Write a program to input an amount of sales, compute the commission, and print the commission earned.

7.  A salesman is assigned a commission on the following basis:

| SALE | COMMISSION |
|------|------------|
| $ 00–$500 | 1% |
| $500–$5000 | 5% |
| over $5000 | 8% |

Write a program to enter an amount of sales and calculate the commission.

8.  Enter an amount in cents between 0 and 100. Write a program to break down the amount read into the least number of quarters, nickels, and pennies as is possible, for example, 76 cents = 3 quarters and 1 penny.

9.  The metric system is upon us! Some simple approximation rules for metric conversions are listed as follows:

   a.  Fahrenheit to centigrade: Take half and subtract 15.

   b.  Inches to centimeters: Double and add half (40 inches − 2 · 40 + 20 = 100 cms).

   c.  Miles to kilometers: Add 60 percent (100 miles − 100 + 60% of 100 = 160 kms).

   d.  Pounds to kilograms: Take half and then some (60 lbs − 60/2 = 30 − 10% of 30 = 27 kgs).

   Write a program to enter a Fahrenheit temperature, a number of inches, a number of miles, and a number of pounds, and convert to corresponding metric measures. Identify all results with appropriate headers. Then go from metric to Fahrenheit, inches, etc.

10. A store owner can buy speckled bangles (bracelets) at a base price of $30.00 a piece. If he purchases the bangles with blue speckles, $1 is added to the price of the bangles. If he purchases the bangles with green speckles, $2 is added to the base price. Write a program to accept from the terminal the number of bangles ordered, the base price, the price for blue speckles, and the price for green speckles. Print with appropriate headings: the number ordered, the total base price, the total price if ordered with blue speckles, and the total price if ordered with green speckles.

11.  The store owner has a 40 percent markup. Modify program 10 to compute and print with appropriate headings the sales price of the various types of bangles, the gross profit made from the sale of one of each type, and the unit cost of each type.

12.  Input a grade $N$ between 0 and 99 and write a program using the ON/GO TO statement to print out appropriate letter grade defined by the following table:

| GRADES | LETTER GRADE |
|---|---|
| 0–49 | F |
| 50–59 | D |
| 60–79 | C |
| 80–89 | B |
| 90–99 | A |

(*Hint:* For the expression in the ON/GO TO make use of $N/10$.)

13.  The Wastenot Utility Company charges customers for electricity according to the following scale:

| KILOWATT-HOURS (KWH) | COST |
|---|---|
| 0–300 | $ 5.00 |
| 301–1000 | 5.00 + .03 for each kwh above 300 |
| 1001– and over | 35.00 + .02 for each kwh above 1000 |

Write a program to accept as input the old and the new meter readings and calculate the amount of the customer's bill.

14.  Consider the polynomial $P(x) = x^2 - 1.596x + .266$ which has a root between 1.3 and 1.4. Find by trial and error an approximation $r$ to that root such that $|P(r)| < .001$. (Recall that a root $s$ of $P(x)$ is such that $P(s) = 0$.)

15.  Write a program to compute and print the absolute value of $x$ to be entered via an INPUT statement. Recall that $|x| = x$ if $x \geqslant 0$ and $|x| = -x$ if $x < 0$.

16.  Input three values and determine if they represent the three sides of a right triangle.

17.  Write a program to compute the area of a triangle given three sides a, b, and c using the formula:

$$\text{area} = \sqrt{s(s-a)(s-b)(s-c)}$$

where $s = \dfrac{a + b + c}{2}$

(*Caution:* Not all possible values of a, b, and c represent a triangle. How could your program detect such values?)

## 4-6-3   Projects

1.

XYZ CORPORATION
Balance Sheet
April 30, 1976

| *Assets* | | *Liabilities and Stockholders' Equity* | |
|---|---|---|---|
| Cash | $ 3,500 | Liabilities: | |
| Accounts receivable | 500 | Accounts payable | $ 3,000 |
| Supplies | 100 | | |
| Land | 2,000 | Stockholders' equity: | |
| Buildings | 10,000 | Capital stock | 18,100 |
| Machines and equipment | 3,000 | | |
| Patents | 2,000 | Total Liabilities and | ——— |
| Total Assets | $21,100 | Stockholders' Equity | $21,100 |

a.  Write a program to duplicate this balance sheet. Define each asset and liability by a variable name as in LET C = 3500 (for cash = $3,500). Variables for the various entries should appear in the PRINT statements. Do not print commas or dollar signs.

b.  Write a program to generate a balance sheet as described previously for the Triple Star Corporation for the month of September 1976, given the following data:

| | | | |
|---|---|---|---|
| Cash | = $3,200 | Accounts receivable = $1,300 | |
| Capital stock | = $5,000 | Repair supplies | = $ 700 |
| Accounts payable = $2,500 | | Land | = ? |

Use variable names to define these entries and let the computer determine the value of the land in such a way that Total Assets = Liabilities + Stockholders' Equity.

2.  Write a program to print a balance sheet as shown in Project 1 for each of the following three companies for the month of May 1979. The data read for each company should be entered at execution time using the INPUT statement. Use the following tables for data:

| | Company 1 | Company 2 | Company 3 |
|---|---|---|---|
| Cash | $ 3,900 | $ 2,069 | $ 6,642 |
| Accounts receivable | — | 500 | 517 |
| Supplies | 600 | 3,530 | 801 |
| Land | 3,000 | 1,000 | 1,300 |
| Buildings | — | 2,400 | 8,500 |
| Machines and equipment | — | — | 9,948 |
| Patents | — | 110 | 1,500 |
| Accounts payable | 2,800 | 470 | 4,106 |
| Capital stock | 7,500 | 9,127 | 25,000 |

Three balance sheets should be printed with respective headings: Company 1, Company 2, and Company 3. In case assets do not equal liabilities plus equities, print a message stating that the balance sheet for that company is incorrect.

3.  Salaries at the XYZ Corporation are based on job classification, years of service, education, and merit rating. The base pay for all employees is the same; percentage of the base pay is added according to the following schedule:

| JOB CLASSIFICATION | PERCENTAGE OF BASE PAY | EDUCATION | PERCENTAGE OF BASE PAY |
|---|---|---|---|
| 1 | 0 | 1 (high school) | 0 |
| 2 | 5 | 2 (junior college) | 10 |
| 3 | 15 | 3 (college) | 25 |
| 4 | 25 | 4 (graduate degree) | 50 |
| 5 | 50 | 5 (special training) | 15 |

| MERIT RATING | PERCENTAGE OF BASE PAY | YEARS OF SERVICE | PERCENTAGE OF BASE PAY |
|---|---|---|---|
| 0 (poor) | 0 | 0–10 years | 5 |
| 1 (good) | 10 | each additional year | 4 |
| 2 (excellent) | 25 | | |

Write a program to accept numerical codes for each of the four variables and calculate the employee's salary as a percentage of a base pay.

4.  Write a program to make daily weather reports. Each input record should contain nine integer values giving the following information: current month, day, and year; high temperature for the day, low temperature for the day; year in which the record high for this day was set, record high temperature; year of record low, record low temperature. After entering an input record, print a message of one of the following three types, depending on the data:

|   |   |   |   |
|---|---|---|---|
| 1. | 10/23/76 | HIGH TODAY | 52 |
| | | LOW TODAY | 23 |
| | | | |
| 2. | 10/24/76 | HIGH TODAY | 71* |
| | | LOW TODAY | 38 |

*(BEATS RECORD OF 70 SET IN 1906)

|   |   |   |   |
|---|---|---|---|
| 3. | 10/25/76 | HIGH TODAY | 73* |
| | | LOW TODAY | −10** |

*(BEATS RECORD OF 68 SET IN 1938)
**(BEATS RECORD OF −8 SET IN 1918)

Stop reading data cards when you come to one whose month number is zero.

5. Write the BASIC code to simulate a conversation between a physician and yourself. The physician should introduce himself to you and ask your name, age, and problems that you might have had lately. You should respond to these questions and possibly also ask him some questions.

## Games

The statement LET I = INT(RND(1) * 10) will generate a random integer number between 0 and 9; i.e., as a result of executing that statement, the value of I will be a random number (whole number) between 0 and 9.

6. Write a program to play a guessing game with the computer, as follows:

   a. The computer thinks of a number between 0 and 9, and you have to guess his number by entering your guess at the terminal. If you guess it, the computer should print a complimentary remark and ask you whether you desire to play another game; if not, you must continue guessing.

   b. To help you guess the number more quickly, the computer should print either of the following messages: "GUESS HIGHER" or "GUESS LOWER" depending on whether your guess was high or low.

   c. Reverse the roles. You think of a number and the compute must guess your number. Play both games ten times. Why are you winning over the long run?

7. Simulate a dice game. The computer throws two dice for itself and then throws two for you. The one who wins is the one who throws the first pair. A congratulatory message should be addressed to the winner. To simulate one throw of dice use the statement LET K = INT(RND(1) * 6) + 1. Change variable name (K) to simulate other throws.

8. The square root of a number A can be computed by successive approximations using the iterative formula $x_{n+1} = \frac{1}{2} (x_n + A/x_n)$. This formula can be expressed in BASIC as X = .5*(X + A/X). Starting with an initial approximation X = 1, a new approximation X to the square root of A is computed using the above formula. This new approximation, in turn, can be substituted in the above formula to compute a newer approximation X. This process can be continued until the square of the new approximation X is close to A within a prescribed degree of accuracy $\epsilon$ (where $\epsilon$ = .1, .01, .001, etc. depending on the accuracy needed); that is,

$$|X - A| < \epsilon.$$

Write a program to read A and E ($\epsilon$) to compute $\sqrt{A}$. Write an error message if A < 0.

9.    Systems of equations can be solved by iterative techniques. For example, the system

$$\begin{cases} 2x + y = 3 \\ x - 3y = 2 \end{cases}$$

can be solved by solving for $x$ in terms of $y$
in the first equation and for $y$ in terms of $x$
in the second equation to obtain:

$$\begin{cases} x = (3 - y)/2 \\ y = (x - 2)/3 \end{cases}$$

Starting with an initial approximate solution XOLD = YOLD = 1, we refine this approximation by computing XNEW and YNEW as follows:

$$\begin{cases} \text{XNEW} = (3 - \text{YOLD})/2 \\ \text{YNEW} = (\text{XOLD} - 2)/3 \end{cases}$$

This procedure is repeated by letting the old approximations become the new approximations (XOLD = XNEW and YOLD = YNEW) and computing new values for XNEW and YNEW in terms of XOLD and YOLD. The process can be terminated by substituting XNEW and YNEW in the original equation and verifying that:

$$\begin{array}{ccc} 2\text{XNEW} + \text{YNEW} \simeq 3 & 2\text{XNEW} + \text{YNEW} - 3 \simeq 0 & |2\text{XNEW} + \text{YNEW} - 3| < \epsilon \\ \text{XNEW} - 3\text{YNEW} \simeq 2 & \text{XNEW} - 3\text{YNEW} - 2 \simeq 0 & |\text{XNEW} - 3\text{YNEW} - 2| < \epsilon \end{array}$$

or                            or

where $\epsilon$ is a prescribed degree of accuracy ($\epsilon$ = .01, .0001, etc.).

Write a program to solve the following system of equations using the above iterative technique:

$$\begin{array}{l} 2.56x - .034y = -.56 \\ 3.14x + 1.32y = 50.76 \end{array} \quad \text{and set } \epsilon = .01$$

## 4-6-4  Answers to Self Test

1.    a.  IF S < 3 THEN 1
          IF S > 3 THEN 3
          GO TO 5

      b.  IF X = Z − 4 THEN 15
          IF X > Z − 4 THEN 3
          GO TO 5

      c.  IF X + Y > SQR(3) THEN 6
          IF X + Y = SQR(3) THEN 1
          GO TO 3

2.  a.  10  IF A $>$ = B THEN 40
    20  LET C = C + 1
    30  PRINT A
    40  · · ·

b.  10  IF A $<$ 3 THEN 40
    20  LET D = D + 1
    30  LET S = S + A
    35  GO TO 4
    40  LET C = C + 1
    45  GO TO 4

3.  a.

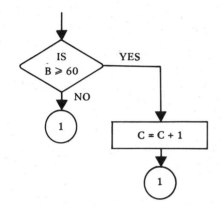

10  IF B $<$ 60 THEN 1
20  LET C = C + 1
30  GO TO 1

b.

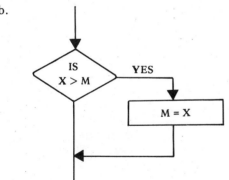

10  IF X $<$ = M THEN 30
20  LET M = X
30  · · ·

c.

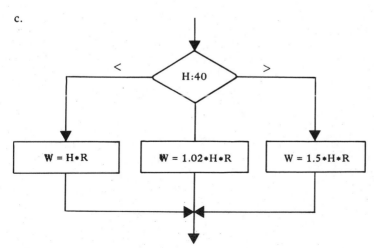

10  IF H $<$ 40 THEN 50
20  IF H $>$ 40 THEN 70
30  LET W = 1.02*H*R
40  GO TO 80
50  LET W = H*R
60  GO TO 80
70  LET W = 1.5*H*R
80  · · ·

d.

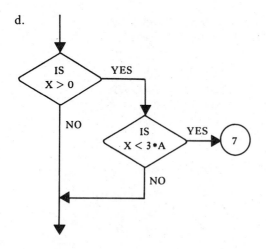

10   IF X > 0 THEN 30
20   GO TO 40
30   IF X < 3∗A THEN 7
40   • • •

e.

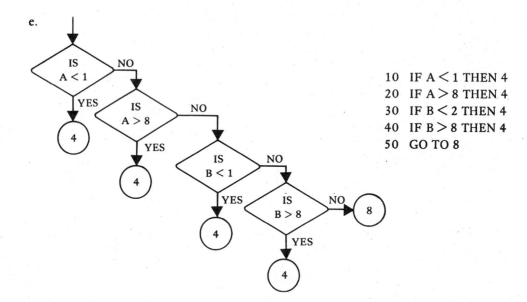

10   IF A < 1 THEN 4
20   IF A > 8 THEN 4
30   IF B < 2 THEN 4
40   IF B > 8 THEN 4
50   GO TO 8

f.

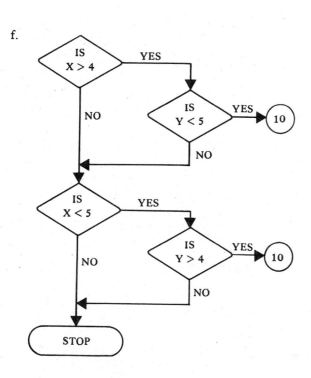

```
10  IF X > 4 THEN 40
20  IF X < 5 THEN 60
30  STOP
40  IF Y < 5 THEN 10
50  GO TO 20
60  IF Y > 4 THEN 10
70  GO TO 30 .
```

# THE COUNTING PROCESS
# AND BASIC STATEMENTS
# READ/DATA, RESTORE,
# PRINT USING

## 5-1   Problem Example

A poll was conducted in a political science class to determine student feelings about isolationism. The code used to record students' opinions was as follows:

| CODE | MEANING |
|------|---------|
| 2 | For isolationism |
| 1 | Neutral |
| 0 | Against isolationism |

All responses were gathered (e.g., 0, 1, 1, 0, 2, 0, 0, 1, 2, 2, 0, 0, 0, 1, 2, 9) with the special code 9 as the last data item to indicate the physical end of the results. Write a program to determine the number of students in favor of isolationism. A program to solve the problem is shown in Figure 5-1.

Note the two new types of BASIC statements introduced in the program shown in Figure 5-1:

1.   The READ statement.

2.   The DATA statement, which is always used in conjunction with a READ statement.

This chapter also introduces a new programming concept, *counting*, which is of great importance in writing programs.

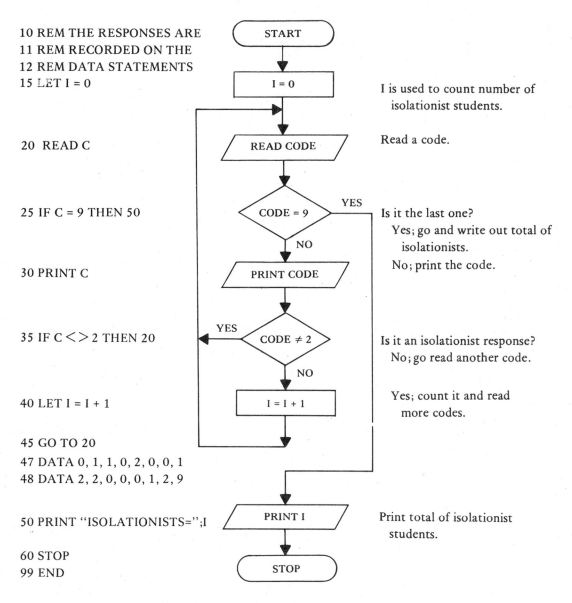

```
10 REM THE RESPONSES ARE
11 REM RECORDED ON THE
12 REM DATA STATEMENTS
15 LET I = 0
```
I is used to count number of
  isolationist students.

```
20  READ C
```
Read a code.

```
25 IF C = 9 THEN 50
```
Is it the last one?
  Yes; go and write out total of
    isolationists.
  No; print the code.

```
30 PRINT C
```

```
35 IF C < > 2 THEN 20
```
Is it an isolationist response?
  No; go read another code.

```
40 LET I = I + 1
```
Yes; count it and read
  more codes.

```
45 GO TO 20
47 DATA 0, 1, 1, 0, 2, 0, 0, 1
48 DATA 2, 2, 0, 0, 0, 1, 2, 9
```

```
50 PRINT "ISOLATIONISTS=";I
```
Print total of isolationist
  students.

```
60 STOP
99 END
```

**Figure 5-1**    Counting and end-of-file checking.

# 5-2    BASIC Statements

## 5-2-1    DATA Statement

The general form of the DATA statement is

$$statement\text{-}number \text{ DATA } constant\text{-}list$$

where DATA is a key word. The *constant-list* consists of numeric constants, or character type
data enclosed in quotes (''). Items in the list must be separated by commas.

DATA is a nonexecutable statement, unlike all other BASIC statements — except REM — encountered so far. It is not translated into a machine-language instruction and thus is never executed. DATA statements may be placed anywhere in the program (before the END statement).

The DATA statement informs the BASIC system that the numbers specified in its constant-list are to be stored in memory until the user decides to process these numbers during program execution. BASIC collects all numbers or string literals specified in all the DATA constant-lists of the program and stores them in a memory area (a DATA block) in the order in which the DATA statements were encountered in the program. For example, the DATA statements in examples 1, 3, and 3 of Figure 5-2 all produce the same memory arrangement or DATA block. The values in the DATA block can be retrieved only by the READ statement.

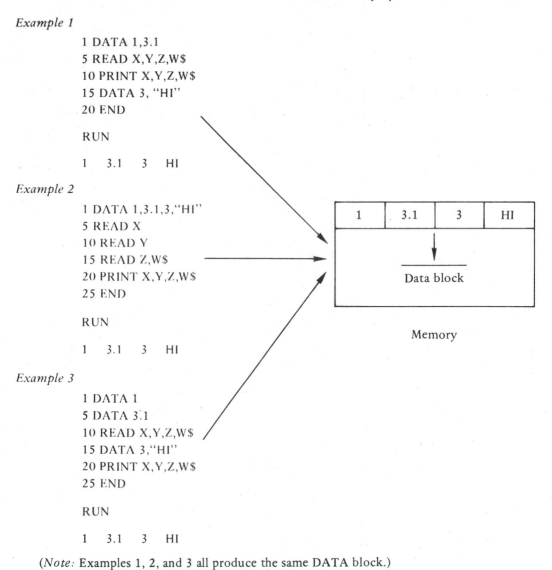

*Example 1*

```
1 DATA 1,3.1
5 READ X,Y,Z,W$
10 PRINT X,Y,Z,W$
15 DATA 3, "HI"
20 END

RUN

1    3.1    3    HI
```

*Example 2*

```
1 DATA 1,3.1,3,"HI"
5 READ X
10 READ Y
15 READ Z,W$
20 PRINT X,Y,Z,W$
25 END

RUN

1    3.1    3    HI
```

*Example 3*

```
1 DATA 1
5 DATA 3.1
10 READ X,Y,Z,W$
15 DATA 3,"HI"
20 PRINT X,Y,Z,W$
25 END

RUN

1    3.1    3    HI
```

| 1 | 3.1 | 3 | HI |

Data block

Memory

(*Note:* Examples 1, 2, and 3 all produce the same DATA block.)

**Figure 5-2**    Examples of use of READ/DATA.

## 5-2-2   READ Statement

The general form of the READ statement is

*statement-number* READ *variable-list*

where READ is a key word. The *variable-list* consists of variables separated from one another by commas.

The READ statement causes as many values to be fetched from the DATA block as there are variables in the READ list. The assignment of values to variables is made in the order in which variables appear in the READ list. Consider the following example and note assignments of values to variables:

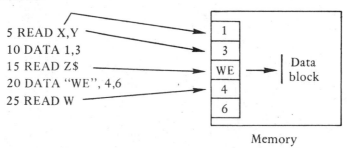

Memory

In examples 1, 2, and 3 of Figure 5-2, the values read for X, Y, Z, and W$ are respectively 1, 3.1, 3, and HI. Note that all three programs produce the same output.

## 5-2-3   Counting

Counting is an essential technique in programming. Counting may be used to read a specified number of data items from a DATA list, to repeat a certain procedure so many times (*loop control*), to count the occurrence of specific events, or to generate sequences of numbers for computational uses. In any event, the computer cannot count by itself, and therefore the programmer must resort to certain counting techniques. Such techniques can best be illustrated by means of examples. Consider the problem example in Section 5-1, where it is desired to count the number of occurrences of the code 2 in the DATA list. A variable acting as a counter ($I$ in the example) is set (*initialized*) to zero before the counting process starts. A code $C$ is read and tested to determine whether it is equal to 2. If $C$ equals 2, the statement $I = I + 1$ is processed, that is, the value 1 is added to the counter $I$. That result then becomes the new value for $I$, reflecting the fact that another code 2 has been found.

The statement $I = I + 1$ is of such paramount importance that we reemphasize its meaning:

$I = I + 1$  means add 1 to $I$ and call this the new value $I$ or
the new value for $I$ is equal to the old value plus 1.

Internally, this statement causes the computer to fetch the contents of memory location $I$, add 1 to it, and store the result back into location $I$. This, of course, causes destruction of the value that was previously stored in $I$.

Note that in the problem example of Section 5-1, the statement $I = I + 1$ is bypassed whenever $C$ is not equal to 2, which means that for any code other than 2 the counter $I$ will not be incremented by 1. Other examples of counting are discussed in Section 5-4.

## 5-2-4   Loop Control

An important application of counting is loop control. Loop control allows the programmer to repeat a procedure a predetermined number of times by making use of a counter to keep track of the number of times the procedure is being carried out (loop). Exiting or branching out of this loop is achieved when the counter has reached its predetermined value. Consider, for example, the following problem: A data file contains six grades. Write a program to read these six grades, and print those greater than 90. Also print the number of occurrences of grades over 90.

There are many ways to solve this problem; we offer two methods shown in Figures 5-3 and 5-5. In Figure 5-3, a counter is used to control the number of times a grade is read and tested. The counter is initially set to 0 and incremented by 1 each time after the READ statement (keeping track of each time a grade is read).

In Figure 5-3, the statements 30 through 60 constitute a loop. To better visualize the mechanism of the loop process, we can trace through the loop and, for each cycle through the loop, record the values assumed by the different variables. A table of values can then be constructed. This process is called *tabulation*. The table corresponding to the program in Figure 5-3 is shown in Figure 5-4 with the given DATA statement.

In Figure 5-5, the counter is initially set to 6 and is decremented by one each time the statement $J = J - 1$ is processed after the READ statement.

To visualize the counting (decrementing) process in the problem of Figure 5-5, see Figure 5-6.

## 5-2-5   Number Generation

Another important application of counting is number generation. To generate the even positive integers 2, 4, 6, 8, . . . , the statement $I = I + 2$ is repeatedly processed with $I$ set initially to 0. To generate the odd positive numbers, the same formula could be used, with $I$ set initially to 1. The program shown in Figure 5-7 prints a 12's addition and multiplication table. The numbers 1, 2, 3, . . . , 10 can be generated by the statement $I = I + 1$, with $I = 0$ initially. There is no need to read these numbers, since they can be easily generated. Each time a new value for $I$ is generated, it is immediately included in the computational formulas $12 * I$ and $12 + 1$. The value of $I$ is then compared to 10 to determine the end of the program (see Figure 5-7).

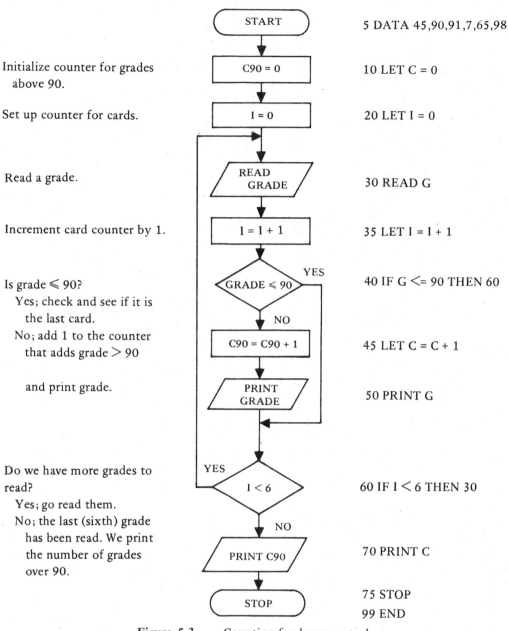

Initialize counter for grades above 90.

Set up counter for cards.

Read a grade.

Increment card counter by 1.

Is grade ≤ 90?
  Yes; check and see if it is the last card.
  No; add 1 to the counter that adds grade > 90

  and print grade.

Do we have more grades to read?
  Yes; go read them.
  No; the last (sixth) grade has been read. We print the number of grades over 90.

START

5 DATA 45,90,91,7,65,98

C90 = 0

10 LET C = 0

I = 0

20 LET I = 0

READ GRADE

30 READ G

I = I + 1

35 LET I = I + 1

GRADE ≤ 90   YES

40 IF G <= 90 THEN 60

NO

C90 = C90 + 1

45 LET C = C + 1

PRINT GRADE

50 PRINT G

YES

I < 6

60 IF I < 6 THEN 30

NO

PRINT C90

70 PRINT C

STOP

75 STOP
99 END

**Figure 5-3**    Counting for loop control.

*Input data*

| C | I | G | |
|---|---|---|---|
| 0̸ | 0̸ | | |
| | 1̸ | 45̸ | |
| | 2̸ | 90̸ | |
| 1̸ | 3̸ | 91̸ | Grade is printed. |
| | 4̸ | 7̸ | |
| | 5̸ | 65̸ | |
| 2 | 6 | 98 | Grade is printed. |

DATA 45,90,91,7,65,98

**Figure 5-4**    The tabulation process.

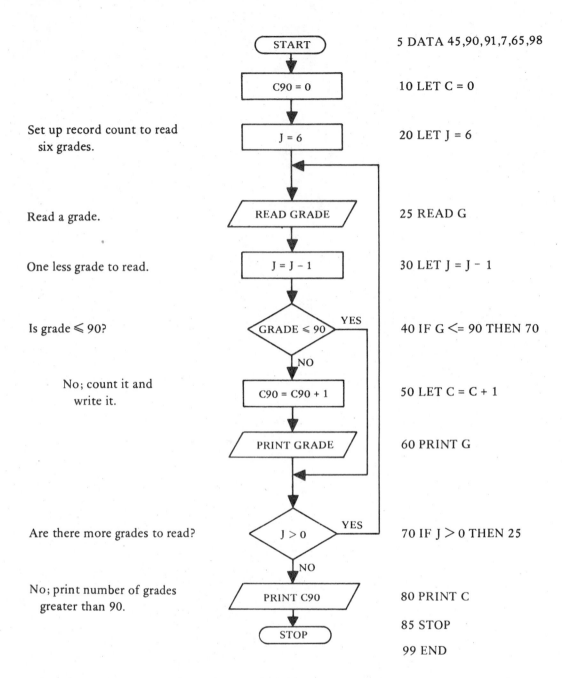

| | |
|---|---|
| | START |
| | 5 DATA 45,90,91,7,65,98 |
| | C90 = 0 |
| | 10 LET C = 0 |
| Set up record count to read six grades. | J = 6 |
| | 20 LET J = 6 |
| Read a grade. | READ GRADE |
| | 25 READ G |
| One less grade to read. | J = J – 1 |
| | 30 LET J = J – 1 |
| Is grade ≤ 90? | GRADE ≤ 90   YES |
| | 40 IF G <= 90 THEN 70 |
| | NO |
| No; count it and write it. | C90 = C90 + 1 |
| | 50 LET C = C + 1 |
| | PRINT GRADE |
| | 60 PRINT G |
| Are there more grades to read? | J > 0   YES |
| | 70 IF J > 0 THEN 25 |
| | NO |
| No; print number of grades greater than 90. | PRINT C90 |
| | 80 PRINT C |
| | STOP |
| | 85 STOP |
| | 99 END |

**Figure 5-5**    Decrementing a counter.

Input data

| C | J | G | |
|---|---|---|---|
| 0̸ | 0̸ | 4̸5 | |
| | 8̸ | 90 | |
| | 4̸ | 9̸1 | Grade is printed. |
| 1̸ | 3̸ | 7̸ | |
| | 2̸ | 6̸5 | |
| | 1̸ | 98 | Grade is printed. |
| 2 | 0 | | Exit is taken. |

DATA 45,90,91,7,65,98

**Figure 5-6**    Tabulation of a loop.

01 REM MULTIPLICATION TABLE

05 LET I = 0

10 LET I = I + 1

15 PRINT "12 X ";I;"=";12 * I,
20 PRINT "12 +";I;"=";12 + I

25 IF I < 10 THEN 10

27 STOP

30 END

RUN

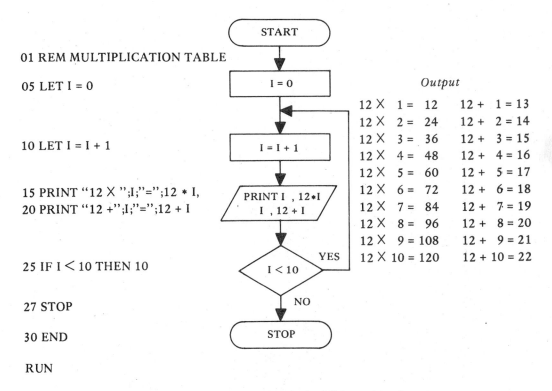

*Output*

| | | |
|---|---|---|
| 12 X  1 =  12 | 12 +  1 = 13 |
| 12 X  2 =  24 | 12 +  2 = 14 |
| 12 X  3 =  36 | 12 +  3 = 15 |
| 12 X  4 =  48 | 12 +  4 = 16 |
| 12 X  5 =  60 | 12 +  5 = 17 |
| 12 X  6 =  72 | 12 +  6 = 18 |
| 12 X  7 =  84 | 12 +  7 = 19 |
| 12 X  8 =  96 | 12 +  8 = 20 |
| 12 X  9 = 108 | 12 +  9 = 21 |
| 12 X 10 = 120 | 12 + 10 = 22 |

**Figure 5-7**    Multiplication and addition tables for 12.

## 5-2-6    End-of-File Checking

As noted in Chapter 1, computers can read and write data from a variety of devices or mediums: punched card, magnetic tape, or terminals. Data on such mediums is generally organized by fields. For example, if the DATA statement is used, a field is defined as a group of related digits (characters). A field, then, contains a particular fact about some entity. A record is a group of related fields and describes many facts about an entity. A file is a collection of related records. Consider the fields in each of the following records:

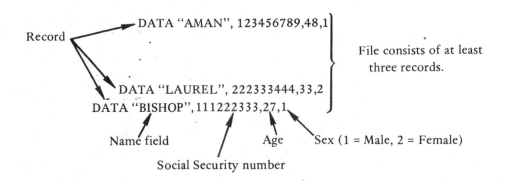

Note that in BASIC the data fields can be strung together in one DATA statement as follows:

DATA "BISHOP", 111222333,27,1, "LAUREL", 222333444,33,2, "AMAN", 123456789,48,1

$\underbrace{\qquad\qquad\qquad}$   $\underbrace{\qquad\qquad\qquad}$   $\underbrace{\qquad\qquad\qquad}$

Record 1                   Record 2                   Record 3

When one reads a file, it is important not to attempt to read more records than are present in the file. Thus some ways to avoid reading records indefinitely must be decided upon. We have discussed a method based on counting that can be used when the number of records is known. However, in most cases it is impractical to count the number of records a file contains before processing them. A commonly used technique to take care of such a situation is the last-record check, which is also called the *trip record* method.

### 5-2-7   Trip Record Method

When using the trip record method to detect end-of-file, it is the programmer's responsibility to tell the computer system when it is reading the last data record. The program must then be written to simulate an end-of-file condition. A special end-of-file code called a *trip code*, purposely different from any of the data items read, is placed on the last record of the data file. Every time a record is read, the content of the data field is checked to determine if it contains the trip code.

**Problem**

Draw a flowchart to read a data file with an unknown number of records; each record contains a name and a grade. Print each name and grade. The flowchart to solve this problem is shown in Figure 5-8.

In the flowchart of Figure 5-8, G is used as a trip code. Every time a record is read, G is compared to zero. If G is not less than zero, then the record read is not the last one, and more records are read. If G is negative, reading is terminated, and the last record (trip code) is not printed. Note that N$ could just as well have been chosen for the trip code. It is important that

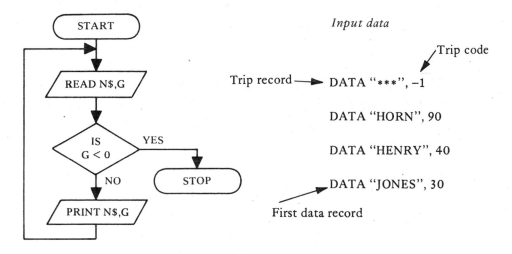

**Figure 5-8**    End-of-file detection using a trip record.

the last record contain as many fields as the previous records, even if these fields are not processed. The selection of a trip code depends on the nature of the data. Generally the data will fall within a certain range of values; a trip code can be any value outside the known range for the data values.

It should be emphasized that when one is using the trip record method for end-of-file condition the test for trip code should immediately follow the READ statement; otherwise the trip code itself may be processed as part of the original data. Consider, for example, the flowchart in Figure 5-9, using the data of the preceding problem.

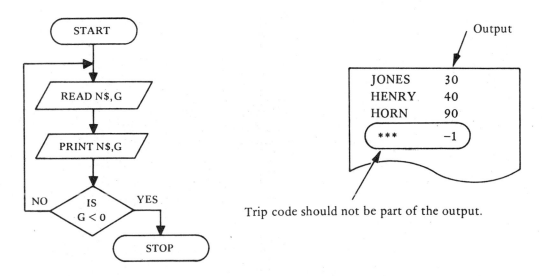

**Figure 5-9**    Incorrect use of the trip record method.

# 5-3  You Might Want To Know

1.  What is the difference between the INPUT and READ statements?

    *Answer:*  Both allow the user to enter data in memory. The INPUT statement causes the program to stop at run time to request data. This allows the user to respond with data that is not necessarily predetermined, such as playing games with the computer. For any application that requires transcription of masses of data, the READ statement would be preferable.

2.  What happens if the READ statement runs out of data elements in the DATA list?

    *Answer:*  An error message is printed to the effect that the READ is out of data. On many systems, the program is aborted when a data interruption is encountered.

    *Action:*

    1.  Check the logic of the program.
    2.  If the DATA statement is at fault because it contains too few items, retype another DATA statement with added items, press RETURN, and type RUN to start the program from the beginning.

3.  What happens if control is passed to a nonexecutable statement such as DATA?

    *Answer:*  Since these statements cannot be executed, control is passed to the next executable statement following the DATA statement.

4.  When counting for loop control, is it always necessary to initialize the counter to zero?

    *Answer:*  No. Any value will do as long as the difference between the terminal and initial value of the counter is equal to the number of times it is desired to process the loop. Normally, though, as a matter of habit you would initialize the counter to zero.

5.  Suppose I can't get all my data items on one DATA statement. What do I do?

    *Answer:*  Continue with another DATA statement as follows:

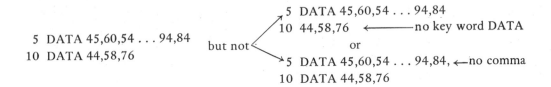

```
                                          5  DATA 45,60,54 ... 94,84
                                         10  44,58,76   ←————no key word DATA
  5  DATA 45,60,54 ... 94,84                        or
 10  DATA 44,58,76           but not
                                          5  DATA 45,60,54 ... 94,84, ←no comma
                                         10  DATA 44,58,76
```

# 5-4    Programming Examples

## 5-4-1    Computing a Percentage of Passing Grades

A data file consists of several sets of records (see Figure 5-10), each containing grades obtained by different class sections of an "Introduction to Management" course. Each set is identified by a header record specifying the section number and the number of grades for a particular section. Write a program to determine the percentage of passing grades for each section (passing grades are grades above 60). Provide a listing of grades by section number with appropriate heading, as shown in Figure 5-10.

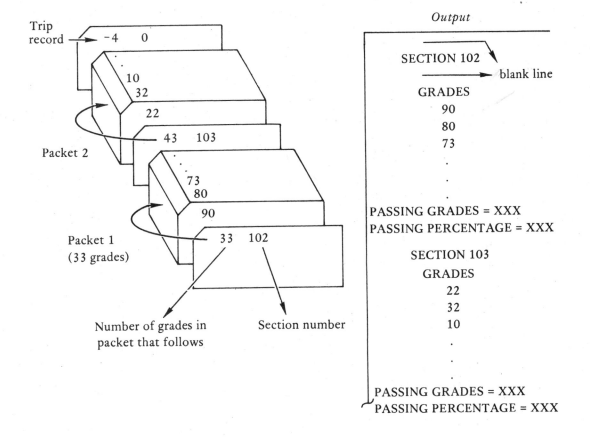

Figure 5-10    Sample input/output.

To transcribe the data onto DATA statements, we have different choices. For example, we can list all data items one after the other on one DATA statement. But in so doing we lose the nature of the physical arrangement and make it more difficult to verify the correctness of the input. We can also preserve the arrangement, as follows:

| | |
|---|---|
| DATA 33, 102 | Header DATA statement for set 1. |
| DATA 90, 80, 73, . . . | Grades for set 1. |
| DATA 43, 103 | Header DATA statement for set 2. |
| DATA 22, 32, 10, . . . | Grades for set 2. |
| DATA -4, 0 | Trip record. |

A program to solve this problem is shown in Figure 5-11.

## 5-4-2   Short-Term Interest

The formula to compute a simple interest INTDUE on a loan of $L$ dollars at an interest rate $R$ for $T$ days is

$$INTDUE = L * R * T/360$$

Write a program to read a dollar amount and an interest rate and produce a table showing the interest to be paid at the end of each month for a period of 12 months (assume each month is 30 days). The program to solve this problem is shown in Figure 5-12. The interest is first computed when $T = 30$. $T$ is then incremented by 30 before a new interest is calculated (see statement 50).

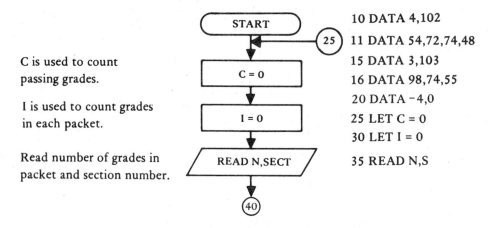

**Figure 5-11**   Computing percentage of passing grades.

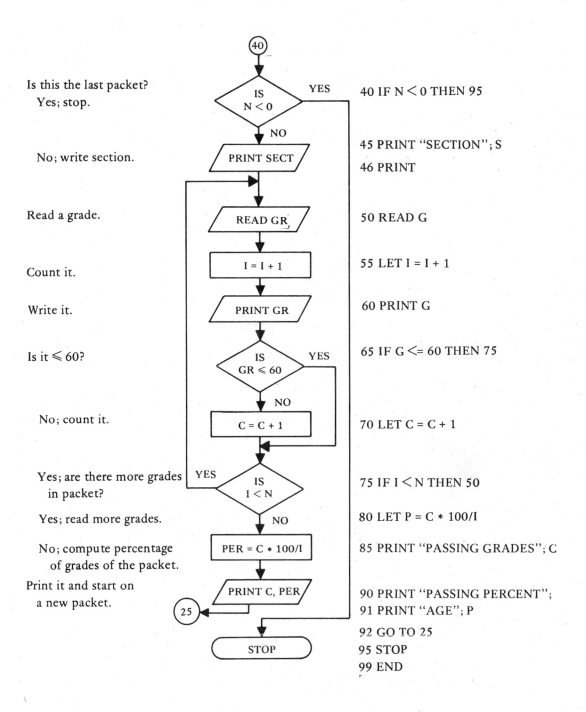

Is this the last packet?
   Yes; stop.

40 IF N < 0 THEN 95

No; write section.

45 PRINT "SECTION"; S
46 PRINT

Read a grade.

50 READ G

Count it.

55 LET I = I + 1

Write it.

60 PRINT G

Is it ≤ 60?

65 IF G <= 60 THEN 75

No; count it.

70 LET C = C + 1

Yes; are there more grades
   in packet?

75 IF I < N THEN 50

Yes; read more grades.

80 LET P = C * 100/I

No; compute percentage
   of grades of the packet.

85 PRINT "PASSING GRADES"; C

Print it and start on
   a new packet.

90 PRINT "PASSING PERCENT";
91 PRINT "AGE"; P

92 GO TO 25
95 STOP
99 END

**Figure 5-11**     Computing percentage of passing grades. (continued)

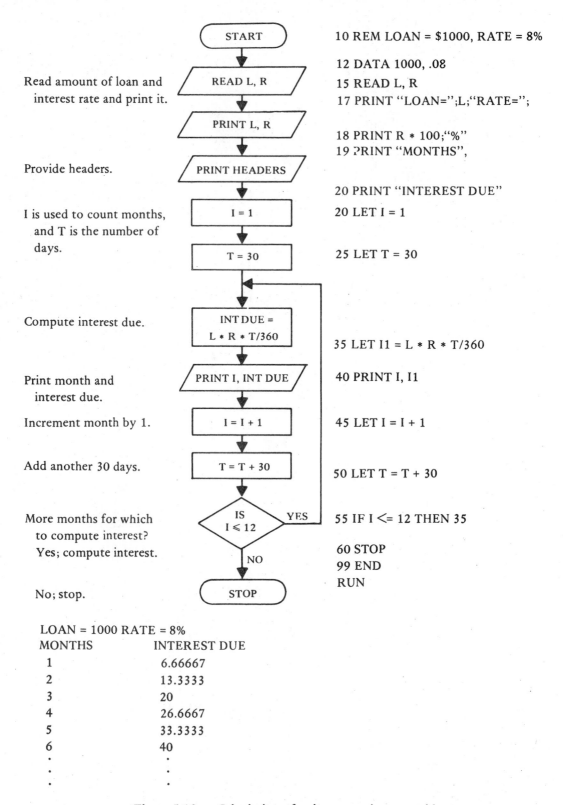

Read amount of loan and
interest rate and print it.

Provide headers.

I is used to count months,
and T is the number of
days.

Compute interest due.

Print month and
interest due.

Increment month by 1.

Add another 30 days.

More months for which
to compute interest?
Yes; compute interest.

No; stop.

```
10 REM LOAN = $1000, RATE = 8%

12 DATA 1000, .08
15 READ L, R
17 PRINT "LOAN=";L;"RATE=";

18 PRINT R * 100;"%"
19 PRINT "MONTHS",

20 PRINT "INTEREST DUE"
20 LET I = 1

25 LET T = 30

35 LET I1 = L * R * T/360

40 PRINT I, I1

45 LET I = I + 1

50 LET T = T + 30

55 IF I <= 12 THEN 35

60 STOP
99 END
RUN
```

LOAN = 1000 RATE = 8%

| MONTHS | INTEREST DUE |
|--------|--------------|
| 1 | 6.66667 |
| 2 | 13.3333 |
| 3 | 20 |
| 4 | 26.6667 |
| 5 | 33.3333 |
| 6 | 40 |
| . | . |
| . | . |
| . | . |

**Figure 5-12**    Calculation of a short-term interest table.

## 5-4-3   A Computer Assisted Instructional (CAI) Unit

Johnnie needs to be drilled on his addition tables (1 through 10). For reinforcement purposes, random congratulatory messages should be printed whenever Johnnie gets the right answers; otherwise Johnnie keeps responding until he gets the correct answer. Figure 5-13 shows the program as well as the ensuing dialogue.

```
 5  PRINT "WHAT'S YOUR NAME"
10  INPUT N$
15  LET X = INT (RND(1)*10 + 1)
20  LET Y = INT (RND(1)*10 + 1)
25  PRINT N$; "WHAT'S" ;X; "+" ;Y
30  INPUT A
35  IF A = X + Y GO TO 50
40  PRINT "SORRY" ;N$; "TRY AGAIN"
45  GO TO 30
50  LET I = RND(1)
55  IF I > .5 GO TO 70
60  PRINT "GEE" ;N$; "YOU ARE TERRIFIC!"
65  GO TO 15
70  PRINT "GREAT" ;N$; ". BEAUTIFUL!"
75  GO TO 15
80  END
```

Generate the two random numbers between 1 and 10.
Enter the response.
If the answer is correct, print congratulatory message; otherwise enter another response.
Generate a random number.

Choose between two messages

and keep drilling Johnnie.

```
    RUN

WHAT'S YOUR NAME
?
?JOHNNIE
JOHNNIE WHAT'S 7 + 5
?12
GEE JOHNNIE YOU ARE TERRIFIC!
JOHNNIE WHAT'S 6 + 10
?7
SORRY JOHNNIE TRY AGAIN
?16
GREAT JOHNNIE. BEAUTIFUL!
JOHNNIE WHAT'S 8 + 10
?
```

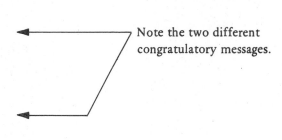

Note the two different congratulatory messages.

**Figure 5-13**   A CAI unit with dialogue.

# 5-5  Probing Deeper

### 5-5-1  RESTORE Statement

Usually elements from a DATA list are processed by a READ statement only once. If it is desired to reread the data from a DATA list, the RESTORE statement can be used. The RESTORE statement causes the next READ statement to start at the *beginning* of the list in the DATA block. The RESTORE statement is shown in Figure 5-14.

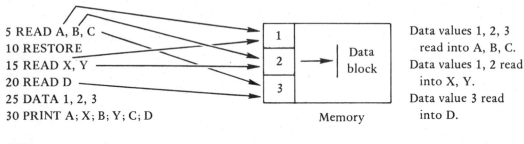

```
5 READ A, B, C
10 RESTORE
15 READ X, Y
20 READ D
25 DATA 1, 2, 3
30 PRINT A; X; B; Y; C; D

RUN

1 1 2 2 3 3
```

Data values 1, 2, 3 read into A, B, C. Data values 1, 2 read into X, Y. Data value 3 read into D.

Figure 5-14    RESTORE illustration.

The RESTORE can be very convenient when it is needed to process items in a DATA statement more than once, although arrays (see Chapter 7) can be even more convenient, due to their ease of manipulation. A problem is offered to illustrate the use of the RESTORE statement.

**Problem**

The final grades for an "Introduction to Management" class have already been recorded on a DATA statement in descending order. The instructor is allowed 10 percent A's in his class. Write a program to list all A scores for that class (round off percentage of grades to next whole number, i.e., 9.1 = 10). A program to solve this problem is shown in Figure 5-15. First we must determine the number of grades (this implies reading the list once); then we need to reread the list to print the first 10 percent scores. In the accompanying flowchart, the RESTORE command is placed in an input/output block, since it is an operation related to input/output.

### 5-5-2  The PRINT USING Statement

By now you probably have found out that to generate an elegant output with titles, headings, and subheadings and to align numeric fields properly under headings, etc., requires a great deal of "print position" counting with the TAB statement. A very convenient way to "dress up" your output, or to make it attractive, can be achieved through the PRINT USING statement. It should be noted that the implementation of the PRINT USING will vary from one BASIC system to another. The following discussion, however, is general enough that you can attempt to use the PRINT USING on your system.

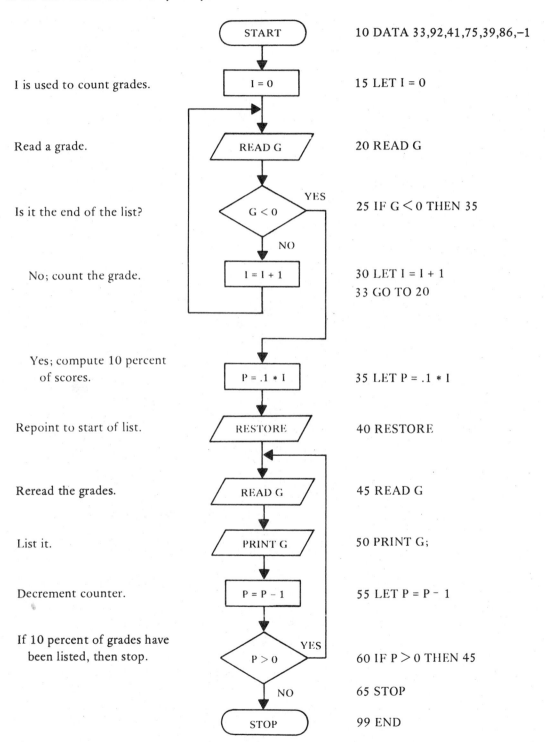

| | |
|---|---|
| | 10 DATA 33,92,41,75,39,86,–1 |
| I is used to count grades. | 15 LET I = 0 |
| Read a grade. | 20 READ G |
| Is it the end of the list? | 25 IF G < 0 THEN 35 |
| No; count the grade. | 30 LET I = I + 1<br>33 GO TO 20 |
| Yes; compute 10 percent<br>of scores. | 35 LET P = .1 * I |
| Repoint to start of list. | 40 RESTORE |
| Reread the grades. | 45 READ G |
| List it. | 50 PRINT G; |
| Decrement counter. | 55 LET P = P – 1 |
| If 10 percent of grades have<br>been listed, then stop. | 60 IF P > 0 THEN 45 |
| | 65 STOP |
| | 99 END |

**Figure 5-15**    Rereading a list of scores.

The general form of the PRINT USING IS

*statement-number* PRINT USING *image-statement-number, [expression-list]*

where *image-statement-number* is the number of a BASIC statement that describes the format (image, layout) of the data items (*expression-list*) to be printed. Special "format-control-characters" are used at the *image-statement-number* to describe the output image and to control spacing and strategic positioning of data fields on the output line.

The *expression-list* consists of a sequence of variables and expressions separated by commas, similar to the expression-list specified in any PRINT statement.

The general form of the "image" is

*image-statement-number : sequence-of-format-control-characters*[1]

where the colon (:) is a required key word which identifies this type of statement. To better understand the use of the PRINT USING, consider the following cases.

**Case 1**

*Numeric, alphabetic, and literal images: The L and # format-control-characters.*

Suppose you were to write a payroll program to read employee names, their rate of pay, and hours worked to produce a report similar to the following:

| NAME | RATE OF PAY | HOURS | GROSS PAY |
|------|-------------|-------|-----------|
| JONES P. | 36.45 | 84.00 | 3061.80 |
| ARDAMAN J. | 98.00 | 37.00 | 3626.00 |
| GRIZZI M. | .50 | .50 | .25 |

Note that the first line consists solely of literal data (headings) and would be produced by executing statement 10 in Figure 5-16. The succeeding lines are produced by statement 22, which references image-statement-number 40. This image is used to print alphabetic and numeric data. The format-control-character *L* is used for alphanumeric data, and the pound sign (#) is used for numeric data (see Figure 5-16). At run time the field of *L*'s and fields of #'s will be replaced by the values to be printed.

Note that image-statement-number 50 solely specifies headings. The image consists only of literal data and there are no format-control-characters such as the pound sign or the *L* control character.

---

[1] In many BASIC systems, the image itself is described within the PRINT USING statement as

*statement-number* PRINT USING *sequence-of-format-control-characters, expression-list.*

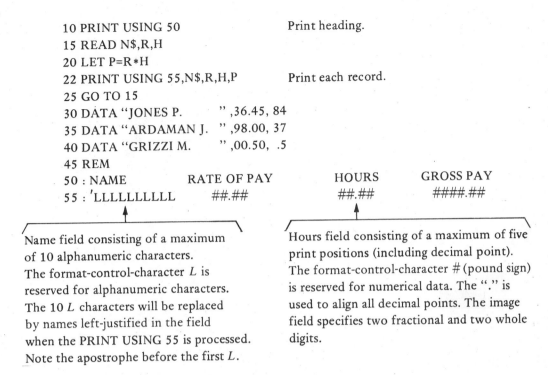

```
10 PRINT USING 50                    Print heading.
15 READ N$,R,H
20 LET P=R*H
22 PRINT USING 55,N$,R,H,P           Print each record.
25 GO TO 15
30 DATA "JONES P.      " ,36.45, 84
35 DATA "ARDAMAN J.   " ,98.00, 37
40 DATA "GRIZZI M.    " ,00.50, .5
45 REM
50 : NAME            RATE OF PAY        HOURS          GROSS PAY
55 : 'LLLLLLLLLL       ##.##           ##.##           ####.##
```

Name field consisting of a maximum of 10 alphanumeric characters. The format-control-character $L$ is reserved for alphanumeric characters. The 10 $L$ characters will be replaced by names left-justified in the field when the PRINT USING 55 is processed. Note the apostrophe before the first $L$.

Hours field consisting of a maximum of five print positions (including decimal point). The format-control-character # (pound sign) is reserved for numerical data. The "." is used to align all decimal points. The image field specifies two fractional and two whole digits.

**Figure 5-16    The pound format-control-character.**

## Case 2

*The $ and C format-control-characters.*

In many financial statements or transactions, a leading $ is sometimes required at the beginning of the dollar amount field. In BASIC, the format-control-character $ is placed at the beginning of the numeric image field (# characters) to print the dollar sign at whatever print position the $ is typed. For example, see statements 30, 40, and 55 in Figure 5-17.

Also, subheadings may have to be centered beneath other headings. This task can be accomplished automatically in BASIC with the format-control-character $C$. A field of $C$'s is typed in the image statement, and the character string to be printed in that field will be centered. For example, see statements 15 and 25 of Figure 5-17 and note the apostrophe before the first $C$.

Figure 5-17 computes an adjusted balance for a bank reconciliation statement.

On some systems, it is possible to incorporate the comma in dollar amount fields to facilitate readability of results. For example, if in Figure 5-17 we changed images 30 and 55 to

```
30 :BALANCE PER BOOKS    . . . . . . . . . . . . . . . . $#,###.##
55 :ADJUSTED BALANCE . . . . . . . . . . . . . . . . . . $#,###.##
```

we would obtain the following results:

```
BALANCE PER BOOKS    . . . . . . . . . . . . . . . . $3,290.37
ADJUSTED BALANCE  . . . . . . . . . . . . . . . . . . $3,226.07
```

```
15 :                              'CCCCCCCCCCCCCCCCCCC
20 :                              BANK RECONCILIATION
25 :                              'CCCCCCCCCCCCCCCCCCCC
30 : BALANCE PER BOOKS . . . . . . . . . . . . . . . . . . . . . . . . . . . . . . . . $####.##
35 : DEDUCT BANK'S CHARGES NOT ON THE BOOKS:
40 :     EXCHANGE . . . . . . . . . . . . . . . . . . . . . . . $##.##
45 :     COLLECTION . . . . . . . . . . . . . . . . . . . . . . . . . . .##
50 :     N.S.F. CHECK–JON GUMP . . . . . . . . . . . . . . . . . . . ##.##           ##.##
55 : ADJUSTED BALANCE . . . . . . . . . . . . . . . . . . . . . . . . . . . . . . $####.##
56 REM
60 READ N$,D$,B,E,C,N
65 LET A=B−(E+C+N)
70 PRINT USING 15,N$
75 PRINT USING 20
80 PRINT USING 25,D$
85 PRINT USING 30,B
90 PRINT USING 35
95 PRINT USING 40,E
100 PRINT USING 45,C
105 PRINT USING 50,N
110 PRINT USING 55,A
115 DATA "M.C.HOOTEN COMPANY","JUNE 27 1979"
120 DATA 3290.37,.10,.25,63.95
130 END
RUN
```

M.C. HOOTEN COMPANY
BANK RECONCILIATION
JUNE 27 1979

```
BALANCE PER BOOKS  . . . . . . . . . . . . . . . . . . . . . . . . . . . . . . . . . $3290.37
DEDUCT BANK'S CHARGES NOT ON THE BOOKS:
    EXCHANGE . . . . . . . . . . . . . . . . . . . . . . . . . . . . . $   .10
    COLLECTION  . . . . . . . . . . . . . . . . . . . . . . . .          .25
    N.S.F. CHECK–JON GUMP . . . . . . . . . . . . . . . . . . .        63.95
ADJUSTED BALANCE . . . . . . . . . . . . . . . . . . . . . . . . . . . . . . $3226.07
```

**Figure 5-17**    The $ and C format-control-characters.

**Case 3**

*The C, L, and R format-control-characters.*

Sometimes it may be required to write programs to print multilevel structures of headers, identifiers, etc., or organizational charts such as follow:

BOARD OF TRUSTEES

| INTERNAL AUDITOR | PRESIDENT | ASSISTANT TO PRESIDENT |
|---|---|---|
|  | VICE PRESIDENT |  |
| DEAN1 | DEAN2 | DEAN3 |

The program shown in Figure 5-18 can be used to produce this chart. Note that the program will center all fields except the internal auditor and assistant to president fields. The former is left-justified (the L format-control-character), while the latter is right-justified in its field (the R format-control-character). See statement 15. Note also how literals are part of the PRINT USING statement at statements 50 and 60.

Other format-control-characters exist such as the dollar sign (asterisk) protection feature, the negative or positive dollar/amount fields, etc. The user is advised to check these features in his or her BASIC technical reference manual.

```
10 : 'CCCCCCCCCCCCCCCCCCCCCCCCCCCCCCCCCCCCCCCCCCCCCCCCCCCCCCCCCCCCCCC
15 : 'LLLLLLLLLLLLLLLLLLLLLLLL'CCCCCCCCCCCCCCCCCC'RRRRRRRRRRRRRRRRRRR
20 : 'CCCCCCCCCCCCCCCCCCCCCCCCCCCCCCCCCCCCCCCCCCCCCCCCCCCCCCCCCCCCCCC
25 : 'CCCCCCCCCCCCCCCCCCCCCCC'CCCCCCCCCCCCCCCCCC'CCCCCCCCCCCCCCCCCCCC
30 REM
35 LET A$="BOARD OF TRUSTEES"
40 LET B$="VICE PRESIDENT"
45 PRINT USING 10,A$
50 PRINT USING 15,"INTERNAL AUDITOR","PRESIDENT","ASSISTANT TO PRESIDENT"
55 PRINT USING 20,B$
60 PRINT USING 25,"DEAN1","DEAN2","DEAN3"
65 END
```

**Figure 5-18** The C, L, R format-control-characters.

# 5-6 Assignments

## 5-6-1 Self Test

1. How many data items will be read by the following flowcharts?

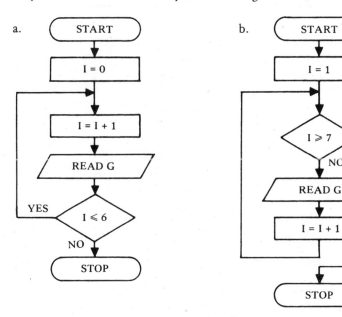

c.

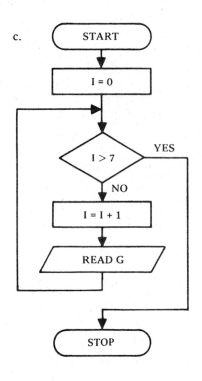

d.

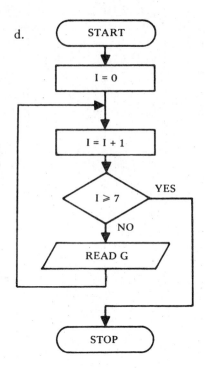

e.

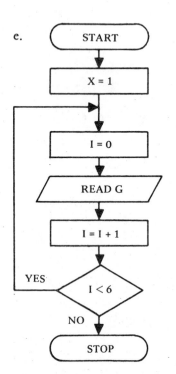

f.

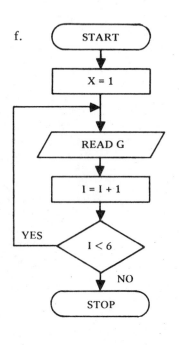

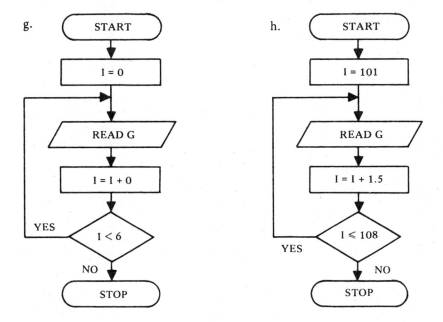

2. A certain file contains 10 data records. Which of the following flowcharts will read 10 and only 10 data records?

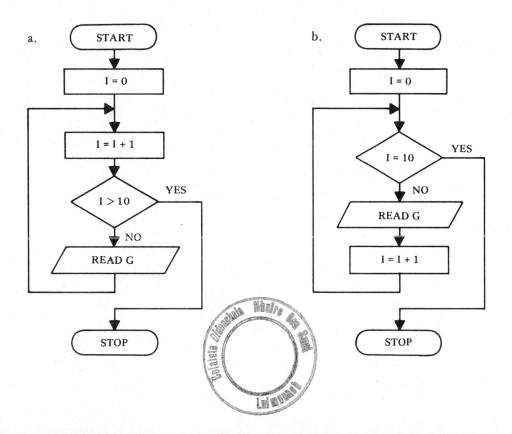

c.
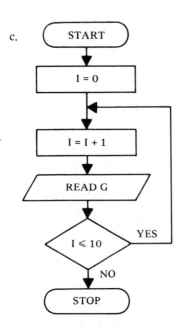

d.
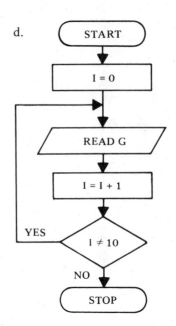

3.  Complete each IF statement so that the program will read 10 data items.

a.  10  LET I = 0
    15  READ J
    20  IF I ⬜ THEN 35
    25  LET I = I + 1
    30  GO TO 15
    35  STOP
    99  END

b.  10  LET I = 0
    15  LET I = I + 1
    20  READ J
    25  IF I ⬜ THEN 15
    30  STOP
    99  END

c.  10  LET I = 0
    15  READ J
    20  IF I ⬜ THEN 30
    25  GO TO 40
    30  LET I = I + 1
    35  GO TO 15
    40  STOP
    99  END

d.  10  LET I = 0
    15  IF I ⬜ THEN 35
    20  READ G
    25  LET I = I + 1
    30  GO TO 15
    35  STOP
    99  END

e.  10  LET I = 10
    15  IF I ⬜ THEN 35
    20  READ T
    25  LET I = I - 1
    30  GO TO 15
    35  STOP
    99  END

f.  10  LET I = 10
    15  LET I = I - 1
    20  READ J
    25  IF I ⬜ THEN 15
    30  STOP
    99  END

## 5-6-2   Exercises

1.  A file consists of an unknown number of records; each record contains a Social Security number, a sex code (1 = male, 2 = female), and an earning. Write a program using the sex as a trip record to count the number of males earning above $30,000 and a list of females, by Social Security numbers, earning less than $5,000.

2.  A DATA statement contains numbers supposedly arranged in numerical ascending order. Write a program to print a message if they are in order and another message if they are not.

3.   A DATA statement contains 10 pairs of grades. Write a program to compute and print each pair and its sum. Now, suppose that the first number in the DATA statement is a number that tells how many pairs of grades follow that first number. Write a program to process this type of file.

4.   A DATA statement contains an unknown number of positive and negative numbers varying from −1,000 to +1,000. Write a program to determine how many positive, how many negative, and how many zero numbers there are in the list.

5.   A DATA statement contains numbers thought to be in numerical ascending order. Write a program to identify those numbers not in sequence. For example, given:

DATA 10, 15, 12, 19, 16, 18, 22

the output should be similar to ⟶

```
10
15
12    OUT OF SEQUENCE
19
16    OUT OF SEQUENCE
18    OUT OF SEQUENCE
```

6.   Each data record in a file contains two items: an age and a code for marital status (1 = single, 2 = married, 3 = divorced, 4 = widowed). There are an unknown number of data records. A code of 9 in the marital status field signifies that it is the last record. Write a program to compute and print the following:

a.   The percentage of people over 30 years of age

b.   The number of people who are either widowed or divorced

c.   The number of people who are over 50 or less than 30 and who are not married

7.   Write a program to print out multiplication tables from 2 to 10 as follows:

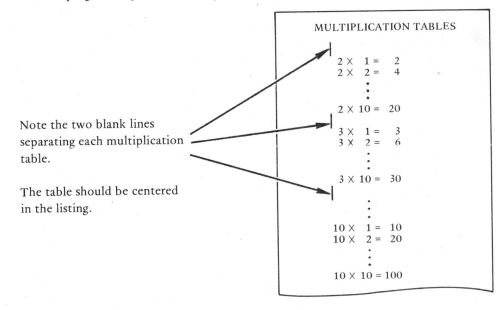

Note the two blank lines separating each multiplication table.

The table should be centered in the listing.

```
        MULTIPLICATION TABLES

        2 X   1 =    2
        2 X   2 =    4
               .
               .
               .
        2 X 10 =   20


        3 X   1 =    3
        3 X   2 =    6
               .
               .
               .
        3 X 10 =   30
               .
               .
               .
       10 X   1 =   10
       10 X   2 =   20
               .
               .
               .
       10 X 10 = 100
```

8.  Write a program to compute how much a person would weigh on the following planets, based on the following table:

| PLANET | PERCENTAGE OF EARTH WEIGHT |
|---|---|
| Moon | 16 |
| Jupiter | 264 |
| Venus | 85 |
| Mars | 38 |

Create a table with weights ranging from 50 to 250 pounds in steps of 10 pounds.

9.  Make your family a temperature conversion chart that displays the temperatures in Fahrenheit and centigrade starting at $-35°$F up to $125°$F ($F = 9/5 * C + 32$).

10. Write a program to print out the following board (exactly):

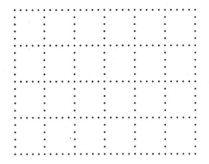

11. Write a program to simulate octal counting up to $27_8$, that is, print the numbers 1, 2, $\cdots$, 7, 10, 11, $\cdots$, 17, 20, 21, $\cdots$ 27. Can you generalize your program for counting in octal up to any number?

12. Write a program to read a positive value for $J$ and print:

    a.  The even integers from 2 to $J$.

    b.  The first $J$ odd positive integers.

    c.  A message if $J$ is a prime number.

13. A data file consists of 14 positive or negative numbers. Write a program to stop reading the file whenever two numbers of the opposite sign follow one another. Print the number of items read up to this point.

14. Read $N$ grades already sorted in ascending order ($N$ is accepted from input) and compute the median. The median is the mark that divides a distribution of scores in two equal parts. (To determine whether $N$ is even or odd, evaluate $2 * INT(N/2) - N$. For example, $INT(3.8) = 3$ and $INT(15.01) = 15$.)

    10, 11, 12, 13, 14, 15, 16        The median is 13.

    10, 11, 12, 13        The median is $\dfrac{11 + 12}{2} = 11.5$.

15. A data file consists of records containing an employee number, a number of hours worked, and an hourly rate of pay. Overtime is time and a half for each hour over 40. Federal and state taxes are 18 and 5 percent of gross earnings respectively. Your program should produce an output with the following headings:

PAYROLL REPORT

| EMPLOYEE | GROSS | OVERTIME PAY | FED. AND ST. TAXES | NET PAY |
|----------|-------|--------------|--------------------|---------|

16. Cards have been punched for a store showing daily sales for corresponding days of succeeding years. The first value on the card is the amount of sales for a given day in the first year; the second value is the amount of sales for the corresponding day in the second year. Find the number of days in which the second year's daily sales exceeded the first year's daily sales by more than 10 percent of the first year's sales. The output should be similar to the following (transcribe data on DATA statements):

Sample input                         Output

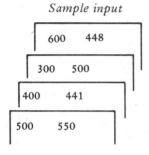

FIRST YEAR   SECOND YEAR

| FIRST YEAR | SECOND YEAR | |
|------------|-------------|------|
| 500 | 550 | |
| 400 | 441 | ** |
| 300 | 500 | ** |
| 600 | 448 | |

Superior sales days number 2

(Note that "**" identifies those records for which the second year's daily sales exceeds the first year's daily sales by more than 10 percent.)

17. A wholesaler accepts a $5,000 promissory note from a retailer at 7 percent in lieu of cash payment for delivered goods. Write a program to compute the maturity value of the note for a 30-, 60-, and 90-day short-term loan. (Formula for maturity value is $S = P(1 + I \cdot N)$. $S$ is the maturity value, $P$ is principal, $I$ is interest rate, and $N$ is the number of years, or if less than 1 year, number of days/360.)

18. Each employee working at Manpower, Inc., is paid at a regular hourly rate of $5.00 for the first 40 hours. The overtime rate is 1.5 times the regular rate. The number of hours worked by each employee is entered on DATA statements.

   a. Write a program to read the number of hours worked by each employee and compute each employee's pay. The output should be similar to the following:

| HOURS | RATE | OVERTIME HOURS | PAY |
|-------|------|----------------|-----|
| 10.00 | 5.00 | 0 | 50.00 |
| 50.00 | 5.00 | 10 | 275.00 |
| . | . | . | . |
| . | . | . | . |

b.  Same as part a, except that the number of hours and the rate of pay are read from DATA statements. Also, 6.1 percent of each employee's pay up to the first 30 hours is subtracted from the pay to go into a pension plan. The produced output should be similar to

| HOURS | RATE | PENSION PLAN | PAY |
|-------|------|--------------|-----|
| 50.00 | 10.00 | 18.30 | 531.70 |
| . | . | . | . |
| . | . | . | . |

c.  Same as part b, except that a bonus amount in addition to the hours and rate of pay is recorded for each employee on the DATA statement. If the employee's pay exceeds $500, the bonus is added to the employee's pay; otherwise the bonus field is left blank on the output as follows (not included in pay):

| HOURS | RATE | PENSION PLAN | BONUS | PAY |
|-------|------|--------------|-------|-----|
| 50.00 | 10.00 | 18.30 | 100 | 631.70 |
| 10.00 | 5.00 | 3.05 | | 46.95 |
| . | . | . | | . |
| . | . | . | | . |

Note blank field.

d.  Same as part a, except that overtime hours are converted into corresponding regular hours. For instance, 10 hours of overtime at time-and-a-half rate of $8.00 per hour is equivalent to 15 straight hours (regular hours at $8.00/hour).

19.  Compute the monthly payment for a $45,000 loan at interest rates varying from 8.75 percent to 9.25 percent in increments of .25 for 15-, 20-, 25-, and 30-year mortgages. The output should be similar to the following:

| PRINCIPAL | INTEREST | DURATION | MONTHLY PAYMENT | TOTAL |
|-----------|----------|----------|-----------------|-------|
| 45000 | 8.75 | 15 | XXX | |
| | | 20 | XXX | |
| | | 25 | XXX | |
| | | 30 | XXX | XXX |
| | 9.00 | 15 | XXX | |
| | | 20 | XXX | |
| | | 25 | XXX | |
| | | 30 | XXX | XXX |
| | 9.25 | 15 | XXX | |
| | | 20 | XXX | |
| | | 25 | XXX | |
| | | 30 | XXX | XXX |

The formula to compute the monthly payment is

$$M = \frac{i \cdot P/12}{1 - (i/12 + 1)^{12 \cdot \text{Years}}}$$

where $i$ and $P$ are interest and principal.

20.  Write a program that would produce the following report:

TYPE YOUR NAME AND ACCOUNT NUMBER
?
MAT HARRIS 11-57
TYPE THE PRINCIPAL, THE ANNUAL INTEREST RATE, THE NUMBER OF
INTEREST PERIODS PER YEAR, AND THE NUMBER OF YEARS
?
100, 5, 4, 2

                         MAT HARRIS 11-57
THE PRINCIPAL IS 1000 AND THE ANNUAL RATE OF INTEREST IS 5%
THE PRINCIPAL WILL BE COMPOUNDED 4 TIMES PER YEAR FOR 2 YEARS
THE PERIODIC RATE OF INTEREST IS 1.25% FOR 8 PERIODS

| PERIOD | OLD BALANCE | CURRENT INTEREST | INTEREST TO DATE | NEW BALANCE |
|--------|-------------|------------------|------------------|-------------|
| 1 | 1000 | 12.5 | 12.5 | 1012.5 |
| 2 | 1012.5 | 12.65625 | 25.15623 | 1025.156 |
| 3 | 1025.156 | 12.81445 | 37.97067 | 1037.97 |
| 4 | 1037.97 | 12.97462 | 50.94528 | 1050.945 |
| 5 | 1050.945 | 13.13681 | 64.08208 | 1064.081 |
| 6 | 1064.081 | 13.30101 | 77.38309 | 1077.382 |
| 7 | 1077.382 | 13.46727 | 90.85035 | 1090.849 |
| 8 | 1090.849 | 13.63561 | 100.486 | 1104.485 |

21.  The simple discount is the amount deducted from the maturity value $S$ (see problem 26) of an obligation when the latter is sold before its date of maturity. The formula is $SD = S \cdot D \cdot N$. $SD$ = simple discount, $S$ = maturity value, $D$ = discount rate, and $N$ = term of loan, that is, time remaining before maturity.

    A wholesaler receives a \$10,500 promissory note for goods sold to a retailer. The note matures in $N$ months and bears an $I$ percent interest rate. One month later, the wholesaler sells his note to a bank at 9 percent discount rate. Write a program to compute:

a.  The maturity value of the note for $N = 30$, 60, and 90 days with interest rate of $I = 4$ percent, 5 percent, and 6 percent. That is, $N = 30$ for $I = 4$ percent, 5 percent, and 6 percent; $N = 60$ for $I = 4$ percent, 5 percent, and 6 percent; and so forth.

b.  The proceeds received by the wholesaler as a result of selling the note to the bank for $N = 30$, 60, and 90 days with interest rate of 4 percent, 5 percent, and 6 percent.

22. Mr. Small is thinking of borrowing $5,000 to purchase a new automobile for $N$ months at 8 percent simple discount rate. Write a program to compute the proceeds of this loan for the following values of $N$: 6 months, 1 year, 2 years, and 3 years. The proceeds ($P$) is the sum remaining after the discount is deducted: $P = S(1 - D - N)$ (see exercise 30).

23. The Kiddie Up Company manufactures toys for adults. The company expects fixed costs for the next year to be around $180,000. With the demand for adult toys increasing, the company is looking for sales of $900,000 in the year to come. The variable costs are expected to run at about 74 percent of sales.

   a. Write a program to determine the break-even point (BEP) (the dollar amount of sales that must be made to incur neither a profit nor a loss) and compute the expected profit. The formula to compute the BEP is

   $$\text{BEP} = \frac{\text{total fixed costs}}{1 - \dfrac{\text{variable costs}}{\text{sales}}}$$

   b. The Kiddie Up Company management is arguing that, with the current rate of inflation, variable costs will run higher for the next year—probably anywhere from 75 to 83 percent of sales. With sales still projected at $900,000, the management directs its DP staff to generate the following report to determine the break-even point and the profits and losses for varying variable costs. Sales and fixed costs remain constant.

   KIDDIE UP COMPANY
   OPERATIONS FORECAST (1979)

   | SALES | FIXED COSTS | VARIABLE COST | PERCENT VARIABLE COST OF SALES | BREAK-EVEN POINT | PROFIT | DEFICIT |
   |---|---|---|---|---|---|---|
   | 900,000 | 180,000 | . | 75 | . | . | . |
   | . | . | . | 76 | . | . | . |
   | . | . | . | . | . | . | . |
   | . | . | . | . | . | . | . |
   | 900,000 | 180,000 | . | 83 | . | . | . |

   Write a program to complete this report. Place three stars (∗∗∗) in the profit column if there is no profit. Do the same for deficit.

c.   The company employees have just won a new contract. As a result, variable costs are expected to reach 80 percent or 81 percent of next year's projected $900,000 sales. A recent internal study carried out by the company on the various aspects of the manufacturing operations disclosed production inefficiencies. Corrective measures could significantly lower fixed costs. Determine the extent to which present fixed costs could be reduced to satisfy the projected variable costs figures for the coming year.

24.   The first DATA statement in a set of DATA statements contains the current date. Each succeeding DATA statement contains the date of the last time an item was sold, the number of items on hand, the cost per item, and the regular selling price for the item. A store plans a sale to try to sell slow-moving items. The purpose of the program is to produce a report showing recommended sale price as follows:

   If item has not been sold in the last 30 days, discount is 10 percent.
   If item has not been sold in the last 60 days, discount is 20 percent.
   If item has not been sold in the last 90 days, discount is 40 percent.

However, any item that has sold in the last 30 days is not to be placed on sale. Also, if there is only one item left in stock, it should not be placed on sale, no matter what the last date of sale. The amount of discount allowed should never be such that sales price is lower than cost.

   The report should have page headings (page contains 60 lines) and all necessary identifiers.

25.   One method for calculating depreciation is to subtract a fixed percentage of the original value of the item each year. Thus, a $100 item depreciated at 10 percent would be valued at $90 at the end of the first year, $80 at the end of the second, and so forth. Another method for calculating depreciation is to subtract a fixed percentage of the present value of the item. A $100 item depreciated at 10 percent would be valued at $90 at the end of the first year, $90 - .1 \times 90 = \$81$ at the end of the second year, and so forth. Write a program to accept as input the original value $(V)$, the depreciation rate $(R)$, and a number of years $(N)$, and produce a table showing the value of the items for the first, second, third, . . . $N$th year using both depreciation methods.

26.   The number $e$ can be defined as the limit of $(1 + 1/n)^n$ as $n$ gets larger and larger. Write a program to approximate a value for $e$. Stop when the difference between two successive approximations is less than .001. Print out the values for $e$ and $n$.

## 5-6-3   Projects

1.   The following is a bank statement. Write a program using the PRINT USING to duplicate the statement. Do not use the READ statement. Generate the numbers internally by assigning them variable names and by adding fixed increments.

|  | | |  |
| --- | --- | --- | --- |
| M.H. GUNSON<br>146 N.E. 35 ST.<br>CHICAGO, ILLINOIS | STATEMENT OF ACCOUNT<br>POUREMS STATE BANK | | |
| CHECKS | DEPOSITS | DATE | BALANCES |
|  |  | May 31, 1978 | 4,000.00 |
|  | 100.00 | June 1, 1978 | 4,100.00 |
|  | 200.00 | June 2, 1978 | 4,300.00 |
|  | 300.00 | June 3, 1978 | 4,600.00 |
|  | 400.00 | June 4, 1978 | 5,000.00 |
|  | 500.00 | June 5, 1978 | 5,500.00 |
| 600.50 |  | June 6, 1978 | 4,899.50 |

2.   Write a program using PRINT USING to design checks and read dollar amounts to write out the checks.

3.   You have probably cut out, completed, and sent off coupons as shown below. Write a program using the PRINT USING to design such a form and then read sets of test data of your own to complete the form.

```
CAMCOT
CAMOUFLAGE COMPANY, INC.
1715 N.W. ST., MIDDLAND, NY 11797

_____  Please send me the CAMCOT KIT @ $2.95 per kit

_____  Please have a representative call me

Name _____  Phone _____

Organization _____

Address _____

City/State _____  Zip _____

Amount Enclosed  $____.____
```

4.  The following is an organizational chart of a major corporation. Names of executive officers are shown within parentheses. Write a program using the PRINT USING to design such a chart and read a list of names that are to replace the current names of the executive officers.

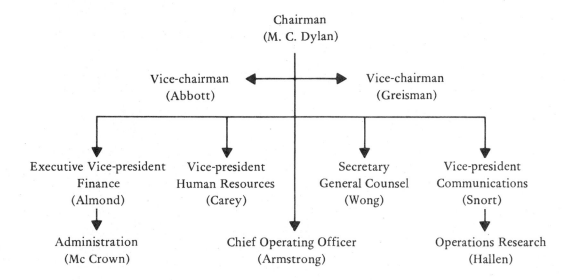

5.  You have been hired by E. Naddor, Inc., a world-famous firm specializing in inventory control problems, to write a computer program for one of Naddor's largest customers, The Shopping Basket. This firm would like to computerize part of its reordering system to cut down on the cost of replenishing inventories.

    Each Friday, at the close of business, the ending inventory of each product is compared to the fixed reorder point for that product. If the ending inventory is equal to or below the reorder point for that product, The Shopping Basket orders enough of the item to bring the amount on hand up to a predetermined order level. Any order placed on Friday is delivered over the weekend so that the company can begin a new week of business with well-stocked shelves. It is possible that the ending inventory could be negative, indicating that demand exceeded supply during the week and some orders were not filled. Shopping Basket policy is to order enough to cover this back-ordered demand.

    Your task is to write a program to read five DATA statements corresponding to the five different products to determine which products must be ordered and how much of each product to order. The program should also calculate the cost of ordering each item and the total cost for all products ordered. Design the program to make the correct reorder decision for an unknown number of items.

    To aid you in your task, you have been given some old records that illustrate how the reorder system works. You should use the sample data in the *Inventory Summary* below to test your program. Note that the only output required from your program is an *Order Report* similar to the one on page 120.

Some helpful formulas and decision rules:

a. Order an item only if the ending inventory is less than or equal to the reorder point for that item.

b. Amount to order = order level − ending inventory.

c. Cost of ordering an item = amount ordered * unit price.

### INVENTORY SUMMARY (WEEK ENDING OCTOBER 1, 1979)

| ITEM NUMBER | 15202 | 67180 | 51435 | 49415 | 24361 |
|---|---|---|---|---|---|
| DESCRIPTION | TUNA FISH | LIGHTER FLUID | BODY SOAP | PIZZA MIX | TURTLE SOUP |
| Unit price (per case) | 4.27 | 8.48 | 12.29 | 9.27 | 15.32 |
| Order level (cases) | 30 | 25 | 55 | 75 | 15 |
| Reorder point (cases) | 5 | 8 | 10 | 25 | 2 |
| Ending inventory (cases) | 9 | 5 | 7 | −10 | 6 |

The description of each DATA statement is as follows (tuna, for example):

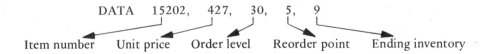

DATA    15202,    427,    30,    5,    9

Item number    Unit price    Order level    Reorder point    Ending inventory

The output report should be similar to:

### THE SHOPPING BASKET

### ORDER REPORT

| ITEM NUMBER | UNIT PRICE | ORDER LEVEL | REORDER POINT | ENDING INVENTORY | ORDER | COST |
|---|---|---|---|---|---|---|
| 15202 | 4.27 | 30 | 5 | 9 | 0 | 0.00 |
| 67180 | 8.48 | 25 | 8 | 5 | 20 | 169.60 |
| 51435 | 12.29 | 55 | 10 | 7 | 48 | 589.92 |
| 49415 | 9.27 | 75 | 25 | −10 | 85 | 787.95 |
| 24361 | 15.32 | 15 | 2 | 6 | 0 | 0.00 |

Total cost        $1,547.47

### Games

Recall that the RND function can be used to generate random numbers. This, in turn, allows us to simulate processes or systems. For example, to simulate the toss of a coin we might agree that 1 represents heads and 2 tails and use the statement LET J = INT(RND(1) * 2) + 1 to generate either a 1 or a 2. To simulate the throw of a die, we would use LET K = INT(RND(1) * 6) + 1. $K$ will then take on any value between 1 and 6.

To determine the probable outcome of a particular event, a program can be written to simulate that event a great number of times and to count the various outcomes. The more the event is simulated, the more accurate the projection of the frequency of the different outcomes. For example, to determine the probability of Johnnie's tossing a 5 with an "honest" die, we would simulate tosses and count the number of times a 5 came out. One thousand tosses would probably result in an answer close to 167, representing 1/6 of the time.

6. Write a program to check the "honesty" of your random number generator by generating randomly a whole number between 1 and 4 (LET K = INT(RND(1) * 4) + 1) and counting the occurrence of each of the numbers (use the ON/GO TO if you have that feature).

7. Write a program to create modern art as follows. Associate with the number 1 a line consisting of, say, 10 consecutive stars (asterisks), with the number 2 a line with 15 consecutive stars, and so on up to the number 6 with a line of so many stars. Then generate a random number between 1 and 6 and print out its corresponding pictorial representation (line of so many stars). Repeat the process 10 or 15 times. You may want to experiment with symbols other than asterisks for the graphic display.

8. A dog is lost in a tunnel at node 0 (see diagram). It can move one node at one time in either direction right or left with equal probability (1 = right, 2 = left). When the dog hits node $L_2$, however, a force of nature always propels him directly to node $L_4$. The dog escapes from the tunnel when he either hits $L_5$ or $R_4$. Write a program to determine:

   a. Whether the dog has a better chance to exit from the right or the left; in fact, what are the odds that he will exit from $R_4$?

   b. How long, on the average, the dog stays in the tunnel (each node takes one minute to cover).

   c. Whether he might stay in the tunnel forever.

   Restart the dog at node 0 a thousand times and count the number of times he escapes through $R_4$ or $L_5$.

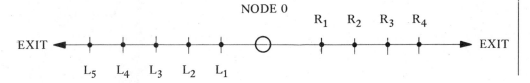

9.  Same as Item 8, except that node $L_2$ propels the dog to $L_4$ only when traveling in a left direction. If node $L_2$ is reached when traveling to the right, the node $L_2$ has no effect.

10. Marc and Laura each toss a die. What is the chance that they each toss the same number? (Simulate 100 throws.)

11. Sue and Tom each toss a pair of dice. What is the chance that both toss out a 2, i.e., a pair of 1's each? a 3? a 4 (2 and 2 or 3 and 1)? a 5? a 12? Express the chance as "so many" out of 100.

12. Charlie tosses a pair of dice. What number (sum of the face values of both dice) is more likely to be thrown? (A 2 is a face value of 1 and 1; a 7 is a combination of either 4, 3; 5, 2; 6, 1; etc.)

13. Write a second-grade level computer assisted instructional unit on additions and subtractions of numbers ranging from 1 to 10. Subtractions should not give rise to negative numbers. The CAI unit should consist of 10 questions. Numbers as well as the operations should occur in random fashion. Print the percentage of correct answers; if the user cannot get the right answer in three attempts, print a message with the correct answer.

## 5-6-4 Answers to Self Test

1. a. 7    b. 6    c. 8    d. 6    e. infinite    f. I not defined    g. infinite    h. 5

2. a,b,d

3. a. $I = 9$    b. $I < 9$    c. $I < 10$    d. $I = 10$    e. $I = 0$    f. $I > -4$

# THE ACCUMULATION PROCESS AND STATEMENTS FOR/NEXT

## 6-1    Problem Example

An input file consists of five grades. Write a program to compute the grade average. Two programs to solve this problem are shown in Figure 6-1, one with the use of an automatic loop control feature called the FOR/NEXT and the other without it to show you how the FOR/NEXT really works.

| Without FOR/NEXT | With FOR/NEXT | |
|---|---|---|
| 05 DATA 60,70,80 | 05 DATA 60,70,80 | |
| 06 DATA 20,100 | 06 DATA 20,100 | S is used as an accumulator to add |
| 10 LET S = 0 | 10 LET S = 0 | all grades.  It is set to 0 initially. |
| 15 LET I = 1 | | |
| 20 IF I > 5 THEN 45 | 20 FOR I = 1 TO 5 | Process the next two statements 5 times (as |
| 25 READ G | 25    READ G | I ranges from 1 to 5). I is initially 1. |
| 30 LET S = S + G | 30    LET S = S + G | As long as I does not exceed 5 read a grade |
| 35 LET I = I + 1 | | and add it to S (thereby forming a running |
| 40 GO TO 20 | 40 NEXT I | sum of grades). 1 is added to I automatically |
| 45 LET A = S/5 | 45 LET A = S/5 | and the loop is repeated until I > 5 at which |
| 50 PRINT A | 50 PRINT A | time the average is computed and printed. |
| 55 STOP | 55 STOP | |
| 99 END | 99 END | |

**Figure 6-1**    Computing an average of grades.

1

Note the two new types of BASIC statement introduced in Figure 6-1:

1.  The FOR statement, which must always be used in conjunction with

2.  The NEXT statement.

# 6-2   BASIC Statements

## 6-2-1   FOR/NEXT Statements

The statements FOR/NEXT represent no new programming concepts that have not already been discussed; in fact, any BASIC program can be written without the FOR/NEXT statements. The purpose of these two statements is strictly one of convenience to the programmer. They are used primarily for loop control. The usual procedure for loop control is to initialize a counter to a certain value, then increment that counter by a constant, and finally compare the counter to a terminal value for loop exiting. With the FOR/NEXT statements the user specifies in the FOR statement the initial, incremental, and terminal value of the counter (index) and identifies the range of the loop by making the NEXT statement the last statement of the procedure to be repeated.

The general form of the FOR statement is

$$statement\text{-}number \text{ FOR } index = e_1 \text{ TO } e_2 \text{ [STEP } e_3]$$

where FOR, TO, and STEP are key words. The *index* must be a variable name and

$e_1$ is an expression that when evaluated specifies the *initial* value of the index;

$e_2$ is an expression that when evaluated denotes the *test* value of the index;

$e_3$ is an expression that when evaluated specifies the *incremental* value of the index. The STEP phrase is optional.

The general form of the NEXT statement is

$$statement\text{-}number \text{ NEXT } index$$

where NEXT is a key word and *index* is a variable name that must also be specified in a FOR statement. A NEXT statement is used to denote the physical end of a loop initiated by a FOR statement.

The statement 10 FOR I = E1 TO E2 [STEP E3] can be interpreted as follows: the two expressions E1 and E2 are evaluated, and the value E1 is assigned to the index I as the initial value. Then the index is compared to the value of E2. If the index is greater than E2, control is passed to the statement following the NEXT statement. If the index is less than or equal to E2, the statements between the FOR and NEXT statements (called the *body of the loop*) are processed. When the NEXT I statement is reached, the value of the index is incremented by E3 and the program returns to the test in the FOR statement. The flowchart symbol for the FOR/ NEXT in Figure 6-1 can be visualized in Figure 6-2.

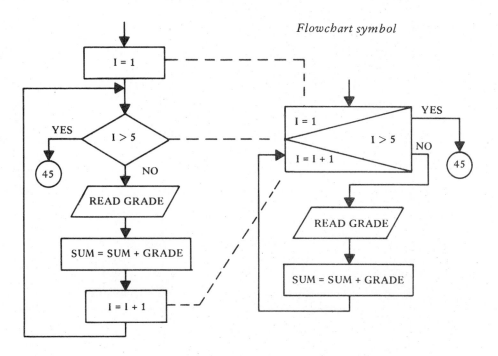

**Figure 6-2**   Flowchart equivalent for the FOR/NEXT symbol.

## 6-2-2   The Accumulation Process

We have already seen how counting in BASIC is made possible by repeated execution of such statements as $I = I + 1$, where $I$ is initially set to a beginning value. Each time $I = I + 1$ is executed, the value 1 is added to the counter $I$, which then takes on successive values 1, 2, 3, 4, and so on, if $I$ is set initially to zero. Counting can be thought of as "accumulating a count." The main difference between "counting" and "accumulating" is that, instead of repetitively adding a constant (1, for example) to a counter, a variable is added[1] repetitively to an accumulator (a special variable used to keep track of running sums or partial sums, products, etc.) (see Figure 6-3).

A review of the program in Figure 6-1 will help you better understand the accumulation process. Recall that five tests grades are recorded on a DATA statement and that it is desired to compute the grade average (see Figure 6-4).

---

[1]Multiplication and other arithmetic operations can also be part of the accumulation process.

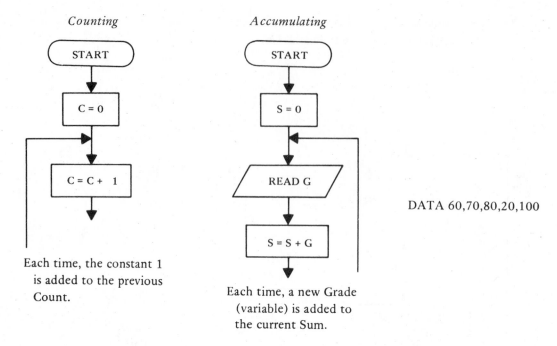

DATA 60,70,80,20,100

Each time, the constant 1 is added to the previous Count.

Each time, a new Grade (variable) is added to the current Sum.

**Figure 6-3**   Comparison between counting and accumulating.

| | |
|---|---|
| 10 LET S = 0 | Initialize Sum to 0. Sum is used as an accumulator to accumulate all grades. |
| 20 FOR I = 1 TO 5 | Process statements 25 and 30 five times. |
| 25    READ G | Read a Grade. |
| 30    LET S=S+G | The new Sum is equal to the old Sum plus the Grade just read. |
| | The first time around the loop, Sum + Grade = 0 + 60, hence new Sum = 60. |
| | The second time around, Sum + Grade = 60 + 70 = 130, hence the new Sum = 130. Each time through the loop, we are adding the grade just read to form a running or partial sum of grades. |
| | When five grades have been read, the sum of five grades will have been computed. |
| 40 NEXT I | Go back to statement 25 until the loop has been processed five times. |
| 45 LET A = S/5 | Now that all the grades have been read, i.e., the loop has gone through its full cycle, we can compute the average and print it out. |
| 50 PRINT A | |
| 45 DATA 60, 70, 80, 20, 100 | |
| 55 STOP | |
| 99 END | |

**Figure 6-4**   Average of five grades.

Note the importance of setting $S$ initially to 0 outside the loop, and note how the partial sums of grades are formed each time a Grade is read using the statement $S = S + G$. The statement $Y = S + G$ could not be used to accumulate the sum. The accumulation process may be better understood or visualized if we tabulate the values for $I$ and $G$ and $S$ as follows:

| INPUT DATA | SEQUENCE OF PARTIAL SUMS $(S)$ | COUNTER $(I)$ | GRADES READ $(G)$ |
|---|---|---|---|
| DATA 60,70,80,20,100 | 0 | 1 | 60 |
|  | 60 (0 + 60) | 2 | 70 |
|  | 130 (60 + 70) | 3 | 80 |
|  | 210 (130 + 80) | 4 | 20 |
|  | 230 (210 + 20) | 5 | 100 |
|  | 330 (230 + 100) |  |  |

## 6-2-3  The FOR/NEXT Revisited

The FOR/NEXT statement can be quite convenient when it is desired to execute one or more statements a specified number of times as in example 1, where 303 records are read and printed.

Example 1

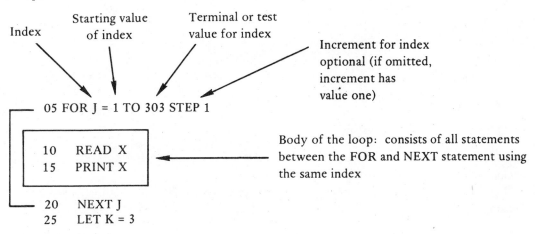

All statements in the body of the loop (statements 10 and 15) will be processed 303 times as $J$ ranges from the starting value of 1 to 304 in steps of 1. When $J$ is 304, the statements in the body of the loop are not processed and control is passed to the statement following the NEXT statement (statement 25).

Sometimes it may be convenient to use the index not just as a counting mechanism for loop control but also as a variable (number generator) within the body of the loop. Suppose, as in example 2, it is desired to sum the first 100 positive integers, as in

$$SUM = 1 + 2 + 3 + 4 + \cdots + 100$$

The index *I* can be used to generate these numbers, as follows:

**Example 2**

```
10 LET S = 0
15    FOR I = 1 TO 100
20    LET S = S + I
25 NEXT I
30 PRINT S
```

The sum is initially 0.
I generates the numbers 1, 2, 3, . . . 100.
As these numbers are generated, keep adding
them to Sum to form a running Sum.
Print the final sum.

To generate and print the sequence of numbers 10, 9, 8, 7, . . . 2, 1, the following code might be used:

**Example 3**

```
10 FOR I = 10 TO 1 STEP -1
15 PRINT I;
20 NEXT I
```

Note that the constants in the FOR/NEXT can take on fractional values, as in example 4:

**Example 4**

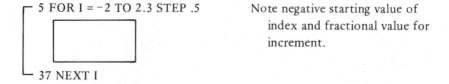

Note negative starting value of
index and fractional value for
increment.

The values assumed by the index I are -2, -1.5, -1, -.5, 0, .5, 1, 1.5, 2, and hence the statements in the body of the loop will be executed 9 times.

It is often convenient to express the terminal value of a FOR/NEXT loop as a variable, as in example 5:

**Example 5**

```
10 READ N
```

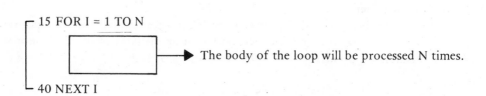

The body of the loop will be processed N times.

The programmer may also wish to express the initial and step values as variables, as in example 6:

**Example 6**

10 READ L,K

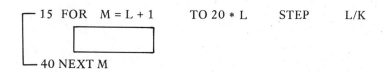

15 FOR M = L + 1     TO 20 * L     STEP     L/K

40 NEXT M

However, care should be exercised *not* to change either the index, the initial, the terminal, or the step variable within the FOR/NEXT loop. Avoid the following common pitfalls:

<table>
<tr><td>
5 FOR J = K TO 10<br>
10     READ X,J<br>
15 NEXT J
</td><td>
5 FOR I = 1 TO L<br>
10 LET L = L+1<br>
15 NEXT I
</td></tr>
<tr><td>
The index J is redefined by the READ statement.
</td><td>
The value of L should remain fixed within the loop.
</td></tr>
</table>

**Transfer Into and Out of Loops**

*Case 1: Permissible*

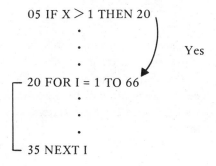

05 IF X > 1 THEN 20

Yes

20 FOR I = 1 TO 66

35 NEXT I

Transfer can be made to a loop as long as the transfer target is the FOR/NEXT statement.

*Case 2: Not permissible*

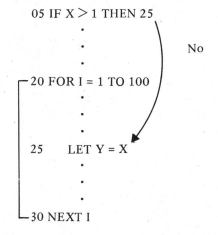

05 IF X > 1 THEN 25

No

20 FOR I = 1 TO 100

25     LET Y = X

30 NEXT I

Cannot transfer from outside a loop into a statement within the body of a loop. The value of I would be undefined.

*Case 3: Permissible*

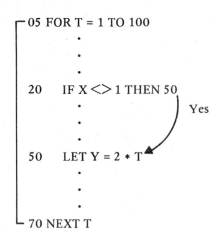

Transfer can be made from one statement to another within the same loop.

*Case 4: Permissible*

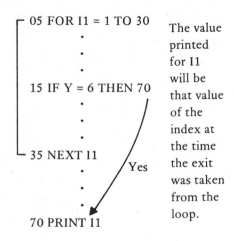

The value printed for I1 will be that value of the index at the time the exit was taken from the loop.

Transfer from a statement within a loop outside the loop is legitimate.

*Case 5: Permissible*

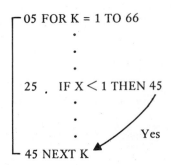

Stay in loop but bypass statements between 25 and 45.

*Case 6: Logical error*

```
   05 FOR I = 1 TO 10          No
   10    LET X = I ** 2 - 7 * I + 12
   15    IF X <> 0 THEN 5
   20    PRINT I
   25 NEXT I
```

A transfer from within a loop to the FOR statement will cause a resetting of the index rather than a continuation of the loop process; the result will be an infinite loop. A transfer to the NEXT statement should be made.

## Nested Loops

When writing programs, it is often necessary to repeat a loop a certain number of times. This is an example of a loop within a loop, or, more exactly, a complete loop is part of the body of another loop. In such cases, each pass in the outer loop causes the inner loop to run through its complete cycle. The following code illustrates the mechanism of the so-called nested loop.

OUTER LOOP

Since *I* varies from 1 to 3, the inner loop will be processed three times.

```
10 FOR I = 1 TO 3
12    FOR J = 1 TO 4
14    PRINT I,J
16    NEXT J
20 NEXT I
```

INNER LOOP

The inner loop will cause the PRINT statement to be processed 4 times. Since the outer loop is processed 3 times, the PRINT statement will be processed altogether 12 times.

The result produced by the above code is

| *I* | *J* | |
|---|---|---|
| 1 | 1 | |
| 1 | 2 | First time through the inner loop |
| 1 | 3 | (outer loop index *I* = 1) |
| 1 | 4 | |
| 2 | 1 | |
| 2 | 2 | Second time through the inner loop |
| 2 | 3 | (outer loop index *I* = 2) |
| 2 | 4 | |
| 3 | 1 | |
| 3 | 2 | Third time through the inner loop |
| 3 | 3 | (outer loop index *I* = 3) |
| 3 | 4 | |

As an application of nested loops, Figure 6-5 prints the first five multiplication tables.

```
05  FOR J = 1 TO 10
10      FOR K = 1 TO 5
15          PRINT K; "X"; J;
20          PRINT "="; K * J,
25      NEXT K
30    PRINT
40  NEXT J
50  RUN
```

This innermost loop controls the horizontal length of each line. It will print
$1 \times J = \Box \ 2 \times J = \Box \cdots 5 \times J = \Box$ for values of J ranging 1 to 10

The outer loop controls the number of rows printed.

| | | | | |
|---|---|---|---|---|
| 1 X 1 = 1 | 2 X 1 = 2 | 3 X 1 = 3 | 4 X 1 = 4 | 5 X 1 = 5 |
| 1 X 2 = 2 | 2 X 2 = 4 | 3 X 2 = 6 | 4 X 2 = 8 | 5 X 2 = 10 |
| 1 X 3 = 3 | 2 X 3 = 6 | 3 X 3 = 9 | 4 X 3 = 12 | 5 X 3 = 15 |
| 1 X 4 = 4 | 2 X 4 = 8 | 3 X 4 = 12 | 4 X 4 = 16 | 5 X 4 = 20 |
| 1 X 5 = 5 | 2 X 5 = 10 | 3 X 5 = 15 | 4 X 5 = 20 | 5 X 5 = 25 |
| 1 X 6 = 6 | 2 X 6 = 12 | 3 X 6 = 18 | 4 X 6 = 24 | 5 X 6 = 30 |
| 1 X 7 = 7 | 2 X 7 = 14 | 3 X 7 = 21 | 4 X 7 = 28 | 5 X 7 = 35 |
| 1 X 8 = 8 | 2 X 8 = 16 | 3 X 8 = 24 | 4 X 8 = 32 | 5 X 8 = 40 |
| 1 X 9 = 9 | 2 X 9 = 18 | 3 X 9 = 27 | 4 X 9 = 36 | 5 X 9 = 45 |
| 1 X 10 = 10 | 2 X 10 = 20 | 3 X 10 = 30 | 4 X 10 = 40 | 5 X 10 = 50 |

**Figure 6-5** Example of a nested loop.

When using nested loops, it is important to keep in mind that each nested loop must lie totally within the body of the outer loop. For example, consider the following illustrations of valid and invalid nested loops.

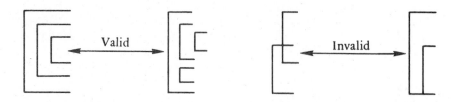

# 6-3 You Might Want To Know

1. To what depth or level can loops be nested?

   *Answer:* It depends on the manufacturer's BASIC. It is safe to assume that all BASIC systems will allow a depth of three nested loops. (Check with BASIC technical reference manual.)

2. What happens to the FOR/NEXT loop in the following cases?

   a.   FOR I = 5 TO 5

   b.   FOR J = 100 TO 1

   c.   FOR K = 2, 10, – 1

   In most systems the following actions will be taken:

   *Case a:* The loop is executed only once.

   *Case b:* The loop is not executed and control is passed to the statement following the NEXT statement.

   *Case c:* Same as case b since value of K is less than test value and increment is negative.

3. Can the programmer count on the value of the index to be the same as the terminal value specified in the FOR/NEXT statement when exiting out of the loop through the NEXT statement?

   *Answer:* No. If that value is desired, use another variable in the loop to keep track of it.

4. When I write a program to compute some dollar amount the result often gets printed with seven or more significant digits. Now, I'm only interested in dollars and cents and need only two digits to the right of the decimal point. How can I essentially round off and truncate excess digits?

   *Answer:* To round off $X = 41.829$ to two fractional digits, do the following:

   a.   Multiply $X$ by 100 to get 4182.9.

   b.   Add .5 to $X$ to get 4183.4 (round off).

---

c.  Take integer part to get 4183 (truncate).

d.  Divide by 100 to get 41.83.

These four steps can be accomplished by the statement LET X = INT (X * 100 + .5)/100, where INT is the integer function (see Chapter 9), which truncates all digits to the right of the decimal point, i.e., INT (2.99) = 2.

5.  How can I determine whether an integer $N$ is even or odd?

*Answer:* Use the integer function INT by computing the expression

$$2 * INT(N/2) - N$$

If $N$ is even, $N = 4$, the result of the expression is always zero (2 * 2 − 4).

If $N$ is odd, $N = 7$, the result of the expression is always negative (2 * 3 − 7 = −1).

6.  Is there a formula that can tell me how many times a FOR/NEXT loop will be executed depending on the value of the parameters?

*Answer:* Given positive *integer values* for the initial value ($I$), step value ($S$), and terminal value ($T$) of the FOR/NEXT statement, the formula to compute the number of times ($NT$) the loop will be executed is given by

$$NT = \frac{T - I}{S} + 1 \qquad \text{Here, only the integer result of the division is kept.}$$

*Example:*

$$\overset{I}{\underset{\downarrow}{\phantom{x}}} \quad \overset{T}{\underset{\downarrow}{\phantom{x}}} \quad \overset{S}{\underset{\downarrow}{\phantom{x}}}$$
FOR K = 3 TO 10 STEP 2

The number of times the body of the loop is executed is given by

$$NT = \frac{10 - 3}{2} + 1 = \frac{7}{2} + 1 = 3 + 1 = 4.$$

# 6-4  Programming Examples

## 6-4-1  Transfer Within and Out of a Loop

A DATA statement contains an unknown number of grades (0—100) with a maximum of 100 entries in the DATA statement including the trip record. An out-of-range grade terminates the input data. Passing grades are grades above 73. Print a list of passing grades and determine the percentage of passing grades. A program to solve this problem is shown in Figure 6-6.

10 DATA ∿,∿,∿

15 LET I7 = 0

20 FOR I = 1 TO 100

25 READ G

30 IF G < 0 THEN 55

35 IF G > 100 THEN 55

40 IF G <= 73 THEN 50

45 LET I7 = I7 + 1

50 NEXT I

55 LET A = I7/(I − 1) * 100

60 PRINT A

65 STOP

99 END

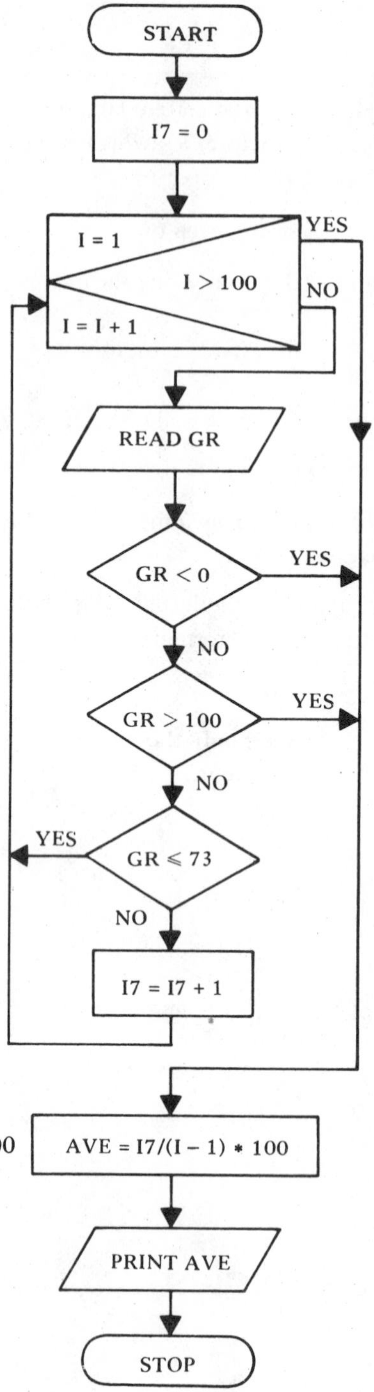

**START**

I7 = 0

I = 1    YES

I > 100    NO

I = I + 1

READ GR

GR < 0    YES

NO

GR > 100    YES

NO

YES    GR ≤ 73

NO

I7 = I7 + 1

AVE = I7/(I − 1) * 100

PRINT AVE

**STOP**

I7 is the counter to count grades >73

Process at most 100 grades in the DATA statement. The YES branch will never be taken, since exiting from the loop will be as a result of the trip record.
Read a grade.

Is it outside the range 0−100?

No; is the grade ≤73? If yes, go back and read more grades. Note that the transfer is made to the NEXT statement (50).

Count grade if above 73.

The trip record has been found and exiting from the loop takes place.

**Figure 6-6** Transfer within a loop.

Note that the index I is used to keep track of the number of grades read. In computing the percentage, note the division by I − 1, since the last record read is the trip record.

## 6-4-2 Standard Deviation

The general formula to compute the standard deviation for $n$ grades $x_1, x_2, x_3, \ldots, x_n$ is:

$$SD = \sqrt{\frac{n(x_1^2 + x_2^2 + x_3^2 + \ldots + x_n^2) - (x_1 + x_2 + x_3 + \ldots + x_n)^2}{n(n-1)}}$$

Write a program to read 30 grades from a DATA list and compute the average and the standard deviation. In this particular case, $n$ is 30. To compute the standard deviation it is necessary to

1. Accumulate the sum of the grades $(x_1 + x_2 + \ldots + x_{30})$.
2. Accumulate the sum of the square of each grade $(x_1^2 + x_2^2 + \ldots + x_{30}^2)$.

The program shown in Figure 6-7 could be used.

| | |
|---|---|
| 1 LET N = 30 | Set number of grades to 30 for this problem. |
| 5 LET Q = 0 | Set variable to accumulate the sum of the square of each grade to 0. |
| 10 LET S = 0 | Set variable to accumulate the sum of the grades to 0. |
| 15 FOR K = 1 TO N | Start loop. |
| 20    READ G | Read one grade each time through the loop. |
| 25    LET S = S + G | Accumulate the sum of the grades, one at a time. |
| 30    LET Q = Q + G * G | Accumulate the sum of the square of each grade. |

```
35 NEXT K
37 REM COMPUTE THE STANDARD DEVIATION D
40 LET D = ((N * Q - S * S)/(N * (N - 1))) ** .5
45 PRINT "STANDARD DEVIATION =";D
50 PRINT "AVERAGE GRADE =";S/N
55 DATA 10,20,30,40,50,60,70,80,90,100,90,80,70,60,50
60 DATA 11,22,33,44,55,66,77,88,99,12,34,40,30,2,1
99 END


RUN


STANDARD DEVIATION = 29.8752
AVERAGE GRADE = 50.4666
```

**Figure 6-7** Calculation of a standard deviation.

### 6-4-3   War Game

A submarine has been trapped into an enemy bay with only one escape channel leading out of the bay. The bay is surrounded by mines as shown below. All navigating equipment is malfunctioning, and the blind submarine is now moving randomly in any of the four cardinal directions one square at a time. If the sub hits any of the mines, it is instantly destroyed. Write a program to determine the sub's escape chances from its present position of row 4 and column 2. The sub escapes when it reaches row 2 column 5.

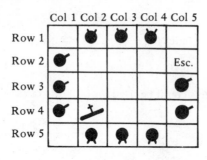

| 10 LET E=0 | E counts the escapes. |
| 15 LET D=0 | D counts the destroys. |
| 20 FOR I=1 TO 10000 | Simulate 10,000 trips for the sub, each trip |
| 25    LET R=4 | originating at Row 4 and Column 2. |
| 30    LET C=2 | |
| 35    LET J=INT(RND(1)*4+1) | J = 1 move up; J = 2 move left; J = 3 move |
| 40    ON J GO TO 45,60,75,90 | down, J = 4 move right. |
| 45    LET R=R−1 | Go and calculate the new coordinates (R,C). |
| 50    IF R=1 GO TO 105 | Sub moves up. |
| 55    GO TO 35 | If R = 1 sub is destroyed; otherwise continue |
| 60    LET C=C−1 | the journey. |
| 65    IF C=1 GO TO 105 | |
| 70    GO TO 35 | Repeat same technique for other directions. |
| 75    LET R=R+1 | |
| 80    IF R=5 GO TO 105 | |
| 85    GO TO 35 | |
| 90    LET C=C+1 | |
| 95    IF C<>5 GO TO 35 | |
| 100    IF R=2 GO TO 115 | If C = 5 and R = 2 sub escapes. |
| 105    LET D=D+1 | |
| 110    GO TO 120 | |
| 115    LET E=E+1 | |
| 120 NEXT I | |
| 125 PRINT"% ESCAPE=";E/100 | Print percentage of escapes. |
| 130 END | |
| RUN | |
| % ESCAPE= 1.33 | |

Figure 6-8    Naval warfare simulation.

To solve this problem we identify the position of the sub by setting R = 4 and C = 2. A random number (1-4) is used to determine the direction; depending on that number, we change the row R or the column C. If either R or C is 1 or 5 the sub is destroyed. If the R = 2 and C = 5, the sub escapes and appropriate counters are incremented. When the sub has been destroyed or has escaped, it is repositioned at R = 4 and C = 2 and the entire process is repeated 10,000 times. The sub's escape chances are then E out of 10,000. A program to solve this problem is shown in Figure 6-8.

## 6-4-4    Bar Graph (Nested Loops)

We often need programs to print graphic output. A scientific problem might require the graph of a function; a business problem might require a bar graph. Consider, for example, the following problem. Data regarding company sales for a week have been tabulated as follows:

To visualize graphically the sales trend, we would like to write a program to produce the following output:

| DAY | SALES |
|-----|-------|
| 1 | 15 |
| 2 | 19 |
| 3 | 23 |
| 4 | 16 |
| 5 | 21 |
| 6 | 25 |
| 7 | 28 |

```
DAY    SALES

 1      15    ***************
 2      19    ******************
 3      23    **********************
 4      16    ***************
 5      21    ********************
 6      25    *************************
 7      28    ****************************
```

Such a program is illustrated in Figure 6-9.

10 DATA 15,19,23,16

14 DATA 21,25,28
15 PRINT "DAY"; TAB(5);
16 PRINT "SALES"

20 PRINT

25 FOR I = 1 TO 7

30 READ S

35 PRINT I; TAB(6); S,

40 FOR J = 1 TO S

45 PRINT "*";

50 NEXT J

60 PRINT

65 NEXT I

70 STOP

99 END

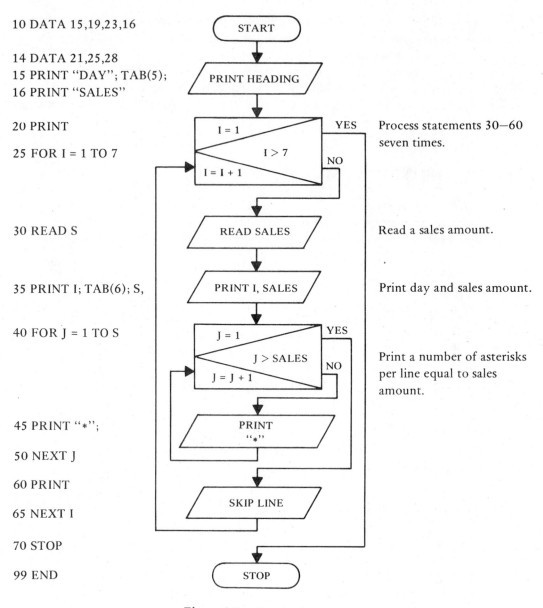

Figure 6-9   Bar graph program.

# 6-5 Assignments

## 6-5-1 Self Test

1. State whether the following are valid or invalid FOR/NEXT loops and give reasons if invalid.

    a. FOR I = 1 TO 10
       FOR I = 1 TO 6
       PRINT I
       NEXT I

    b. FOR K = K TO 5
       .
       .
       NEXT K

    c. FOR K + 1 = 1 to -9
       .
       .
       NEXT K

    d. FOR J = 1 TO 10
       LET J = I * I + 1
       NEXT I

    e. FOR K2 = -3 TO 2
       FOR K = 2 TO 15
       .
       .
       NEXT K2
       .
       .
       NEXT K

    f. FOR K = 1 TO 6
       READ K1, K
       LET S = S + K1
       LET S2 = S2 + K
       NEXT K

    g. FOR L = 8 TO 1 STEP -1
       FOR K = 1 TO 3
       FOR L = L + 1
       NEXT K
       NEXT L

    h. FOR I = 1 TO 4
       .
       .
       NEXT I
       FOR I = 2 TO 10
       .
       .
       NEXT I

    i. FOR I = 1 TO L
       .
       .
       IF Q = 6 GO TO 5
    5  FOR K = 1 TO 10
       .
       .
       NEXT K
       LET L = L - 1
       NEXT I

2.   What output will be produced by each of the following code segments?

a.   FOR I = 1 TO 10 STEP 2          b.   FOR J = 6 TO 18 STEP 3
     PRINT I                              PRINT J;
     NEXT I                               NEXT J

c.   FOR K = 4 TO 1
     PRINT K
     NEXT K

3.   Assuming all loops go through their complete cycle, how many times will the statement
     LET X = 1 be processed?

a.   FOR I = 1 TO 3               b.   FOR I = 2 TO 20 STEP 3
     FOR J = 1 TO 4                    FOR J = 3 TO 17 STEP 5
     FOR K = 1 TO 10                   LET X = 1
     LET X = 1                         NEXT J
     NEXT K                           NEXT I
     NEXT J
     NEXT I

c.   FOR I = 2 TO 8 STEP 2
     FOR J = I TO 10
     LET X = 1
     NEXT J
     NEXT I

4.   Which of the following code segments will compute the average (A) of 10 grades?

a.   LET S = 0                    b.   LET S = 0
     FOR I = 1 TO 10                   FOR I = 1 TO 10
     READ G                            READ G
     LET S = S + G                     LET S = S + G
     NEXT I                            LET A = S/I
     LET A = S/I                       NEXT I
     PRINT A                           PRINT A

## 6-5-2   Exercises

1.   Write a program to accumulate and print each of the following:

a.   $1 + 3 + 5 + 7 \cdots + 225$   Is accumulation necessary in this problem?

b.   $1^2 + 2^2 + 3^2 + 4^2 \cdots + 100^2$

c.   $2 * 4 * 6 * 8 \cdots * 100$

d.   $2 + 4 + 8 + 16 + 32 \cdots + 1024$

e.   $1 + 1/2 + 1/3 + 1/4 \cdot \cdot \cdot + 1/100$

f.   $1 - 2 + 3 - 4 + 5 \cdot \cdot \cdot - 100$

g.   Print the ordered triples for $x,y,z$ for $z = x^2 + y^2$ where $y$ takes on values 1,2,3 for each value of $x$ equal to 2, 4, 6, and 8.

2.   A data statement contains a list of positive and negative numbers varying from $-100$ to $+100$. The last item on the list is a special code 999. Write a program to compute the sum of the positive values and the sum of the negative values (exclusive of the special code). Print both sums.

3.   Grades (100 at most) are recorded on a DATA statement. A special code of 999 terminates the list. Write a program using the FOR/NEXT to determine the largest and smallest grade. Print both these grades.

4.   Write a program to compute the following sequences of sums:

$$S_1 = 1$$
$$S_2 = 1 + \frac{1}{2}$$
$$S_3 = 1 + \frac{1}{2} + \frac{1}{3}$$
$$S_4 = 1 + \frac{1}{2} + \frac{1}{3} + \frac{1}{4}$$

.

.

.

How many different sums would you have to compute before the sum exceeds 3.9?

5.   A data file consists of records each containing the following information concerning items produced at the XYZ manufacturing plant: a department number, an item number, a quantity, and a cost per item. Assume the file has been sorted into order by ascending department number. Write a program to produce a summary report as follows:

| DEPARTMENT | ITEM NO. | QUANTITY | COST/ITEM | VALUE | TOTALS |
|---|---|---|---|---|---|
| 15 | 1389 | 4 | 3.20 | 12.80 | |
| 15 | 3821 | 2 | 7.00 | 14.00 | |
| | | | | | 26.80 |
| 16 | 0122 | 8 | 2.50 | 20.00 | |
| | | | | | 20.00 |
| 19 | 1244 | 100 | .03 | 3.00 | |
| 19 | 1245 | 20 | 4.00 | 80.00 | |
| 19 | 2469 | 4 | 16.00 | 64.00 | |
| | | | | | 147.00 |
| | | | | GRAND TOTAL | 193.80 |

Could you alter the program to write each subtotal on the same line as the last transaction line of each department? Make your own data file.

6.  The *mode* of a set of scores is that score which occurs most frequently. For example, in the set:

    $$13, 13, 15, 20, 20, 31, 31, 46, 46, 46, 50$$

    the mode is 46. Write a program to read a set of scores already arranged in numerical ascending order and print the scores and the mode.

7.  The SLY company convinced Mr. Jones to work for them for 30 days as follows: The first day Mr. Jones gets paid 1 cent, the second day 2 cents, the third day 4 cents, the fourth day 8 cents, etc., in general, twice the previous day's pay. Print a table showing Mr. Jones's earnings during the last 10 days. (Make sure these earnings are displayed in dollar figures.)

8.  Every time a meal is sold at Charlie's Eatery, the cost of the order and a meal code (1 = breakfast, 2 = lunch, 3 = dinner) is entered at a terminal. Write a program to compute and print:

    a.  Today's total sales

    b.  Average cost of breakfasts

    c.  Minimum dinner order

9.  You are the owner of a bookstore that sells both paperback and hardback books. For every book you sell, you have a record with two numbers: the amount the book cost and either a 0 or a 1 (0 if the book is a paperback; 1 if the book is hardback). You want to know the following information:

    a.  Total amount taken in              d.  Minimum price of a hardback book

    b.  Total number of books sold          e.  Average price of a paperback book

    c.  Average price per book

10. Accept a number $N$ with five digits to the right of the decimal point and round it off to a number with three digits to the right of the decimal point (see Section 6-3, question 4).

11. The Post Office charges 15¢ for the first ounce or part thereof for a first class letter and 13¢ for each additional ounce or part thereof. Write a program to accept letter weights in ounces and print the required postage.

12. Write a program to calculate the amount of change to be given from a dollar in amounts accepted from input, for example:

    Purchase of 17¢   Change = 1 half dollar, 1 quarter, 1 nickel, 3 pennies
    Purchase of 65¢   Change = 1 quarter, 1 dime

13. Write a program to compute the value of $\pi/4$ using the following formula:

    $$\frac{\pi}{4} = 1 - \frac{1}{3} + \frac{1}{5} - \frac{1}{7} + \frac{1}{9} - \cdots$$

    1st approximation is $\pi/4 = 1$;
    2nd approximation is $\pi/4 = 1 - 1/3$;
    3rd approximation is $\pi/4 = 1 - 1/3 + 1/5$; etc.

    Stop when the difference between two successive approximations is less than .01.

14.  A prime number is any number which can be divided only by itself and 1. Write a program to input a number $N \leqslant 5000$ and determine whether N is prime.

15.  The sine of an angle can be computed from its series expansion:

$$\sin x = x - \frac{x^3}{3!} + \frac{x^5}{5!} - \frac{x^7}{7!} \cdots \qquad \text{where } x \text{ is expressed in radians.}$$

If $x = 1$, compute the number of terms required to produce sin 1 with a truncation error less than $5 \times 10^{-5}$. The truncation error is equal to the first term neglected. For example if the first two terms are used to compute sin $x$, the truncation error is $x^5/5!$ (the first term not used).

16.  The number $e$ can be approximated by the formula

$$e_4 \simeq 1 + \frac{1}{1}\left(1 + \frac{1}{2}\left(1 + \frac{1}{3}\left(1 + \frac{1}{4}\right)\right)\right)$$

however, a better approximation would be

$$e_{100} \simeq = 1 + \frac{1}{1}\left(1 + \frac{1}{2}\left(1 + \frac{1}{3}\left(1 + \frac{1}{4}\left(1 + \frac{1}{5}\left(1 + \frac{1}{6}\left(\cdots \frac{1}{99}\left(1 + \frac{1}{100}\right)\right)\cdots\right)\right.\right.\right.\right.$$

Write a program to compute $e_{100}$.

## 6-5-3  Projects

1.  You would like to buy a new car on credit. You decide what the monthly payment is to be (maximum you can afford). That monthly payment must remain constant throughout the loan schedule. The interest is also calculated monthly and added to the balance each month. Compute and print out a formatted table containing (1) the number of months the loan has been in effect, (2) the remaining balance after adding the interest and subtracting the payment, and (3) the total amount paid to your loan company so far. The interest is calculated on the balance *before* the payment is subtracted. Be sure that you don't overpay on the last payment. Enter three values: Total car cost, monthly payment, and interest rate. The output should be as shown in the following example:

THE BALANCE OF A CAR LOAN

| COST OF CAR = $5,000 | INTEREST = 1.00% | PAYMENT = $100.00 |
|:---:|:---:|:---:|
| MONTH | BALANCE | TOTAL TO DATE |
| 1 | 4950.00 | 100 |
| 2 | 4899.50 | 200 |
| 3 | 4848.49 | 300 |
| . | . | . |
| . | . | . |

2.  Write a program to compute the area under a curve $y = f(x)$:

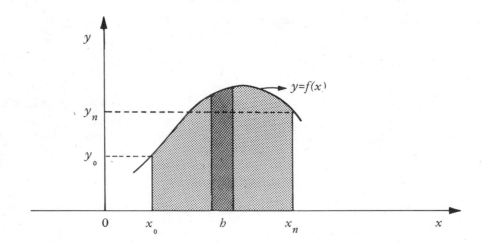

The darkened area under a curve $y = f(x)$ can be approximated by breaking the interval $(x_0, x_n)$ into $n$ equal intervals of size

$$h = \frac{x_n - x_0}{n}$$

and computing the sum of the $n$ areas of the trapezoids with base $h$. The smaller the interval $h$ the closer the approximation is to the exact area. The formula to compute the sum of the areas of the $n$ trapezoids is

$$A = \frac{h}{2}\left(y_0 + 2y_1 + 2y_2 + \cdots + 2y_{n-1} + y_n\right)$$

where $y_0, y_1, y_2, \cdots, y_n$ are the values of the function at the points $x_0, x_1, x_2, \cdots, x_n$. Your program should approximate the area under the curve $y = e^{-x^2/2}$ for $x$ between 1 and 2 for three different values of $h$: .1, .01, .001. (This is equivalent to obtaining an approximation for $\int_1^2 e^{-x^2/2}$.)

3.  A study was conducted to determine whether different communication modes to computers could affect a student's attitude towards programming. In a computer-related course, thirteen students used batch processing mode to solve problems on the computer while twelve other students used conversational mode to solve the same problems. The following entries reflect the average score obtained by each student across all the twenty questions of the Attitude Test Toward Programming (ATTP) given at the end of the semester:

*Mode of Communication*

| *Batch Processing* | *Conversational* |
|---|---|
| 2.75 | 4.15 |
| 2.95 | 3.70 |
| 3.00 | 3.55 |
| 3.10 | 4.45 |
| 4.50 | 4.20 |
| 4.75 | 3.95 |
| 2.50 | 3.80 |
| 3.35 | 4.00 |
| 4.00 | 3.00 |
| 3.05 | 3.65 |
| 2.00 | 4.00 |
| 3.35 | 4.35 |
| 4.10 | |

Conversational students had a higher average score than batch processing students. Write a program to determine if this difference is significant. The difference is significant if $t > 2.069$, where $t$ is given by the following formula:

$$t = \frac{\bar{X}_c - \bar{X}_b}{\sqrt{\frac{\left((N_c - 1)S_c^2 + (N_b - 1)S_b^2\right)}{(N_c + N_b - 2)} \cdot \frac{(N_c + N_b)}{N_c \cdot N_b}}}$$

where: $\bar{X}_c$ and $\bar{X}_b$ are the averages of the conversational and batch scores respectively

$S_c$ and $S_b$ are the standard deviations for conversational and batch modes respectively (See Section 6-4-2 for the programming example of a standard deviation.)

$N_c$ and $N_b$ are the number of scores for conversational and batch processing respectively

4. The Meals on Wheels Company operates a fleet of vans used for the delivery of cold foods at various local plants and construction sites. The management is thinking of purchasing a specially built $18,000 van equipped to deliver hot foods. This new addition to the fleet is expected to generate after-tax earnings $E_1, E_2, \ldots, E_6$ (as displayed below) over the next six years, at which time the van's resale value will be zero. Projected repair and maintenance costs $C_0, C_1, C_2, \ldots, C_6$ over the six years are shown as follows:

PROJECTED EARNINGS

PROJECTED COSTS

| | | | |
|---|---|---|---|
| | | $C_0$ | $18,000 (purchase cost of the van) |
| $E_1$ | $2,500 | $C_1$ | 610 |
| $E_2$ | 2,500 | $C_2$ | 745 |
| $E_3$ | 3,000 | $C_3$ | 820 |
| $E_4$ | 4,500 | $C_4$ | 900 |
| $E_5$ | 6,000 | $C_5$ | 950 |
| $E_6$ | 6,000 | $C_6$ | 1,000 |

a. Write a program to determine whether or not the company should acquire the van. The decision depends on the benefit/cost ratio ($BCR$) (grossly speaking, earnings/ expenditures) given by the formula

$$BCR = \frac{E_1(1 + i)^1 + E_2(1 + i)^2 + \cdots + E_6(1 + i)^6}{C_0 + C_1(1 + i)^1 + C_2(1 + i)^2 + \cdots + C_6(1 + i)^6}$$

where $i$ is the rate of investment of earnings by the company (6 percent in this problem). If $BCR < 1$, then the company should not acquire the van. Use the accumulation process to compute the $BCR$. Accumulate the numerator by reading all earnings $E_1, E_2, \ldots, E_6$ from one DATA statement, and then accumulate the denominator by reading all costs $C_1, \ldots, C_6$ from another DATA statement. (The statement READ E and READ C should be processed six times.)

b. When shown the projected maintenance costs for the next six years, the repair and maintenance shop foreman argues that these cost figures are unrealistic and proposes instead the following costs starting with the first year: 1,000, 1,500, 2,000, 2,000, 2,100, 2,400. Using these figures, determine whether the company should purchase the van.

c. Finding that the van cannot be purchased with the foreman's cost projections, but still determined to acquire the vehicle, the management decides to determine how high their investment rate ($i$) would have to be raised to permit the purchase of the vehicle. Write a program to compute the $BCR$ for investment rates starting at 6 percent and increasing in amounts of .1 percent. The output should be as follows:

| BENEFIT/COST RATIO | INVESTMENT RATE |
|:---:|:---:|
| . | 6 % |
| . | 6.1 |
| . | . |
| . | . |

Stop whenever the $BCR$ is greater than 1 and print the message "purchase of the van requires that the investment rate be XX.XX percent." (Make use of the RESTORE statement.)

d. Having decided that the foreman's cost projections were realistic (part b of the problem), the management decides to recompute the $BCR$ allowing for a resale value of $1,000 for the van, the investment rate being fixed at 6 percent. Determine whether or not the van should be purchased. (Note that the sale of the van represents an earning.)

## Games

5. You are now at the famous Monte Carlo casino and you have $1,000 to burn. You are not a sophisticated roulette player, and so you decide to place bets on the even or odd. The roulette ball lands on any of 36 numbers (1–36). The number 33 is the house's lucky

number, and the croupier rakes in everything on the board. Correct bets double your input. Write a program to continuously accept bets (in amounts of either $100, $400, or $800), to spin the wheel (LET K = INT(RND(1) * 36 + 1), and print your remaining balance. The game should go on till you have either run out of cash or doubled your initial investment. Play 10 such games and keep track of how many you win and how many you lose. What are your chances of doubling your initial investment?

The following exercises (6–9) relate to the submarine program illustrated in Figure 6-8 of Section 6-4.

6. Change the program of Figure 6-8 to allow the submarine to travel in either diagonal direction. Do you expect the sub's chances of escape are improved with the sub's increased versatility?

7. Compute the submarine's chances of escape for each of the squares in the grid of Figure 6-8.

8. Allow the submarine to restart at row 4, column 2, 10,000 times. In those 10,000 attempts, determine the least number of steps the submarine took to escape. Do you think the answer is 5?

9. Assume there is another blind submarine in row 3, column 4. What are the chances of the submarines' colliding with each other?

10. a. The following diagram represents an island surrounded by water (shaded area). One bridge leads out of the island. A mole is placed at the black square. Write a program to make the mole take a walk through the island. The mole is allowed to travel only one square at a time, either horizontally or vertically. A random number between 1 and 4 should be used to decide which direction the mole is to take. The mole drowns when hitting the water and escapes if she crosses the bridge. What is the mole's chance of getting safely out of the island? Restart the mole 100 times at the starting block, and count the number of times she escapes, even if she drowned on some of her prior promenades.

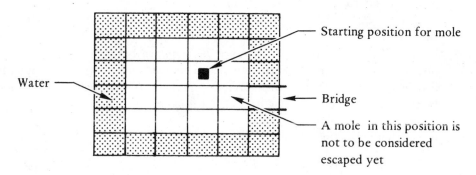

Starting position for mole

Water

Bridge

A mole in this position is not to be considered escaped yet

(*Hint:* To start, use two variables R (row) and C (column) to control movement of the mole. Initially, R = 3 and C = 4. If the mole moves to the right, set C = C + 1 and set C = C − 1 if it moves to the left. Likewise, change R for vertical motion. Then test every time to see if R = 1 or R = 6 for water contact, etc.)

b. The above island (maze) has now been transformed into a closed arena from which no mole can escape. One mole is placed in row 1, column 1 and another mole in row 6, column 6. Moles move about the arena as described in part a above. Upon hitting a wall, the mole bounces back to the position it occupied prior to hitting the wall. Both moles move at the same time. Write a computer program to determine, on the average, how many mole moves are made before a mole collision occurs. (*Hint:* After any collision, restart the moles back in R = 1, C = 1 and R = 6, C = 6 one hundred times.)

11. Write a program to determine the least number of random numbers between 1 and 100 that you should generate so that the average of these numbers lies in the interval 47 to 53.

12. John Jones has $200,000 to invest in speculative gold stock. The gold mines are of such a nature that they either go broke leaving stock worthless or strike gold and make the stockowners wealthy. Mr. Jones's goal is to retire with $2,000,000. He plans to invest $100,000 at a time. He estimates that the probability of losing each $100,000 investment is 75 percent, while the probability of making $1,000,000 from the same investment is 25 percent. In either case, he will sell the stock and make further $100,000 investments of the same nature.

What is the probability of Mr. Jones's retiring with $2,000,000? Write a BASIC program to simulate the behavior of the investment scheme using a random generator to determine whether the stock (the initial investment of $100,000) becomes worthless or valuable. Simulate 100 such investments and count the wins (makes $2,000,000) and losses (goes broke), and from these figures determine the probability for a successful retirement.

## 6-6-4 Answers to Self Test

1. a. Invalid; nested loops may not use the same variable.
   b. Invalid; variable k cannot be used to initialize itself.
   c. Invalid; an expression cannot be used on the left side of the equal sign in the DO statement.
   d. Invalid; NEXT statement must reference the same variable as the FOR statement.
   e. Invalid; body of inner loop must be wholly contained in the body of the outer loop.
   f. Invalid; value of the loop control variable should not be modified inside the loop.
   g. Invalid; syntax of statement FOR L = L + 1 is incorrect.
   h. Valid.
   i. Invalid; limit (L) should not be modified inside the loop.

2. a. 1, 3, 5, 7, 9    b. 6, 9, 12, 15, 18    c. 4

3. a. 120    b. 21    c. 20

4. a,b

# ONE-DIMENSIONAL ARRAYS AND THE DIM STATEMENT

## 7-1    Problem Example

Let us write a program to calculate the average of five grades read from a DATA statement and print the difference between each grade and the average. Up until now, it has been possible to compute an average of grades simply by reading one grade at a time into a variable G using the statement READ G and accumulating the grades as they are read. This procedure cannot be used in this case, however, since each new grade read destroys the previous grade stored in G, thereby making it impossible to compare each grade with the average once the average has been computed. Each grade must therefore be preserved, and for that reason five distinct memory locations (variables) are needed, as shown in Figure 7-1.

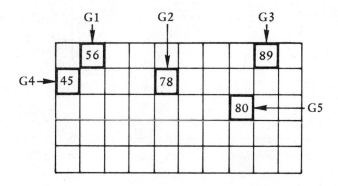

Figure 7-1    Five memory locations.

One method for solving this problem is shown in Figure 7-2. This code is somewhat cumbersome, due to the individual labeling of the five different variable names.

```
10    REM DEVIATION OF FIVE GRADES WITHOUT AN ARRAY
15    READ G1,G2,G3,G4,G5
20    LET A = (G1 + G2 + G3 + G4 + G5)/5
25    PRINT G1, G1 - A
30    PRINT G2, G2 - A
35    PRINT G3, G3 - A
40    PRINT G4, G4 - A
50    PRINT G5, G5 - A
60    DATA 56,78,89,45,80
75    STOP
99    END
```

**Figure 7-2**   Average and deviation without arrays.

Another approach to the problem is to use an array to store the grades. An array is a sequence of consecutive memory locations in which data (elements) are stored. Any element in an array can be referenced by specifying the name of the array and a position number (*subscript*) indicating the position of the desired element with respect to the first element of the array; for example, first, fourth, fifth position, etc. The name for the array of grades might be called G and would consist of five memory locations, as shown in Figure 7-3.

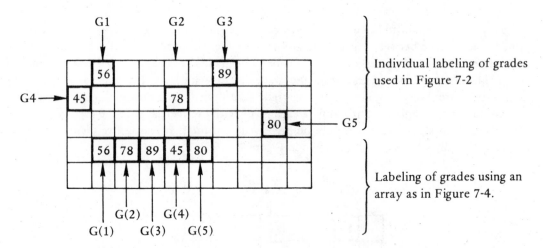

**Figure 7-3**   Array storage.

Allocation of the five memory locations to the array G is made through the DIM statement (see Figure 7-4), which tells the system to reserve five memory locations for the array G.

Both of the methods described to solve the problem of Section 7-1 make use of the same number of memory locations. In the case of the array G, a block of five sequential memory locations is reserved for the five grades. Five memory locations are also used in the case of the individualized labeling of each grade G1,G2,G3, . . . . What makes the array concept different and powerful is that elements within the array can be indexed with a subscript, thereby considerably simplifying the task of manipulating array elements for processing and for input/output considerations (see Figure 7-4).

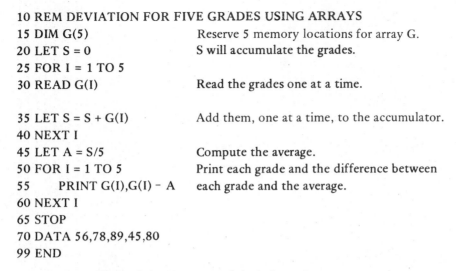

```
10 REM DEVIATION FOR FIVE GRADES USING ARRAYS
15 DIM G(5)                 Reserve 5 memory locations for array G.
20 LET S = 0                S will accumulate the grades.
25 FOR I = 1 TO 5
30 READ G(I)                Read the grades one at a time.

35 LET S = S + G(I)         Add them, one at a time, to the accumulator.
40 NEXT I
45 LET A = S/5              Compute the average.
50 FOR I = 1 TO 5           Print each grade and the difference between
55     PRINT G(I),G(I) - A  each grade and the average.
60 NEXT I
65 STOP
70 DATA 56,78,89,45,80
99 END
```

**Figure 7-4**   Average and deviation using array.

It is the index mechanism that makes the array a convenient and efficient feature. For example, to read the five grades into the array G, storing them into $G(1),G(2), \ldots G(5)$, the program in Figure 7-4 repeatedly processes the statement READ $G(I)$ for values of I ranging from 1 to 5. I is called a *subscript* or an *index*. It is initially set to 1, so that the first time the statement READ $G(I)$ is executed $G(I)$ will refer to $G(1)$, and hence the value read from the DATA statement will be stored in $G(1)$; the second time, I is 2 and $G(I)$ will identify $G(2)$, and a new grade will be stored in $G(2)$. Eventually, I will be 5, and $G(I)$ refers to $G(5)$, and the last grade will be read into $G(5)$. The reading process can be visualized as follows:

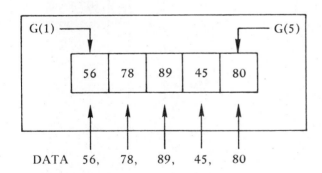

All grades are stored into the array one at a time starting with $G(1), \ldots G(5)$ through the statement READ $G(I)$ as I varies from 1 to 5.

Through the use of indexing, accumulation logic can be used to calculate the sum of the grades. The statement LET $S = S + G(I)$ (see Figure 7-4) accomplishes the accumulation process. The first time through the loop, $I = 1$ and $S = S + G(I) = 0 + G(1) = 56$. The first grade in the array is added to the sum, which is initially zero. The second time through the loop, $I = 2$ and $S = S + G(I) = 56 + G(2) = 56 + 78 = 134$. Finally, when $I = 5$, the fifth grade in the array will have been added to the sum of the four previous grades. Output can be handled in a loop by using a variable subscript on the array G, in much the same way as for input.

In the example of Figure 7-4, the use of an array may not result in a significantly shorter program, but the array technique can be used for many more grades with no increase in the number of statements required and no explicit use of additional variable names.

# 7-2   BASIC Statements

Since many BASIC systems do not allow alphanumeric data (character strings) to be stored into arrays, discussion of arrays for character data is deferred to Section 7-5.

### 7-2-1   DIM Statement

The general form of the DIM statement is

$$\textit{statement-number} \text{ DIM } \textit{variable}_1 \ (\textit{limit}_1) \ [,\textit{variable}_2 (\textit{limit}_2)] \ \ldots$$

where   DIM is a BASIC keyword

$\textit{variable}_1$, $\textit{variable}_2$, . . . are names of the various arrays (any valid variable name)

$\textit{limit}_1$, $\textit{limit}_2$, . . . are unsigned integer constants representing the desired number of memory locations reserved for each array. This does not mean that all reserved locations must be used when processing the array. Array subscripts may vary from 1 to the limit declared in the DIM statement and may not exceed that limit. Any array used in a program must first be declared in a DIM statement. Any number of arrays may be declared in a DIM list. For example, the statement

$$\text{DIM X(10), Z(20), J(107)}$$

declares X and Z and J as arrays. In this case the array X may contain up to 10 elements, the array Z up to 20 elements, and the array J up to 107 values. One might visualize the elements of X, Z, and J as shown in Figure 7-5.

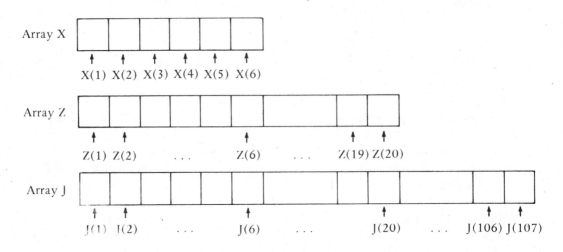

**Figure 7-5**   Representation of linear arrays.

The following DIM statements are invalid:

        DIM A(3.2)     Invalid limit. Should be an integer constant.
        DIM A(N)       N is not a constant.

DIM statements should appear in the program prior to the first executable statement (replacement statement, I/O statement, IF, and GO TO statements). A simple practice is to place the DIM statement at the very beginning of the program. Array names are ordinary variable names that must be declared in a DIM statement. The maximum value that can be specified as a limit to an array size may depend on the size of the memory of the particular computer used.

## 7-2-2   Subscripts

Subscripts are used with array names to locate specific elements of an array. The subscript is an expression enclosed in parentheses following the array name. For example,

$$X(4), Z(I), X(I + 3), Z(R * W), Z(A(2)\uparrow2)$$

are references to arrays X and Z. Note that the subscript can be a single constant, a single variable, or an arithmetic expression. Since subscripts identify the position of an element in an array, it is important that no subscripts evaluate to a negative number; for example, $J(-3)$ is invalid. Note also that $J(I/3)$ where $I = 5$ references the same element at $J(1)$. The result of a subscript division is an integer, that is, the digits to the right of the decimal result are discarded.

It is important to differentiate between the subscript value and the corresponding array element value. The value of A(3) generally has nothing to do with the number 3; for instance, A(3) could well be equal to .0076. Also, the same subscript can be used to reference two different array elements; for example, A(I) and B(I).

Suppose, for example, that the array A and variables I and R contain the following data:

| | 1 | 2 | 3 | 4 | 5 | 6 | | I | | R |
|---|---|---|---|---|---|---|---|---|---|---|
| Array A | 1.3 | 4. | 8.9 | −2.9 | 2.9 | 0. | | 1. | | 5. |
| | A(1) | A(2) | A(3) | A(4) | A(5) | A(6) | | | | |

The following examples illustrate the use and meaning of the subscripts:

| Subscript Form | Example | Meaning |
|---|---|---|
| Constant | A(4) | The value of the fourth location is −2.9. |
| Constant | A(3.7) | The fractional part is dropped. A(3.7) refers then to 8.9. |
| Variable | A(I) | The subscript is evaluated first. Since I=1, this means A(I) refers to the first element of A: 1.3. |

| *Subscript Form* | *Example* | *Meaning* |
|---|---|---|
| Expression | A(24/R−2.3) | The expression evaluates to 4.8 − 2.3 = 2.5. This is truncated to 2 and the variable refers to 4. |
| Subscripted Variable | A(A(2)) | Since A(2) = 4 the variable becomes A(4) which is −2.9. |
| Function | A(INT(A(4)+4)) | A(4) + 4 = 1.1. The integer part evaluates to 1. Hence the variable refers to A(1) = 1.3. |

## 7-2-3 Array Manipulation

When working with arrays, it is often necessary to initialize arrays to certain values, to create duplicate arrays, to interchange elements within arrays, to merge two or more arrays into one, to search or accumulate array entries, to sort arrays, etc. This section illustrates certain commonly used array manipulation techniques so that the reader may better understand the array index mechanism. In the following examples, it is assumed that values have already been read in the arrays.

### Array Initialization and Duplication

The following code sets all elements of array A to zeroes, sets each element of array B equal to the variable X, and then duplicates array D into array S:

```
10 DIM A(100), B(100), S(100), D(100)
15 INPUT N
20 FOR I = 1 TO N

25      LET A(I) = 0
30      LET B(I) = X
35      LET S(I) = D(I)
40 NEXT I
```

Read a value for N. This value must not exceed the size of the arrays declared in the DIM statement.

A(1), A(2), . . . A(N) are set to 0 one at a time as I ranges from 1 to N. Similarly, B(1), B(2), . . .,B(N) are set to the value in X. Finally S(1) = D(1), S(2) = D(2), . . . S(N) = D(N).

Sometimes it might be necessary to set an array C to the sum of two other arrays A and B in such a way that C(1) = A(1) + B(1), C(2) = A(2) + B(2), . . . C(100) = A(100) + B(100). The following code might be used:

```
10 DIM A(100), B(100), C(100)
15 FOR J = 1 TO 100
20      LET C(J) = A(J) + B(J)
25 NEXT J
```

For example,

| | A | | | B | | | C |
|---|---|---|---|---|---|---|---|
| A(1) | 3 | | −1 | B(1) | | 2 | C(1) |
| A(2) | −2 | + | −2 | B(2) | = | −4 | C(2) |
| | · | | · | | | · | |
| | · | | · | | | · | |
| | · | | · | | | · | |
| A(100) | 4 | | .5 | B(100) | | 4.5 | C(100) |

Suppose it is desired to initialize two arrays A and B, as follows:

| | |
|---|---|
| A(1) = B(10) = 1 | 10 DIM A(10), B(10) |
| A(2) = B(9)  = 2 | 15 FOR I = 1 TO 10 |
| A(3) = B(8)  = 3 | 20 LET A(I) = I |
| The code on the right | 25 LET K = 10 − I + 1 |
| could be used: | 30 LET B(K) = I |
| | 35 NEXT I |
| A(10) = B(1)  = 10 | |

The variable K generates the numbers 10,9,8 . . . 1 as I ranges from 1 to 10. If I ranged from 1 to N, the formula K = N − I + 1 would generate the numbers N,N − 1,N − 2, . . . 3,2,1.

## Reversing Arrays

Suppose A is an array of size N where N has been previously defined and it is desired to interchange A(1) with A(N), A(2) with A(N − 1), A(3) with A(N −2), etc. The following code could be used:

```
10 DIM A(100)
15 INPUT N
20 FOR I = 1 TO N/2
25     LET T = A(I)
30     LET K = N − I + 1
35     LET A(I) = A(K)
40     LET A(K) = T
45 NEXT I
```

Since each interchange step involves a pair of array elements, $(A_1, A_N)$, $(A_2, A_{N-1})$, etc., the interchange process need be repeated only N/2 times. If N is odd, the median element remains unchanged. K generates the numbers N, N − 1, . . . 2, 1. T is a temporary location needed to save A(1) before A(1) = A(N) is executed, otherwise, A(1) would be destroyed.

If we used N instead of N/2 in statement 20, the array would "re-reverse" itself and end up as if nothing had been changed.

## Accumulation of Array Elements

To compute the product of the elements of the array A =

| 10 | 20 | 30 | 40 | 50 |
|----|----|----|----|----|

, the following code could be used:

```
10 LET S = 1
15 FOR K = 1 TO 5
20 LET S = S * A(K)
25 NEXT K
```

S is initially set to 1 before the loop is entered.
The first time through the loop, S = S * A(1) = 1 * 10 = 10
The second time through the loop, S = S * A(2) = 10 * 20 = 200

To compute the sum of two arrays S = A(1) + B(1) + A(2) + B(2) + · · · + A(50) + B(50), we could use

```
10 LET S = 0
15 FOR K = 1 TO 50
20 LET S = S + A(K) + B(K)
25 NEXT K
```

### Array Merge

Suppose A and B are two arrays of size 10 and we want the array C to contain the data $A_1$, $B_1$, $A_2$, $B_2$, $\cdots$ $A_{10}$, $B_{10}$ arranged in that order. Any of the following codes could be used:

```
10 LET K = 1            10 FOR I = 1 TO 10        10 LET K = 1
15 FOR I = 1 TO 10      15 LET C(2 * I - 1) = A(I)  15 FOR I = 1 TO 20 STEP 2
20 LET C(K) = A(I)      20 LET C(2 * I) = B(I)     20 LET C(I) = A(K)
25 LET K = K + 1        25 NEXT I                  25 LET C(I + 1) = B(K)
30 LET C(K) = B(I)                                 30 LET K = K + 1
35 LET K = K + 1                                   35 NEXT I
40 NEXT I
```

### Array Search

Assume array A contains 100 grades, and we want to know the number of grades over 60. The following code could be used:

```
10 LET K = 0            K is used to count grades over 60.
15 FOR I = 1 TO 100
20 IF A(I) <= 60 THEN 30   If A(I) <= 60, skip the counting of grades over 60, but
25 LET K = K + 1           stay in the loop by connecting to the NEXT I statement.
30 NEXT I
```

## 7-2-4   Input/Output of Arrays

Arrays can be read and printed out by indexing the array with the index of a FOR/NEXT loop.

**Example 1**

To read 10 data items from a DATA statement, the following code might be used:

```
10 DIM A(10)
15 FOR I = 1 TO 10
20 READ A(I)
25 NEXT I
```

DATA 3, 5, 9, . . . 15

| | |
|---|---|
| 3 | A(1) |
| 5 | A(2) |
| 9 | A(3) |
| . | |
| . | |
| . | |
| 15 | A(10) |

The first time through the loop, I is 1, and A(1) is read from the DATA statement. The second time through the loop, I is 2, and the next data item is read into A(2). Finally, I is 10, and the tenth data item is read into A(10).

**Example 2**

A data file consists of 10 records with two data items per record. To store these items into two different arrays, the following could be used:

```
 5 REM H = HOURS; R = RATE
10 DIM H(10), R(10)
15 FOR I = 1 TO 10
20 INPUT H(I), R(I)



30 NEXT I
```

| | | | | | |
|---|---|---|---|---|---|
| ? 40, 5.1 | 40 | H(1) | 5.1 | R(1) | |
| ? 20, 3 | 20 | H(2) | 3 | R(2) | |
| ? 50, 2.5 | 50 | H(3) | 2.5 | R(3) | |
| · | · | | · | | |
| · | · | | · | | |
| · | · | | · · | | |
| ? 60, −10 | 60 | H(10) | −10 | R(10) | |

**Example 3**

Assume each element of an array Sales contains a daily sales amount and it is desired to print the daily sales with each corresponding day. The following code could be used:

*Output*

| DAYS | SALES |
|---|---|
| 1 | 101.0 |
| 2 | 200.0 |
| 3 | 50.5 |
| 4 | 35.5 |
| 5 | 100.0 |
| 6 | 300.0 |
| 7 | 50.0 |

```
 5 DIM S(7)
10 PRINT "DAYS", "SALES"
15 FOR I = 1 TO 7
20 PRINT I, S(I)
25 NEXT I
```

Note that I represents the day and S(I) represents the day's corresponding sales, i.e., S(I) is the sales for the Ith day.

**Example 4**

Suppose the correct answers to a multiple choice test (maximum of 25 questions) are recorded on a DATA statement with the first entry on that statement reflecting the number of test questions that follow; for example:

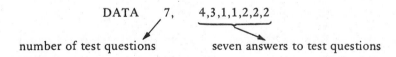

DATA    7,    4,3,1,1,2,2,2

number of test questions          seven answers to test questions

The following code segment would read and print the answers to the test questions:

```
 5 DIM A(25)
10 READ N
15 FOR I = 1 TO N
20 READ A(I)
25 PRINT A(I);
30 NEXT I
```

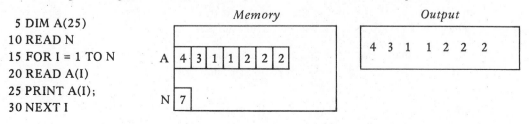

*Memory*

A | 4 | 3 | 1 | 1 | 2 | 2 | 2 |

N | 7 |

*Output*

4  3  1  1  2  2  2

### End-of-File Conditions

Sometimes data may have to be read into arrays from an unknown number of records. For example, someone may give us a large data file to read into an array A. Since the DIM statement must specify an integer constant for the size of the array, the programmer must decide ahead of time what he thinks is the maximum number of locations he will need for the array. He may, of course, never use that many array locations. The programmer *may not* proceed as follows: Declare the array DIM A(N) and then read a value for N. This may sound logical, but the practice is incorrect.

Consider the following problem: Each record of a data file contains a student's number and two test scores. Read into an array N the student's number and store in array SCORE the average of each student's score. Print the number of records processed and the average of all grades (no more than 100 student records are expected). A program to solve this problem is shown in Figure 7-6.

| | |
|---|---|
| 10 DIM S(101), N(101) | Array S is reserved for the scores, N for student numbers. |
| 13 LET S1 = 0 | S1 is used to accumulate all grades. |
| 15 FOR I = 1 TO 101 | 101 because of the trip record. |
| 20     READ N(I), T1,T2 | Read student number and his or her two grades. |
| 25     IF N(I) < 0 THEN 45 | Trip record is the student number (arbitrary decision). |
| 30     LET S(I) = (T1 + T2)/2 | Compute the average of each student and store in array. |
| 35     LET S1 = S1 + S(I) | Accumulate sum of grades. |
| 40 NEXT I | |
| 45 LET A = S1/(I − 1) | Compute average, but don't count trip record. I repre- |
| 50 PRINT "AVERAGE = "; A | sents the number of records read, including the trip |
| 55 PRINT "NO. STUDENTS"; I − 1 | record; hence I − 1 represents the number of students. |
| 60 DATA 99,8,6,98,4,3,−3,0,0 | The trip record is −3, 0, 0. |

**Figure 7-6**    Input of arrays.

# 7-3    You Might Want To Know

1. Is it possible to reference the zero element of an array?

   *Answer:* In most BASIC systems, the lower limit for a subscript is zero; for example, DIM A(10) will allocate 11 memory locations to the array A. These locations are A(0), A(1), A(2), . . ., A(10).

2. In many instances, the use of the subscript zero is inconvenient. Must I always address the first element of an array with a subscript having value zero?

   *Answer:* No. In many instances, the zero element of an array is ignored. The first element of the array can then be addressed with a subscript having value 1.

3.  What are some variations among BASIC systems regarding naming an array?

    *Answer:* Some BASIC systems permit the use of letters of the alphabet and digits for array names; for example, C3(50) is valid. Some systems also allow the use of $, @, and # as valid array names.

4.  Is it always necessary to have a DIM statement when using arrays?

    *Answer:* No. In most systems, it is not required to use a DIM statement for any array not exceeding 10 elements. For example, the following complete program is valid:

$$
\begin{array}{ll}
5 \text{ LET A(1) = 3} & \\
10 \text{ INPUT A(4)} & \qquad \text{Note absence of DIM statement.} \\
15 \text{ PRINT A(4) + A(1)} & \\
20 \text{ END} &
\end{array}
$$

    However, it is probably good programming practice to dimension all arrays.

5.  Is there any limit to the size of an array?

    *Answer:* Yes; the maximum size depends on the memory size of your system.

6.  What happens if in the course of executing a program an attempt is made to use a subscript larger than the limit specified in the DIM statement?

    *Answer:* A run time execution error message will appear to that effect. Either change the size of the array in the DIM statement or check the logic of the program.

7.  Can functions be part of a subscript?

    *Answer:* Yes. For example, T(ABS(X) + 1) is a valid reference to an element of T.

8.  Can you have more than one DIM statement?

    *Answer:* Yes, as many as you want. For example:

$$
\left.\begin{array}{l}
10 \text{ DIM A(3)} \\
15 \text{ DIM B(6)} \\
20 \text{ DIM C(3),D(4)}
\end{array}\right\} \text{equivalent to } 17 \text{ DIM A(3),B(6),C(3),D(4)}
$$

# 7-4    Programming Examples

## 7-4-1    An Array Search

The array G contains 10 grades. It is desired to search the array G to print the largest grade. The following code could be used.

| | |
|---|---|
| 20 LET L = G(1) | Set L initially to the first grade. |
| 30 FOR I = 2 TO 10 | |
| 40    IF L >= G(I) THEN 50 | If the largest grade so far is less than the new grade G(I), replace L by new grade G(I). |
| 45    LET L = G(I) | |
| 50 NEXT I | Otherwise look at the next grade. |
| 60 PRINT "LARGEST VALUE",L | |

The variable L is initialized to G(1); L is then compared successively with the array elements. Any element that is larger than L becomes the new value of L at statement 45. This method, however, does not indicate the position of the largest element witin the array G. It just specifies that L is the largest element.

Another method that indicates the position of the largest element within the array makes use of an index or pointer to locate the largest element. Initially this index is set to the position of the first element (generally 1). Then, as the array elements are compared to one another, the index is changed appropriately to reflect the new location of the largest number found so far. Thus, if K is the pointer to the largest element found so far and $G(K) < G(I)$ (I being the index of the FOR/NEXT loop), then I is now obviously the position (address) of the largest element, and so K is set to I to reflect the position of the largest value so far. Remember, if K is the address of the largest element, then A(K) is the largest element. This search method is illustrated by the following example, given the array G with elements 6, 4, 7, 2, and 8.

array G ────► | 6 | 4 | 7 | 2 | 8 |

1 LET K = 1          K points to the position of the largest element of the array so far.

|  | |
|---|---|
| | K ─► 1 |
| 2 FOR I = 2 TO 5 | \| 6 \| 4 \| |
| | K ──────► 3 |
| 4 IF G(K) >= G(I) THEN 7 | \| 6 \| 4 \| 7 \| |
| | K ──────► 3 |
| 6 LET K = I | \| 6 \| 4 \| 7 \| 2 \| |
| | K ──────► 5 |
| 7 NEXT I | \| 6 \| 4 \| 7 \| 2 \| 8 \| |

Compare G(K) = G(1) with G(2).
K stays 1 since G(1) > G(2).
Compare G(K) = G(1) with G(3).
K becomes 3 since G(1) < G(3).
Compare G(K) = G(3) with G(4).
K stays 3 since G(3) > G(4).
Compare G(K) = G(3) with G(5).
K becomes 5.

8 PRINT K,G(K)          Print the position of the largest element and the largest element.

## 7-4-2  Table Look-Up

The table look-up process is a fast and efficient method to access data directly in an array (table) without any search of the array elements. Consider the following example: Widgets, Inc., manufacturers of widgets of all types, contracts with a trucking company that charges a fixed amount per pound based on a shipping zone. The rate table per pound is as follows:

| ZONE CODE | COST PER POUND | MEANING |
|:---:|:---:|:---:|
| 1 | .50 | The cost to ship one pound of merchandise |
| 2 | .75 | to zone 1 is $.50. |
| 3 | 1.05 | The cost to ship one pound of merchandise |
| 4 | 1.25 | to zone 2 is $.75 |
| 5 | 1.40 | . |
| 6 | 1.70 | . |

Write a program that will accept as input the destination zone and weight of a shipment and print out the corresponding shipping cost. A program for this task is shown in Figure 7-7.

The array R is reserved to store the cost per pound table and is read from a DATA statement. The table of constants is stored in the array R via the READ statement. If a zone (Z) and weight (W) are entered into the system with values 5 and 10 respectively, the corresponding shipping rate is $R(Z) = R(5) = 1.40$. The total cost of shipping a package of W = 10 pounds is then $R(Z) * W = 1.40 * 10 = 14$. More generally, the cost per pound to send a package to a zone Z is R(Z). The total cost for sending a package of W pounds to a zone Z then becomes W * R(Z).

```
10 REM TABLE LOOK-UP EXAMPLE
15 DIM R(6)                                      Cost/pound table array.
20 FOR I=1 TO 6
25     READ R(I)                                 Read the rates.
30 NEXT I
35 PRINT TAB(20);"ZONE","WEIGHT","COST"
40 INPUT Z,W                                     Read a zone and a weight.
42 IF Z<0  THEN 70                               Is this the last input?
45 PRINT TAB(20); Z,W,R(Z)*W
50 GO TO 40
60 DATA .50,.75,1.05,1.25,1.40,1.70
70 STOP
99 END
```

RUN

|  | ZONE | WEIGHT | COST |
|:---:|:---:|:---:|:---:|
| ?5,10 | 5 | 10 | 14 |
| ?4,5 | 4 | 5 | 6.25 |
| ?1,3 | 1 | 3 | 1.5 |
| ?-1,1 | | | |

Figure 7-7   Table look-up example.

### 7-4-3 Frequency Distribution

Write a program to produce a frequency distribution of test grades. Given a list of grades, we must find how many times a grade of 1 appears, how many times a grade of 2 appears, a grade of 3, 4, 5, . . . 100. The grades range from 1 to 100 and are read from DATA statements. For example, suppose you can get 1–10 on a quiz and you have a list of scores in any order. If you wanted to find out the number of each different score by hand, you might draw a chart and count each score as follows:

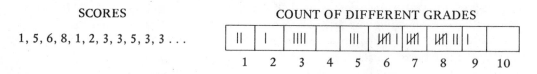

Input of grades is terminated when a value outside the permissible range of grades is encountered. A program to solve this problem for grades ranging from 1 to 100 is shown in Figure 7-8.

```
10  REM FREQUENCY DISTRIBUTION
15  DIM K (100)
20  PRINT "GRADES", "FREQUENCY"
25  FOR I = 1 TO 100                 Initialize the 100 counters to zeroes.
30      LET K(I) = 0
35  NEXT I
40  READ G
45  IF G < = 0 THEN 65               Test for value outside grade range.
50  IF G > 100 THEN 65
55  LET K(G) = K(G) + 1              Increment counter corresponding to grade G.
60  GO TO 40
65  FOR I = 1 TO 100                 If the count of grades for grade I is 0, do not
70      IF K(I) = 0 THEN 80             print it; otherwise, print the grade with its
75      PRINT I, K(I)                   corresponding frequency.
80  NEXT I
85  STOP
90  DATA 12, 23, 45, 12, 98, 12, 98, 98, 23, 98, 0
95  END
```

RUN

| GRADES | FREQUENCY |
|--------|-----------|
| 12 | 3 |
| 23 | 2 |
| 45 | 1 |
| 98 | 4 |

**Figure 7-8**  Frequency distribution.

Since there are 100 possible grades, 100 counters will be required to record all occurrences of grades. The array K will be used for that purpose, with K(1), K(2), . . . , K(100) serving as the 100 counters.

In the first FOR/NEXT loop, the array of counters K is initialized to zero. As each grade is read, it is tested for proper range. If the grade G satisfies the test, the Gth counter is incremented by 1, i.e., K(G) = K(G) + 1. The value of G is used to designate which of the counters should be incremented. Thus, if G has a value of 65, the statement K(G) = K(G) + 1 is the same as K(65) = K(65) + 1. Hence K(65) is incremented by 1—K(65) is the counter used to record occurrences of the grade 65. When a value outside the range is encountered, a listing of all the nonzero grades and their corresponding frequency counts is produced (see Figure 7-8). On output, only the counters with nonzero values are printed. In statement 75 PRINT I, K(I), the variable I represents the grade, while K(I) represents the corresponding grade count (the one counting the grade I). If K(I) = 0, this means that there was no grade I read.

## 7-4-4    Sorting

Two methods for sorting are discussed in this section. One method is called the bubble sort and the other the interchange minimum or maximum sort.

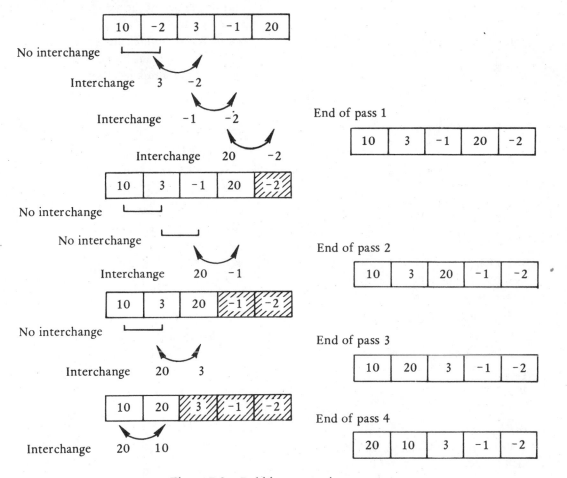

**Figure 7-9**    Bubble sort sorting process.

```
10  REM BUBBLE SORT
15  DIM G(100)
20  PRINT "UNSORTED GRADES";
25  FOR N = 1 TO 100
30      READ G(N)

35      IF G(N) < 0 THEN 45
37      PRINT G(N);
40  NEXT N
45  LET N = N - 1
47  LET K = N - 1




50  FOR I = 1 TO K
55      LET L = N - I


60      FOR J = 1 TO L
65          IF G(J) > G(J + 1) THEN 85




70          LET T = G(J)

75          LET G(J) = G(J + 1)

80          LET G(J + 1) = T
85      NEXT J
90  NEXT I

92  PRINT
95  PRINT "SORTED GRADES";
100 FOR I = 1 TO N
105     PRINT G(I);
110 NEXT I
115 DATA 42, 65, 36, 48, 92, 78, 50, -2
120 STOP
125 END
```

No more than 100 grades expected.

Read grades into the array until there are no more.

Altogether there are N - 1 grades (excluding trip record). K represents the number of passes (one less than the number of grades) required to shift lowest grade into G(N) then into G(N - 1) up to G(2).

L controls the size of the shrinking array. It takes on values N - 1, N - 2, . . . , 3, 2, 1. J is used for the interchange procedure to move the lowest grade into the rightmost position of the shrinking array.

A temporary location is needed to swap G(J) with G(J + 1).

The interchange cycle 1, 2, 3 is shown as follows:

Print sorted grades.

```
RUN
UNSORTED GRADES 42  65  36  48  92  78  50
SORTED GRADES 92  78  65  50  48  42  36
```

Figure 7-10   Bubble sort (descending).

## Bubble Sort

The technique used to sort five numbers is illustrated graphically in Figure 7-9. This method shifts the smallest value to the fifth position of array G, then shifts the next smallest value to the fourth position, then to the third, and so on. The shifting is accomplished by comparing pairs of contiguous array elements, one pair at a time, and interchanging the two numbers whenever necessary to ensure that the smallest value is continuously moved to the right. For instance, the first and second numbers are compared; if the second is less than the first, the second is compared to the third. If the second is larger than the first, these two numbers are interchanged, and the second number (the smaller now) is then compared to the third. Ultimately, the smallest value is moved into the fifth position (see Figure 7-9).

The sorting algorithm requires two loops: An outer loop (statement 50) to control the positioning of the smallest element in the rightmost position of the ever-shrinking array, initially with 5 elements, then 4, then 3, . . . , up to 1, and an inner loop (statement 60) to control the movement of the smallest element to the rightmost position of the shrinking array through the interchange procedure (statements 70, 75, 80). Once again the outer loop controls the number of passes. If the array has N elements, then N − 1 passes will be required.

## Example

Write a program to sort a group of grades into descending sequence. A maximum of 100 grades are to be processed; they will be read from DATA statements, and input will be terminated by an out-of-range value. The program to perform this sort is shown in Figure 7-10.

## Interchange Minimum/Maximum (Mini/Max) Sort

Another method that can be used to sort an array of numbers in ascending order is to determine the location (position) of the smallest element in the array and interchange that element with the first element of the array (see Figure 7-11). At the end of this first search

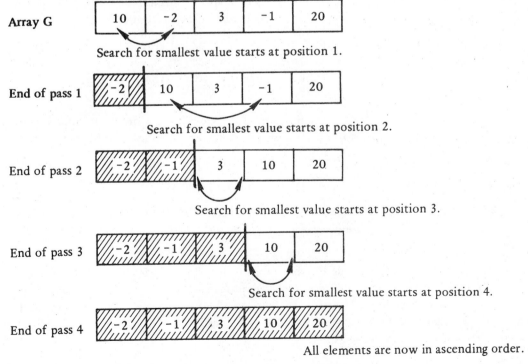

**Figure 7-11**    Mini/max sorting process.

pass, the smallest element is in the first position. The array is then searched for the next smallest element, with the search starting at position 2 of the array; the smallest element is then swapped with the number in position 2 of the array. At the end of this second search pass, the first two elements of the array are already in ascending sequence order. The search for the next smallest number starts in position 3, and the same search and interchange process is repeated until the last two rightmost array elements are processed. Using this sorting procedure, an array of N elements will require N − 1 passes for the search and interchange procedure. The search for the smallest number itself will involve comparing N numbers during the first pass, N − 1 numbers during the second pass, and two numbers during the last pass. Figure 7-11 illustrates the mini/max sort with the data of the bubble sort of Figure 7-9.

To better understand the complete program, let us initially write the code for the first pass, which determines the position of the smallest element of the array and which performs the interchange of the smallest number with the number in the first position of the array. Assume the array G contains N elements.

| | |
|---|---|
| 10 LET K = 1 | Initially, the pointer to the smallest element is 1; that is, A(K) or A(1) is assumed to be the smallest number before entering the loop. |
| 15 LET L = K + 1 | L is 2, since there would be no reason to compare G(1) with G(1) in the following loop if the starting value for I were 1. |
| 20 FOR I = L TO N | Compare N numbers to determine the smallest. |
| 25 IF G(K) <= G(I) THEN 35 | If $G(K) \leqslant G(I)$, then G(K) is still the smallest element, and K still points to the location of the smallest element. |
| 30 LET K = I | If $G(K) > G(I)$, then the smallest element so far is at position I, and so we reset K to I to identify the position of the smallest number, keeping in mind that G(K) is the current smallest number. |
| 35 NEXT I | At the completion of the loop, K identifies the location of the smallest element, and G(K) is the smallest number in the array. |
| 40 LET T = G(1) | Store the value of G(1). |
| 45 LET G(1) = G(K) | Store the smallest number in G(1). |
| 50 LET G(K) = T | Store G(1) in the location that used to contain the smallest number. |

To generalize the preceding code for the complete sort program, K must take on values 1, 2, 3, ... N − 1 (for N − 1 passes). The interchange process will require that T = G(2) on the second pass, T = G(3) on the third pass, etc. Hence an additional loop is required to control K and the positioning of the succeeding smallest values into locations G(1), G(2), G(3), ..., G(N − 1). The complete code is shown in Figure 7-12.

```
10  REM MINI/MAX SORT
15  DIM G(100)
20  PRINT "UNSORTED GRADES";
25  FOR N = 1 TO 100
30      READ G(N)                            Read the grades in the array G.
35      IF G(N) < 0 THEN 50
40      PRINT G(N);
45  NEXT N
50  LET N = N - 1                            There are N = N - 1 elements (trip record).
55  LET N1 = N - 1
60  FOR J = 1 TO N1                          N1 is the number of passes.
65      LET K = J                            K = 1, 2, 3, . . . , N - 1
70      LET L = K + 1                        L = 2, 3, . . . N - 1, N
75      FOR I = L TO N
80          IF G(K) < = G(I) THEN 90         On the last pass, G(N - 1) is compared to G(N).
85              LET K = I                    K identifies position of smallest number.
90      NEXT I
95      LET T = G(J)                         Interchange procedure.
100     LET G(J) = G(K)                      G(K) is smallest element in that pass.
105     LET G(K) = T
110 NEXT J
115 PRINT
120 PRINT "SORTED GRADES";
125 FOR I = 1 TO N
130     PRINT G(I);                          Print sorted grades.
135 NEXT I
140 DATA 42, 65, 36, 48, 92, 78, 50, -2
145 STOP
150 END
```

RUN

UNSORTED GRADES  42  65  36  48  92  78  50
SORTED GRADES  36  42  48  50  65  78  92

**Figure 7-12**    Mini/max sort.

# 7-5   Character Strings

### 7-5-1   Definition

You may have received such personalized form letters as shown in Figure 7-13 with "personal" words underlined. Such letters are, of course, mass produced. The program in Figure 7-14 will keep churning out letters identical to those in Figure 7-13.

THE COCOZZAS
6501 S19 AVE
PENSACOLA                                                    AUGUST 12 1978
FLORIDA

DEAR MR AND MRS COCOZZA

ONLY YOU HAVE BEEN SELECTED IN THE PENSACOLA AREA TO APPLY FOR OUR
ONCE IN A LIFETIME SPECIAL ALUMINUM SIDING BARGAIN OF THE YEAR. THE
COCOZZA FAMILY SHOULD INDEED REJOICE IN HAVING THEIR CHARMING
HOME AT 6501 S19 AVE RESTYLED WITH THE FINEST MATERIAL FROM
FLORIDA.

                                                             SINCERELY

THE DELLA TROCES
11 N 123 ST.
AMARILLO                                                     JULY 12 1978
TEXAS

DEAR MR AND MRS DELLA TROCE

ONLY YOU HAVE BEEN SELECTED IN THE AMARILLO AREA TO APPLY FOR OUR
ONCE IN A LIFETIME SPECIAL ALUMINUM SIDING BARGAIN OF THE YEAR. THE
DELLA TROCE FAMILY SHOULD INDEED REJOICE IN HAVING THEIR CHARMING
HOME AT 11 N 123 ST. RESTYLED WITH THE FINEST MATERIAL FROM TEXAS.

                                                             SINCERELY

Figure 7-13    Personalized form letters.

```
10  REM ENTER NAME, STREET, CITY, STATE, AND DATE
15  INPUT N$, A$, C$, S$, D$
20  PRINT "THE";N$;" 'S"        ⎫
25  PRINT A$                    ⎬  Print address and date.
30  PRINT C$; TAB (36); D$      ⎭
35  PRINT S$
40  PRINT
45  PRINT "DEAR MR AND MRS"; N$
50  PRINT
55  PRINT "ONLY YOU HAVE BEEN SELECTED IN THE ";C$;"AREA TO APPLY FOR"
60  PRINT "OUR ONCE IN A LIFETIME SPECIAL ALUMINUM SIDING BARGAIN OF THE"
65  PRINT "YEAR. THE ";N$;" FAMILY SHOULD INDEED REJOICE IN HAVING THEIR"
70  PRINT "CHARMING HOME AT ";A$;"RESTYLED WITH THE FINEST MATERIAL"
75  PRINT "FROM";S$
80  PRINT
85  PRINT TAB(35); "SINCERELY"
90  GO TO 15
95  END
```

Figure 7-14    Program to produce personalized letters.

Computers can process alphabetic or alphanumeric data just as easily as numerical data. When working with character data (character strings), the reader should keep in mind the following considerations:

1. Character string names are formed by tacking a $ to the variable name. For example, A$, Z$ are valid character string names (also array names). Some systems will allow names such as A1$ or A3$.

2. The number of characters that can be stored in a variable name varies from system to system (at least 15 characters and on some systems up to 256 characters).

3. Character strings may not participate in mathematical operations (addition, multiplication, etc.).

4. Character strings may be compared with the IF statement.

5. Character string constants should always be enclosed in quotes. The length (number of characters) of the string includes any imbedded, leading, or trailing blanks within the quotes.

Character strings can be referenced in a BASIC program in essentially three different ways:

1. Explicit use of a string (literal) in a PRINT statement (no variables are used).

   *Example:* PRINT "COMPARATIVE BALANCE SHEET"

2. Through the READ, INPUT, or LET statement.

   | *Examples:* | 10 LET G$ = "110 ACACIA DR" | The variable G$ consists of 13 characters. |
   |---|---|---|
   | | 20 READ T$ | The variable T$ consists of 11 characters. |
   | | 25 DATA "111-254-179" | |
   | | 30 INPUT G$ | Number of characters depends on |
   | | ? " JOE" | the input data (5 in this case). |

3. Through arrays. Each array element can store a character string of variable length (at least 15 characters per subscripted variable). The character array should be DIMensioned if more than 10 array elements are to be used.

   *Example:*

   | 10 DIM A$(13) | Reserve up to 13 memory locations for character data. |
   |---|---|
   | 20 READ A$(1) | A$(1) contains four characters: A, G, E, and blank. |
   | 25 DATA "AGE " | |
   | 30 LET A$(2) = "SEX" | A$(2) contains three characters. |

   35 PRINT "WHAT ARE YOUR "; A$(1); "AND "; A$(2); "?"
   99 END
   RUN
   WHAT ARE YOUR AGE AND SEX?

Some systems do not allow character strings to be stored into arrays, and the preceding examples would thus be invalid. However, these systems will generally support the character string manipulation features discussed in Section 7-5-4.

## 7-5-2 Character String Comparisons and Input/Output

Since character strings have different internal representation from numbers, no meaningful comparisons can be made between numeric data and character string data. In fact, such an attempt will generally result in an error message. It is, however, possible to compare two character strings.

The ordering of digits and alphabetic characters is as follows:

$$(\text{blank}) < 0 < 1 < 2 \ldots 9 < A < B \ldots < Y < Z$$

If two unequal strings are compared, the shorter string will be padded to the right with blanks (represented by "b" in the following example) to equal the size of the larger string. The comparison process ends at the first unequal character:

| | |
|---|---|
| "DAY" > "DALY" | since Y > L |
| "THAT" < "THIS" | since A < I |
| "PAYROLL" < "PAYROLL12" | since "PAYROLLb" < "PAYROLL1" |

**Example**

```
 5 LET G$ = "13"
10 IF "14" > G$ THEN 40     Control is passed to 40 in this case.
15 IF G$ < 10 THEN 30       Invalid comparison; character string is compared
                              to a number.
```

Input and output of character strings is conducted essentially in the same way as for numeric data.

For INPUT and READ operations, the character string listed in the DATA statement or entered after the ? (resulting from the INPUT statement) may be entered with or without quotation marks. Many systems require quotation marks.

**Example**

```
10 READ N$(1), N$(2), N$(3), N$(4), N$(5), N$6)
20 PRINT N$(1); N$(2); N$(3); N$(4); N$(5); N$(6)
25 DATA IBM, GE, ATT, HAPPY, NEW, YEAR
30 DATA "IBM,", "GE,", "ATT", " HAPPY ", "NEW ", "YEAR"
35 FOR I = 1 TO 6
40     READ N$(I)
45     PRINT N$(I);
50 NEXT I
99 END
RUN
IBMGEATTHAPPYNEWYEAR        No quotation marks in the input data.
IBM,GE,ATT HAPPY NEW YEAR   Quotation marks in the input data.
```

Note blanks

Note how the quotes forced a comma and blanks to be part of the variable read, whereas this was not possible when the data read had no quotation marks. Many systems require that character strings be enclosed in quotation marks, however.

## 7-5-3    Programming Examples

### An Alphabetic Sort

Dr. X., the information science instructor, has assigned a final grade to each of his students. He wishes to prepare a list of his students sorted alphabetically by name in ascending order with their respective final grades. Names and corresponding grades are recorded in DATA statements with the literal "END" indicating the end of the list. The program to produce this listing requires that we sort character strings and at the same time keep track of the students' respective grades as the names are moved around. The logic used for alphabetic sorting is similar to the logic used in the numeric sort (see Section 7-4-4). A program for this task is shown in Figure 7-15.

```
01 REM SORT FOR ALPHABETIC DATA
03 DIM N$ (20), C(20)                        Assume there are no more than 20 students.
05 LET I = 1
10 READ N$(I), C(I)                          Read student names and grades in two arrays.
15 IF N$(I) = "END" THEN 30                  Is it the end of the input?
20 LET I = I + 1
25 GO TO 10                                   Go back and read more data.
30 LET I = I - 1                              I is the number of students.
31 FOR K = 1 TO I - 1                         The outer loop controls the number of passes;
                                              the inner loop finds the "largest" names
35     FOR J = 1 TO I - K                     and after each pass inserts them in locations

50        IF N$(J) < = N$(J + 1) THEN 80
52        LET T$ = N$(J)                      N$(20), N$(19) . . . N$(1), respectively.
54        LET N$(J) = N$(J + 1)
60        LET N$ (J + 1) = T$
65        LET T1 = C(J)                       Every time a name is changed, the
70        LET C(J) = C(J + 1)                 corresponding grade is also changed
75        LET C(J + 1) = T1                   in array C.
80     NEXT J
85 NEXT K
90 FOR J = 1 TO I
95     PRINT N$(J), C(J)                      Print sorted list of names with their
100 NEXT J                                    associated grades.
201 DATA "HOWELL", 97, "JONES", 86, "GLEASON", 84, "END", 0
999 END

RUN

GLEASON        84
HOWELL         97
JONES          86
```

Figure 7-15    An alphabetic sort.

## A File Update Program

Dr. X. is an information science teacher. A file consisting of his students' names and their respective grades is stored in memory as follows:

| STUDENT | GRADE 1 | GRADE 2 | TOTAL |
|---------|---------|---------|-------|
| BOILLOT | 91 | 56 | 147 |
| GLEASON | 40 | 50 | 90 |
| HORN | 50 | 65 | 115 |
| MONISH | 70 | 70 | 140 |
| . | . | . | . |
| . | . | . | . |
| . | . | . | . |
| END$ | 0 | 0 | 0 |

The last entry in the list of names is specified by END$. Write a program to allow Dr. X. to correct his file in the event grades are listed incorrectly. Change of grades is accepted in the following format (for grades that need not be changed, enter in their place a negative number):

INPUT GRADE CHANGE? student-name, grade-1, grade-2

Example

INPUT GRADE CHANGE? "HORN", −1,98

This means change HORN'S second grade to 98 and compute new total.

Figure 7-16 displays the code used for solving this problem. It includes the logic for loading the students' names, grades, and totals and for displaying the data before and after changes. The program terminates when the user enters the name FIN.

```
05  DIM S$(70),G1(70),G2(70),T(70)          Assume no more than 70 students.
08  PRINT "PRESENT GRADES ARE"
09  LET I = 1
10  READ S$(I),G1(I),G2(I),T(I)             Load arrays with names and grades.
11  IF S$(I)= "END$" THEN 20                END$ signifies end of file.
12  PRINT S$(I),G1(I),G2(I),T(I)            Print names, grades, and totals.
13  LET I = I + 1
14  GO TO 10
20  PRINT "INPUT GRADE CHANGE";             Accept name of student and change grades.
21  INPUT N$,S1,S2
22  IF N$ = "FIN" THEN 90                    Are there any more grades to change?
25  LET I = 1
30  IF S$(I) = "END$" THEN 80                Is this the end of the class roster?
35  IF S$(I) = N$ THEN 50                    No. Have we found a matching name?
40  LET I = I + 1
```

Figure 7-16   Grade change program (part 1 of 2).

```
 45  GO TO 30
 50  IF S1 < 0 THEN 60              Which grades need to be changed?
 55  LET G1(I) = S1                 Change first grade.
 60  IF S2 < 0 THEN 70              Change second grade if necessary.
 65  LET G2(I) = S2
 70  LET T(I) = G1(I) + G2(I)       Compute a new total.
 75  GO TO 20
 80  PRINT "NO NAME MATCH FOUND"    In case no matching name is found.
 85  GO TO 20
 90  PRINT
 91  PRINT "* * * * * * * * * * * * * * * * * * * * * * * * *"
 92  PRINT "GRADES AFTER CHANGES ARE"
 93  LET I = 1
 94  IF S$(I) = "END$" THEN 200     Is this the end of the class roster?
 95  PRINT S$(I), G1(I),G2(I), T(I) No; print each student's record.
 96  LET I = I + 1
 97  GO TO 94
100  DATA "BOILLOT", 91, 56, 147
101  DATA "GLEASON", 40, 50, 90
102  DATA "HORN", 50, 65, 115
103  DATA "MONISH", 70, 70, 140
104  DATA "END$", 0, 0, 0
200  END

RUN

PRESENT GRADES ARE
BOILLOT          91          56          147
GLEASON          40          50          90
HORN             50          65          115
MONISH           70          70          140

INPUT GRADE CHANGE? "HORN", -1, 98
INPUT GRADE CHANGE? "GLEASON", 77, 60
INPUT GRADE CHANGE? "BULLIT", 40, 36
NO NAME MATCH FOUND
INPUT GRADE CHANGE? "BOILLOT", 40, -1
INPUT GRADE CHANGE? "FIN", 0, 0

* * * * * * * * * * * * * * * * * * * * * * * * *
GRADES AFTER CHANGES ARE
BOILLOT          40          56          96
GLEASON          77          60          137
HORN             50          98          148
MONISH           70          70          140
```

Figure 7-16    Grade change program (part 2 of 2).

```
10  PRINT "KNOW YOUR NYSE COMPANY STOCK ABBREVIATIONS"
15  LET T$ (1) = "YOU ARE RIGHT"
20  LET T$ (2) = "TAKE ANOTHER GUESS"
25  LET T$ (3) = "NO. THE CORRECT ANSWER IS: "
30  LET S = 0              S is used to compute the number of correct answers.
35  FOR I = 1 TO 4
40       LET J = 1         Initialize pointer to the "you are right" message.
45       READ A$, B$       Read an abbreviation and its interpretation.
50       PRINT A$;         Write the abbreviation and ask what it means.
55       INPUT C$
60       IF C$ = B$ THEN 95    Did the student get it right?
65       LET J = J + 1     The first time, set pointer to the message "take another guess".
70       IF J > 2 THEN 85  The second time, set pointer to "No, the correct answer is".
75       PRINT T$(J);      Print T$(2) i.e., "take another guess".
80       GO TO 55
85       PRINT T$(J); B$   Print T$(3) and the answer.
90       GO TO 100
95       PRINT T$(1)       Print congratulatory message.
97       LET S=S+1         Keep track of correct answers.
100      PRINT
105 NEXT I                 The session consists of four problems in this case.
107 PRINT "YOU GOT"; S/4*100; "PERCENT OF THE QUESTIONS CORRECT"
110 DATA "NCR", "NATIONAL CASH REGISTER"
115 DATA "AMAX", "AMERICAN METAL CLIMAX"
120 DATA "CDC", "CONTROL DATA CORPORATION"
125 DATA "SOB", "SYSTEM OMNI BILATERAL"
130 STOP
135 END

RUN

KNOW YOUR NYSE COMPANY STOCK ABBREVIATIONS

NCR? NATIONAL CASH REGISTER
YOU ARE RIGHT

AMAX? AMERICAN SYNTAX
TAKE ANOTHER GUESS. AMERICAN MEDICAL XRATED
NO. THE CORRECT ANSWER IS: AMERICAN METAL CLIMAX

CDC? CONSOLIDATED DAM CORPORATION
TAKE ANOTHER GUESS. CONTROL DATA CORPORATION
YOU ARE RIGHT

SOB? SON OF A GUN
TAKE ANOTHER GUESS. DONT KNOW
NO. THE CORRECT ANSWER IS: SYSTEM OMNI BILATERAL

YOU GOT 50 PERCENT OF THE QUESTIONS CORRECT
```

**Figure 7-17**    A computer drill program.

**A Computer Drill Program**

A program to teach the company names corresponding to their abbreviations as listed in any business section of a newspaper for the New York Stock Exchange (NYSE) composite transactions is shown in Figure 7-17. The student is asked for the interpretation of a given abbreviation. If he is correct, a congratulatory message is printed. If not, he is asked to try a second time; if still incorrect, the computer prints out the answer and continues with a different abbreviation. At the conclusion of the session, the student is informed of his percentage of correct answers.

## 7-5-4    One-Dimensional Character Strings

Many BASIC systems do *not* allow use of arrays for storage of character strings. They do, however, allow for operation on particular characters within a string. In such systems, character strings can be referenced in either of two ways:

1.  Explicitly, by enclosing the string in quotes, as in

    5 PRINT "WHAT A BEAUTIFUL DAY"

2.  By assigning a string to a dimensioned *character string* variable. The name of a dimensioned character string variable must end with a $ and *must* be specified in the DIM statement. Lengths for strings can vary from 1 character to 255 characters and must be specified in the DIM statement.

**Examples**

| | |
|---|---|
| 5 DIM N$(30) | Thirty characters are reserved for the string N$. |
| 10 LET N$ = "MARC  " | The first four characters of N$ are MARC followed by one blank. |
| 15 PRINT N$; "SIMS" | "MARC SIMS" is printed. |

The name of the above string is N$; an error would occur if N$(1) were used instead of N$. Even though N$ is DIMensioned, it is *not* an array.

**Reference to Characters within a String**

Individual characters or substrings can be extracted from a string as follows:

1.  The variable A$ refers to the entire string. Its length is the length specified in the DIM statement.

2.  The variable A$ (I) refers to the set of characters starting at position I through the last in the string.

3.  The variable A$ (I,J) refers to the segment of the string starting at position I up to and including the Jth position.

Examples

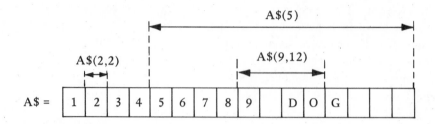

```
10  DIM A$(16)
15  LET A$="123456789 . DOG . . . "
20  PRINT A$                                   123456789  DOG    is printed.
25  PRINT A$(5)                                    56789  DOG    is printed.
30  PRINT A$(9,12)                                     9  DO     is printed.
35  PRINT A$(2,2)                          2                     is printed.
```

## Concatenation of Strings

Strings can be fused or joined together by using the concatenation operator comma (,).

Example

```
0005 DIM A$ (5), B$ (5), C$ (9)
0010 LET A$ = "12345"
0015 LET B$ = "ABCDE"
0020 LET C$ = A$ (3), "999", B$ (3,5)
0024 PRINT C$
0025 END
RUN
345999CDE
```

## Comparison of Strings

Strings can be compared to each other as discussed in Section 7-5-2.

Examples

```
0005 DIM A$ (10), B$ (10)
0010 LET A$ = "BCDEFG"
0015 LET B$ = "36 BCDEFGH"       Note the blank before the letter B.
0020 IF A$ > B$ THEN 60          Transfer will occur; since B > 3.
0030 IF A$ > B$(4) THEN 70       No transfer, since H > (blank).
0040 IF A$(1,4) = B$(4,7) THEN 90 Transfer will occur; substrings are equal.
```

**Programming Example**

Let us code the introductory section of a conversation between a program and a computer terminal user. The program introduces itself and then asks its interlocutor how he or she should be addressed (see Figure 7-18).

```
05  DIM T$(31), F$(31), G$(31)
01  PRINT "MY NAME IS ZAN. WHAT'S YOUR FIRST AND LAST NAME"
15  INPUT T$
17  PRINT
20  FOR I = 1 TO 31
25      IF T$(I,I) = " " THEN 34          Look for a blank to separate first
30  NEXT I                                from last name.
34  PRINT "WOULD YOU PREFER THAT";
35  PRINT "I CALL YOU"; T$(1, I);         T$(1, I) is first name.
36  PRINT "OK MR"; T$(I + 1, 31)          T$(I + 1, 31) is last name.
40  INPUT F$                              F$ is either MR last name
45  PRINT                                 or preferred name of respondent.
50  LET G$ = "MR.", T$(I, 31)             Note concatenation.
55  IF F$ = G$ THEN 70                    If respondent wants to be
65  LET G$ = T$(1,I)                      called Mr . . ., otherwise call
70  PRINT "OK"; G$                        him by his first name.
RUN
```

```
MY NAME IS ZAN. WHAT'S YOUR FIRST AND LAST NAME
? MICHEL EVANS
WOULD YOU PREFER THAT I CALL YOU MICHEL OR MR. EVANS
? MR. EVANS
OK MR. EVANS
```

Figure 7-18   Example of use of character string variable.

# 7-6   Assignments

## 7-6-1   Self Test

1.  Given an array A of size 100, write the partial code to generate the following output:

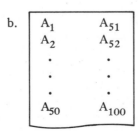

c.

| 1 | $A_{100}$ |
|---|---|
| 2 | $A_{99}$ |
| . | . |
| . | . |
| . | . |
| 100 | $A_1$ |

d.

$A_2$
$A_4$
$A_6$
.
.
.
$A_{100}$

| $A_1$ | $A_2$ | $A_3$ | ... | $A_9$ | $A_{10}$ |
|---|---|---|---|---|---|
| $A_{11}$ | $A_{12}$ | | ... | | $A_{20}$ |

.
.
.

$A_{91}$ $A_{92}$ ... $A_{100}$

2. Write the code to fill successive elements of an array with the values 5, 7, 9, 11, ... 225. Do not use a READ statement.

3. Assume array A with 50 elements has already been loaded. Write the code to compute the sum of the squares of the elements of the array A.

4. A DATA statement contains an unknown number of numbers (at least 51). Write the code to read the first 20 numbers in array A, the next 30 in array B, and the remainder in array C.

5. Array A supposedly contains 20 elements already sorted in ascending order. Write the code to perform a sequence check. Print in sequence if the array is in sequence; otherwise, print ERROR.

6. Array A (10 elements) and array B (16 elements) have already been loaded. Write the code to determine and print the number of identical elements in both arrays.

7. Into an array A of size 11, read 10 numbers already in ascending order from one DATA statement; read another number R from another DATA statement and insert it in proper sequence in array A.

8. A DATA statement contains an unknown number of numbers varying from $-100$ to $100$. Write a program to store the positive numbers in array A and the negative numbers in array B.

9. Write a program to print the following arrangements:

a.

| 1 | 2 | 3 | 4 | 5 | 6 | 7 | 8 | 9 | 10 |
|---|---|---|---|---|---|---|---|---|---|
| 1 | 2 | 3 | 4 | 5 | 6 | 7 | 8 | 9 | |
| 1 | 2 | 3 | 4 | 5 | 6 | 7 | 8 | | |
| 1 | 2 | 3 | 4 | 5 | 6 | 7 | | | |
| 1 | 2 | 3 | 4 | 5 | 6 | | | | |
| 1 | 2 | 3 | 4 | 5 | | | | | |
| 1 | 2 | 3 | 4 | | | | | | |
| 1 | 2 | 3 | | | | | | | |
| 1 | 2 | | | | | | | | |
| 1 | | | | | | | | | |

b.

| 1 | | | | | | | | | |
|---|---|---|---|---|---|---|---|---|---|
| 1 | 2 | | | | | | | | |
| 1 | 2 | 3 | | | | | | | |
| 1 | 2 | 3 | 4 | | | | | | |
| 1 | 2 | 3 | 4 | 5 | | | | | |
| 1 | 2 | 3 | 4 | 5 | 6 | | | | |
| 1 | 2 | 3 | 4 | 5 | 6 | 7 | | | |
| 1 | 2 | 3 | 4 | 5 | 6 | 7 | 8 | | |
| 1 | 2 | 3 | 4 | 5 | 6 | 7 | 8 | 9 | |
| 1 | 2 | 3 | 4 | 5 | 6 | 7 | 8 | 9 | 10 |

## 7-6-2   Exercises

1.   The MILES Furniture store is going out of business. All different store items have been labeled 1, 2, 3, . . . 100 (100 different items in all). The cost per item and the number of items in stock have been recorded as follows: C(I) is the cost of item I and Q(I) is the number of items I. Assume arrays C and Q have already been loaded. Write a program segment to calculate the MILES inventory.

2.   Read in a maximum of 15 account numbers and corresponding amounts deposited (each DATA statement will consist of an account number and an amount deposited) and write the code to:

   a.   Print all the account numbers of those persons who have deposited $50,000 or more.

   b.   THEN print all the account numbers of those persons who have deposited between $10,000 and $50,000.

3.   a.   At the beginning and at the end of each month, members of the U-WATCH-UR-WEIGHT club are weighed in. Each member's name and initial and terminal weights are recorded on a separate DATA statement. The very first DATA statement has the exact number of club members whose weights are recorded on the following DATA statements. Write a program to print each member's name, his or her initial and terminal weight, and weight loss. Additionally, print the number of members whose weight loss is above the total average weight loss. For example the output might be:

| NAME | INITIAL WEIGHT | TERMINAL WEIGHT | LOSS IN WEIGHT |
|---|---|---|---|
| HUBIT | 200 | 180 | 20 |
| MARSINI | 130 | 120 | 10 |
| TODINI | 160 | 154 | 6 |

   AVERAGE WEIGHT LOSS IS 12 POUNDS

   1 MEMBER HAS A WEIGHT LOSS OVER 12 POUNDS

   b.   Same as part a except that an "*" is to be printed alongside each member's name whose weight loss is over the average. Also print a list of these people.

4.   An encyclopedia company has hired saleswomen (20 at most). The name of each girl and the number of encyclopedia sets each girl has sold are recorded on separate DATA statements. Each girl gets paid $90.00 for each set sold, as well as $15.00 extra for each set (and fraction) sold over the average. Write a program to produce the names of the girls, the number of sets sold, and amount earned.

5.   The Triple Star Corporation has its sales (expressed in millions) over the last 10 years recorded on a DATA statement. These figures lie between 0 and 70 (millions), for example, DATA 13, 22, 19, 30, etc. Write a program to produce an output similar to the following:

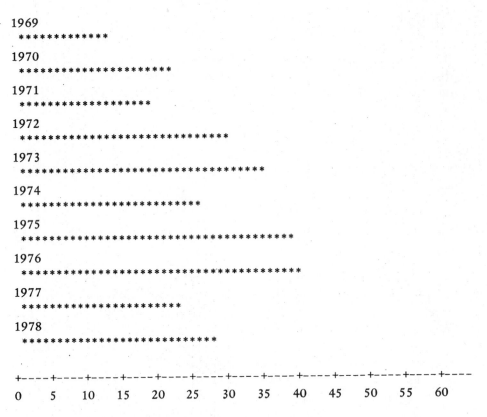

6. For each student in a class, you have one DATA statement with his or her name and 10 test scores. The student's average is based on his or her nine best scores. Write a program to produce an output similar to the following:

GRADE REPORT

NAME: WOODRUFF     AVERAGE = 60
TESTS: 10, 20, 30, 40, 50, 60, 70, 80, 90, 100

NAME: ZIEGLER     AVERAGE = 58.9
TESTS: 100, 50, 60, 40, 35, 65, 80, 20, 30, 70

7. In the bubble sort discussed in Section 7-4-4 it is quite conceivable that in sorting an array of 100 elements, for example, the array becomes sorted by the 60th pass. Therefore, it would be inefficient to continue sorting for the remaining 40 passes. Write a program to discontinue the sorting process as soon as the array elements have become sorted. (*Hint:* If the array is sorted, what happens to the interchange process?)

8. a. Write a program to read a student's schedule from two DATA statements to produce the following geometric arrangement. The first DATA statement contains the student's Monday schedule (identical to Wednesday and Friday), and the second DATA statement contains his Tuesday schedule (identical to Thursday). The meeting time and course description are recorded on the DATA statement in "meeting time" order. For example, given the following data, the printout shown below should be obtained:

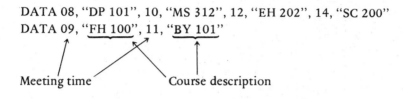

DATA 08, "DP 101", 10, "MS 312", 12, "EH 202", 14, "SC 200"
DATA 09, "FH 100", 11, "BY 101"

Meeting time          Course description

| TIME | MON | TUES | WED | THURS | FRI |
|------|-----|------|-----|-------|-----|
| 8 | DP 101 | | DP 101 | | DP 101 |
| 9 | | FH 100 | | FH 100 | |
| 10 | MS 312 | | MS 312 | | MS 312 |
| 11 | | BY 101 | | BY 101 | |
| 12 | EH 202 | | EH 202 | | EH 202 |
| 13 | | | | | |
| 14 | SC 200 | | SC 200 | | SC 200 |

TOTAL HOURS IS 16

b. Rewrite the preceding program in the event the data is not sorted by ascending "meeting time."

9. Ten DATA statements contain the inventory for 10 items sold by PARTS, Ltd., as of the close of the November 17, 1979, business day. Each card (DATA statement) contains the item number and the number of the specified items in stock. The next day (November 18), some of the items are sold and shipped out; at the close of the November 18 business day, transaction cards are appended to the original 10 cards, each reflecting the item number and the number of items shipped that day. The end of the transaction records is identified by a trailer record with a -1, -1 on it. Write a program to print the original inventory as of the close of November 17, the November 18 transactions and the updated inventory at the close of November 18. The input and output may be visualized as follows (the inventory in this case consists only of four items).

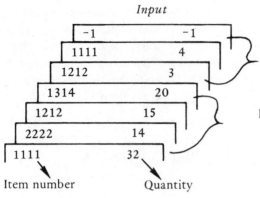

*Input*

Transaction cards from the November
18 business day

Inventory as of the close
of November 17

Item number          Quantity

*Output*

NOV. 17 INVENTORY

| UNIT | QUANTITY |
|------|----------|
| 1111 | 32 |
| 2222 | 14 |
| 1212 | 15 |
| 1314 | 20 |

NOV. 18 TRANSACTIONS

| | |
|------|---|
| 1212 | 3 |
| 1111 | 4 |

NOV. 18 INVENTORY

| | |
|------|----|
| 1111 | 28 |
| 2222 | 14 |
| 1212 | 12 |
| 1314 | 20 |

10.  Write a program to record in an array P the relative ascending order position of each element of array A. For example, if

array A =

| 51 | 20 | 90 | 80 | 100 |
|----|----|----|----|-----|

then

array P =

| 2 | 1 | 4 | 3 | 5 |
|---|---|---|---|---|

This means that:    P(1) points to the smallest element of A
                    P(2) points to the next to smallest element of A
                         .
                         .
                    P(5) points to largest element of A

The following code would then print the elements of A in ascending numerical sequence

```
5 FOR I = 1 TO 5
6 PRINT A(P(I));
7 NEXT I
```

In what programming situation would the above sort algorithm be preferable to the bubble or mini/max sorts?

11. You work for the National Weather Service. They are going to test changes in wind direction by sending up three balloons on each of five different days. Each of the 15 balloons is assigned a unique identification number (ID) between 100 and 999 inclusive (in no particular order). One ballon is released in the morning, one is released at noon, and one is released in the evening of each of the five days. When the ballons are returned, the ID number, day sent up (1,2,3,4, or 5), and distance traveled will be recorded on one DATA statement per balloon.

a. Read the data in three separate arrays (ID, day, and distance).

b. Sort the arrays in ascending order by ID.

c. Print the sorted arrays, one ID, corresponding day sent up, and distance per line.

d. Find the maximum distance that the ballons released on each day traveled (five maximums) and print the ID, day, and maximum distance for each of the five days (you should print the results for the first day, then second, third, etc.).

e. Find the average distance traveled by ballons released on the *first and fifth days combined.*

*Input:*   15 DATA statements (each with an ID, day, and distance traveled)

*Output:*   15 printed lines of sorted ID's and corresponding days and distances (ID, day, distance)

   5 printed lines of maximum distances for each day (1 thru 5) (ID, day, distance)

   1 printed line of the average distance traveled on the first and fifth days

| *Test Data:* | | |
|---|---|---|
| 123 | 2 | 143.7 |
| 269 | 3 | 976.4 |
| 120 | 1 | 370.2 |
| 460 | 5 | 980.8 |
| 111 | 1 | 111.3 |
| 986 | 4 | 1,320.6 |
| 629 | 3 | 787.0 |
| 531 | 2 | 429.2 |
| 729 | 2 | 726.1 |
| 833 | 4 | 433.1 |
| 621 | 3 | 962.4 |
| 143 | 4 | 714.3 |
| 972 | 5 | 320.1 |
| 410 | 5 | 820.4 |
| 511 | 1 | 1,240.0 |

12. At the Kilpatrick Community College, General Mathematics MS 101 has always been offered in the traditional teacher/lecture format. This year, for the first time, students may take MS 101 using a self-paced approach to instruction through a computer assisted instructional method (CAI). Because of the novelty of the CAI approach, the mathematics faculty has formulated the following policies concerning grades and tests for those taking MS 101 in the CAI mode.

a. Students may take one, or two, or three tests during the semester.

b. The final score is based on the student's average score, scaled as follows:
If the CAI class average (AV) is less than 80 (the standardized average for traditional teacher/lecture form), then the difference 80 − AV should be added to each student's average score; otherwise, the difference AV − 80 is subtracted from each student average. The input data is formatted as follows:

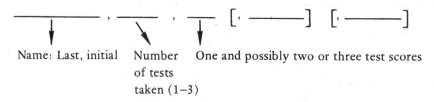

Name: Last, initial    Number    One and possibly two or three test scores
                       of tests
                       taken (1–3)

Write a program to produce the following class-student-score information. For example, the following input data would produce the following output data:

*Output data*

| STUDENT NAME | AVERAGE | SCALED AVERAGE |
|---|---|---|
| BOILLOT M. | 90.5 | 84.5 |
| HORN L. | 87.5 | 81.5 |
| GLEASON G. | 80.0 | 74.0 |
| | | |
| AVERAGE | 86.0 | |

*Input*

DATA "BOILLOT M", 1, 90.5
DATA "HORN L", 2, 86, 89
DATA "GLEASON G", 3, 60, 80, 100

13. On NBC's *Today* show weather report, temperatures from various cities in the United States are listed by geographical areas. Temperature readings are collected from various weather-measuring stations and recorded on DATA statements in no special sequence order. Each card contains the following data:

DATA _____ , _____ , _____

City        Temperature    Section code    { 1 = East Coast    2 = Midwest
                                           { 3 = South         4 = Pacific

a.  Write a program segment to provide the weather reporter with a list of cities and corresponding temperatures by geographical area in the order the cities are encountered in the input. The output should identify each of the geographical areas by name rather than by numeric code. The output should be similar to

EAST COAST
    BOSTON    45
    NEW YORK    51
MIDWEST
    MADISON    – 5
    CHICAGO    57
SOUTHERN STATES
    MOBILE    73
    MIAMI    88
PACIFIC COAST
    FRESNO    66

*Input data*

| | |
|---|---|
| "BOSTON", | 45, 1 |
| "FRESNO", | 66, 4 |
| "NEW YORK", | 51, 1 |
| "MOBILE", | 73, 3 |
| "MADISON", | –5, 2 |
| "CHICAGO", | 57, 2 |
| "MIAMI", | 88, 3 |

HIGHEST TEMPERATURE: 88 : MIAMI

b.  Write another program segment to list cities by ascending temperature order (four cities per printed line), as follows:

| | | | | | | | |
|---|---|---|---|---|---|---|---|
| MADISON | –5 | BOSTON | 45 | NEW YORK | 51 | CHICAGO | 57 |
| FRESNO | 66 | MOBILE | 73 | MIAMI | 88 | | |

14. The BOIHORN company employs a variable number of salesmen. Records of sales by each salesman are recorded on DATA statements, which are already sorted in ascending order by salesman number but not by date. For example, a typical data file might appear as follows:

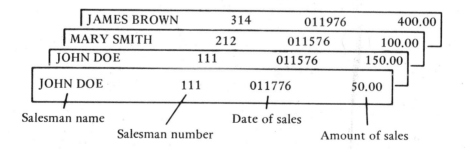

The management wishes to print out a monthly sales report to summarize the total sales for each salesman and the total amount of all sales. Also, a salesman-of-the-month award will go to the salesman with highest sales for the month. Entries are to be listed in ascending order by salesman number. Observe the following output for your data:

| SALESMAN NAME | NUMBER | DATE OF SALES | AMOUNT OF SALES | TOTAL SALES/ SALESMAN |
|---|---|---|---|---|
| JOHN DOE | 111 | 01 15 76 | 150.00 | |
| | | 01 15 76 | 50.00 | 250.00 |
| MARY SMITH | 212 | 01 17 76 | 100.00 | 100.00 |
| JAMES BROWN | 314 | 01 19 76 | 400.00 | 400.00 |
| | | | TOTAL SALES | 750.00 |

**AWARD GOES TO JAMES BROWN**

Write a program to read a transaction file and produce a summary report as shown. Be sure you include more than one transaction for some of the salesmen and note that in such a case you print the number of the salesman only once.

15.  a.  Initialize the three following arrays (PART NUMBER, QUANTITY, and COST/PART) to the values indicated. (Do not read or input data.)

| PART NUMBER | QUANTITY | COST/PART |
|---|---|---|
| 115 | 50 | 90 |
| 120 | 60 | 91 |
| 125 | 70 | 83 |
| 130 | 80 | 93 |
| . | . | . |
| . | . | . |
| . | . | . |
| 160 | 140 | 99 |

For example, there are 50 parts item 115 at a cost of 90 cents each. During the day, sales transactions are recorded on DATA statements (or simulated by a random number generator) as follows:

DATA _____ , _____
Part number      Quantity sold

b.  Write a program to read the day's transaction to produce a parts inventory and

1.  Print a "reorder" message whenever fewer than 20 items are in stock.

2.  Discount the price on any unsold part by 10 percent of its original cost (rounded to the nearest digit).

The inventory report, for example, might be drawn as follows:

| PART NUMBER | STOCK | NUMBER SOLD | COST/PART | |
|---|---|---|---|---|
| 115 | 40 | 10 | 90 | |
| 120 | 0 | 60 | 91 | * * REORDER * * |
| 125 | 70 | 0 | 83 | DISCOUNT |
| 130 | 5 | 75 | 93 | * * REORDER * * |
| . | . | . | . | |
| . | . | . | . | |
| . | . | . | . | |
| 160 | 70 | 70 | 99 | |

c.  In the event a parts number is incorrectly recorded in the transaction data file, generate the same report as in part b with a list of the incorrect part numbers at the bottom of (following) the inventory report. For example:

| PART NUMBER | STOCK | NUMBER SOLD | COST/PART |
|---|---|---|---|
| 115 | 40 | 10 | 90 |
| . | . | . | . |
| . | . | . | . |
| . | . | . | . |
| 160 | 70 | 70 | 99 |

117 ***NO SUCH EXISTING PART. CHECK RECORD***
126 ***NO SUCH EXISTING PART. CHECK RECORD***

d.  To prepare for the following day, recreate a new inventory file by deleting all part numbers with exhausted stock and print the new inventory table as follows:

| PART NUMBER | QUANTITY | COST/PART |
|---|---|---|
| 115 | 40 | 90 |
| 125 | 70 | 83 |
| 130 | 5 | 93 |
| . | . | . |
| . | . | . |
| . | . | . |
| 160 | 70 | 99 |

← Note absence of part number 120.

e.  During the day, a parts salesman persuades the manager to add three new parts to his current line of parts. The parts numbers are numbers between 100 and 170 excluding those already in stock. The manager decides to purchase 300 of each of these new parts. Read three records with new parts number and corresponding costs on each record and produce a new inventory table by inserting the new records in their appropriate ascending position in the file as follows:

| PART NUMBER | QUANTITY | COST/PART |
|---|---|---|
| 100 | 300 | 60 |
| 115 | 40 | 90 |
| 125 | 70 | 83 |
| 130 | 5 | 93 |
| 132 | 300 | 95 |
| . | . | . |
| . | . | . |
| . | . | . |

Note new inserts.

16. Write a program to compute the sum of the squares of the elements of an array with fifty elements.

17. An array contains N elements. Write a program to assign values to an array B such that $B_1 = A_N, B_2 = A_{N-1}, \cdots, B_N = A_1$.

18. Write a program to interchange elements of an array A in such a way that the first and last values are interchanged, the second and next to last are interchanged, and so forth. Use only the array A; do not use a second array.

19. Input two vectors A and B of length 5 and compute their dot product:

$$A_1 B_1 + A_2 B_2 + \cdots + A_5 B_5$$

20. Write a program to read a list of grades from a DATA statement into an array and determine how many grades occur in the intervals:

$$1-9$$
$$10-19$$
$$20-29$$
$$\cdot$$
$$\cdot$$
$$\cdot$$
$$90-99$$

(*Hint:* Use A(1), A(2), . . . , A(10) as counters for the various intervals. Make use of A(G/10 + 1) where G is the grade read.)

21. Modify exercise 20 to account for the intervals

$$0-10$$
$$11-20$$
$$21-30$$
$$\cdot$$
$$\cdot$$
$$\cdot$$
$$91-100$$

22. Write a program to input data and calculate the standard deviation of the input data. The standard deviation may be computed by the formula

$$SD = \sqrt{\frac{\left(X_1 - \overline{X}\right)^2 + \left(X_2 - \overline{X}\right)^2 + \left(X_3 - \overline{X}\right)^2 + \cdots + \left(X_n - \overline{X}\right)^2}{n - 1}}$$

where:   $n$ = number of data items,
$\overline{X}$ = mean of the data items (average), and
$X_1, X_2, X_3, \cdots, X_n$ are the data items.

**Exercises for BASIC Systems Allowing String Manipulation**

23. Read a paragraph of five lines using just one literal string and determine the occurrence of the word "is." Be sure to ignore occurrences of the string "is" imbedded in other words such as "th*is*."

24. Same problem as exercise 23, except count the number of words. Words may be defined as strings separated by commas, periods, or blanks.

25. To facilitate transmission, words in telegrams are usually separated by slashes (/). Regenerate the original line of a telegraph message by substituting blanks wherever slashes appear.

26. Same problem as exercise 25, except compute the cost of the telegram. Each word up to and including the twentieth word costs 15 cents; thereafter, each word costs 12 cents.

27. Addresses in telegrams are transmitted serially. A double slash indicates a new line.

    *Example:* 1301/NORTH12TH/AVE//ATLANTA//GEORGIA/75603//

    Read five such addresses and recreate them as envelope addresses.

28. Write a program to convert military time to civilian time.

    *Example:* 1818 should produce THE TIME IS 18 PAST 6
    1545 should produce THE TIME IS 15 BEFORE 4

29. Write a program to convert civilian time to 24-hour time. Civilian time should contain only the key words P.M. and A.M. The format for the input is

$$\text{DATA hours, minutes,} \quad \left\{ \begin{matrix} \text{"PM"} \\ \text{"AM"} \end{matrix} \right\}$$

    *Example:* DATA 2,15,PM should produce 1415.

30. Translate dates expressed numerically into the usual month and day and year representation.

    *Example:* 11/07/76 should produce NOVEMBER 7 1976

31. Read a word and write it in reverse order.

32.  Write a program to read a five-letter word and generate all possible combinations of two-letter words using those five letters. Can you avoid duplication of two-letter words?

33.  Determine the number of syllables in a word; in a sentence.

34.  Determine the number of sentences and words in a paragraph. An end of sentence identifier is either a . ? ! : ; .

## 7-6-3   Projects

1.  A furniture discount store purchases different types of furniture pieces from a manufacturer; for example, 100 sofas, 200 tables, etc. Each piece of furniture has a classification code; for example, chairs have a code of 21, beds a code of 31, etc. With each item purchased, a manufacturer's suggested retail price (MSRP) is given; the discount store then decides the price to charge the consumer. The store keeps track of its inventory on records that have the following format:

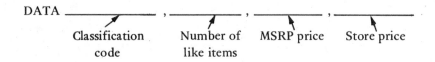

Write a program to read a set of records as defined above to produce the following information:

a.   Give two separate paragraph listings of (1) class of items that are to be sold at or above the MSRP and (2) the class of items that are to be sold below the MSRP. These listings should be printed across the page.

b.   Two consecutive tables listed vertically of items (by name) selling at or above the MSRP and those selling below the MSRP (name of the item and corresponding MSRP and consumer price).

The problem can better be understood with sample data as follows:

| *Input* | *Output* |
|---|---|

Input:

```
DATA 21,  50,  45.99,  43.99
DATA 31, 100,  65.99,  66.95
DATA 41,  50,  45.50,  45.50
DATA 61,  20,  80.00,  70.00
DATA 71,  15, 120.00, 109.00
```

No. items

Store price

Classification code

Manufacturer's retail price

| Chairs | 21 | |
|---|---|---|
| Beds | 31 | |
| Tables | 41 | Code |
| Sofas | 61 | |
| Desks | 71 | |

Output:

```
ITEMS SOLD AT/ABOVE MSRP

     31        41      . . .

ITEMS SOLD BELOW MSRP

     21        61        71      . . .
```

| AT/ABOVE ITEMS | MSRP | PRICE |
|---|---|---|
| Beds | 65.99 | 66.95 |
| Tables | 45.50 | 45.50 |
| . | . | . |
| . | . | . |

| BELOW MSRP ITEMS | MSRP | PRICE |
|---|---|---|
| Chairs | 45.99 | 43.99 |
| Sofas | 80.00 | 70.00 |
| Desks | 120.00 | 109.00 |

## Games

2. Simulate a guessing game between a user and a computer terminal. The user thinks of a number between 1 and 10, and the terminal must guess the number without repeating itself.

3. a. In the game problem 6a of Section 6-6-3, you placed a mole 100 times at position row 3, column 4 of the island and counted each time the number of times the mole escaped. Now, if the mole were clever, the very first time she would find the way out, you'd think she could remember it so that from then on she'd never drown! Write a program to do just that; i.e., keep track in an array of the sequence of steps leading to a safe exit and reject any sequence of paths leading to drowning. Sooner or later the mole will find a way out, and that path will be recorded in an array so that from that point on the mole should always escape.

   b. Of course the mole's first path to freedom may not be the shortest way out. Write a program to force the mole to select the shortest escape path out of some 20 escapes. From then on the mole should remember that particular path. Print the mole's final exit path using a coordinate system as follows:

$$(3,4) \quad (3,3) \quad (4,3) \quad \text{etc.}$$

row      column

4.  Read into an array named W eight of each of the following in random order: nouns, pronouns, verbs, adverbs, adjectives, and articles (repeated, if necessary) and store their corresponding numerical code in an array called C. The word codes are 1 = pronoun, 2 = verb, 3 = adverb, 4 = adjective, 5 = noun, 6 = article. Both the words and numerical codes are recorded randomly as follows:

DATA "HORRIBLE", 4, "MONKEY", 5, "THE", 6, "HE", 1, etc.

Word      Corresponding numerical code

As a result of the input operation, the two arrays W and C might appear as follows:

| W = | HORRIBLE | MONKEY | THE | HE | VERY... | DOLL | A | A |
|-----|----------|--------|-----|-----|---------|------|---|---|
| | W(1) | W(2) | W(3) | | | | | W(48) |

| C = | 4 | 5 | 6 | 1 | 3 | 5 | 1 | 1 |
|-----|---|---|---|---|---|---|---|---|
| | C(1) | C(2) | C(3) | | | | | C(48) |

a.  Write a program to search the word code array to print out all the words of the word array using the following format:

| PRONOUNS | VERBS | ADVERBS | ADJECTIVES | NOUNS | ARTICLES |
|----------|-------|---------|------------|-------|----------|
| HE | LIKES | VERY | HORRIBLE | MONKEY | THE |
| . | . | . | . | . | . |
| . | . | . | . | . | . |
| . | . | . | . | . | A |
| | DRINKS | | | DOLL | A |

b.  Using the random number generator routine to extract entries from the 48-word array (not from the six sorted word arrays), construct two English sentences to fit the following grammatical structure:

Article, noun, verb, adjective. Pronoun, verb, article, adverb, adjective, noun.

For example, the following sentence might be generated:

THE BOY IS TALL. HE IS A VERY BEAUTIFUL MONKEY.

Analyze the selected numerical codes to keep rejecting words until they satisfy the desired grammatical structure. (*Hint:* You might want to store the numerical word codes for the sentence in an array N where $N(1) = 6$, $N(2) = 5$, $N(3) = 2$, ..., $N(10) = 5$, and compare $(N)I$ with $C(J)$, where I varies from 1 to 10, and J is a random number between 1 and 48.)

5.  Write a drill/practice program to randomly generate arithmetic problems of a particular type, accept a solution, and test to see if it is correct. Implement as many of the following optional features as you see fit:

Sign off procedure.

Statistics produced when a user signs off.

Randomized responses to correct and incorrect answers.

Help in the form of a restatement of the problem or a brief tutorial when a number of incorrect answers to a problem have been given.

A "homework" assignment produced when a user signs off.  The problems might consist of all the problems missed by the user during the session.

The program might start with "easy" examples and progress to "harder" problems if the user is successful or remain with easy problems if the user has difficulty. You might be able to identify several levels of difficulty.

Any other feature which you feel would be useful.

## 7-6-4  Answers to Self Test

1.  a.    5 DIM A(100)
         10 FOR I = 1 TO 99 STEP 2
         20 PRINT A(I), A(I+1)
         30 NEXT I

    b.    5 DIM A (100)
         10 FOR I = 1 TO 50
         20 PRINT A(I), A(I+50)
         30 NEXT I

    c.    5 DIM A(100)
         10 FOR I = 1 TO 100
         20 PRINT I, A(101–I)
         30 NEXT I

    d.    5 DIM A(100)
         10 FOR I = 2 TO 100 STEP 2
         20 PRINT A(I)
         30 NEXT I
         40 FOR J=0 TO 9
         50 FOR I = 1 TO 10
         60 PRINT A(J*10 + I);
         70 NEXT I
         80 PRINT
         90 NEXT J

2.  10 DIM X(111)
    20 FOR N = 1 TO 111
    30 LET X(N)=5+(N−1)∗2
    40 NEXT N
    50 FOR I=1 TO 111
    60 PRINT X(I);
    70 NEXT I
    80 END
    RUN

    5 7 9 11 13 15 17 19 21 23 25 27 29 31 33 35 37 39 41
    43 45 47 49 51 53 55 57 59 61 63 65 67 69 71 73 75 77
    79 81 83 85 87 89 91 93 95 97 99 101 103 105 107 109 111
    113 115 117 119 121 123 125 127 129 131 133 135 137 139 141
    143 145 147 149 151 153 155 157 159 161 163 165 167 169 171
    173 175 177 179 181 183 185 187 189 191 193 195 197 199 201
    203 205 207 209 211 213 215 217 219 221 223 225

3.  5 DIM A(50)
    10 FOR I=1 TO 50
    20 LET S=S+A(I)∗A(I)
    30 NEXT I

4.  10 DATA . . .
    20 DIM A(20), B(30), C(100)
    30 FOR I=1 TO 20
    40 READ A(I)
    50 NEXT I
    60 FOR I = 1 TO 30
    70 READ B(I)
    80 NEXT I
    90 FOR I=1 TO 100
    100 REM THE VALUE 0 IS ASSUMED TO BE THE LAST VALUE IN THE DATA
    110 READ C(I)
    120 IF C(I) = 0 THEN 140
    130 NEXT I
    140 END

5.  10 DIM A(20)
    20 FOR I = 1 TO 19
    30 IF A(I) > A(I+1) THEN 70
    40 PRINT A(I)
    50 NEXT I
    60 PRINT A(20)
    65 STOP
    70 PRINT "ERROR"
    80 END

6.  5 DIM A(10),B(16)
    10 FOR I=1 TO 10
    20 FOR J=1 TO 16
    30 IF A(I) <> B(J) THEN 50
    40 LET M=N+1
    50 NEXT J
    60 NEXT I
    70 END

7.
```
100 DIM A(11)
200 DATA 2,3,5,6,7,8,9,10,12,14
300 DATA 4
400 FOR I=1 TO 10
500 READ A(I)
600 NEXT I
700 READ R
800 FOR I=1 TO 10
900 IF A(I) > R THEN 1100
1000 NEXT I
1100 FOR J=11 TO I+1 STEP −1
1200 LET A(J)=A(J−1)
1300 NEXT J
1400 LET A(I)=R
1500 FOR I=1 TO 11
1600 PRINT A(I);
1700 NEXT I
1800 END
RUN
2 3 4 5 6 7 8 9 10 12 14
```

8.
```
100 DATA . . .
200 DIM A(100),B(100)
250 LET I=0
260 LET J=0
300 READ X
400 IF X > 100 THEN 1000
500 IF X >= 0 THEN 800
600 LET J=J+1
700 LET B(J)=X
750 GO TO 300
800 LET I=I+1
900 LET B(I)=X
950 GO TO 300
1000 END
```

9. a.
```
100 FOR J=10 TO 1 STEP −1
200 FOR I=1 TO J
300 PRINT I;
400 NEXT I
500 PRINT
600 NEXT J
700 END
RUN
1 2 3 4 5 6 7 8 9 10
1 2 3 4 5 6 7 8 9
1 2 3 4 5 6 7 8
1 2 3 4 5 6 7
1 2 3 4 5 6
1 2 3 4 5
1 2 3 4
1 2 3
1 2
1
```

b.
```
100 FOR J=1 TO 10
200 FOR I=1 TO J
300 PRINT I;
400 NEXT I
500 PRINT
600 NEXT J
700 END
RUN
1
1 2
1 2 3
1 2 3 4
1 2 3 4 5
1 2 3 4 5 6
1 2 3 4 5 6 7
1 2 3 4 5 6 7 8
1 2 3 4 5 6 7 8 9
1 2 3 4 5 6 7 8 9 10
```

# TWO-DIMENSIONAL ARRAYS AND THE MAT STATEMENTS

## 8-1    Problem Example

Widgets, Inc., manufacturer of widgets of all kinds, utilizes three identical shops in its production facilities. Each shop is composed of five machines required in the manufacture of widgets. The company has compiled the repair records on all machines and has tabulated the number of hours lost on each machine in each shop as follows:

MACHINE

| SHOP | 1 | 2 | 3 | 4 | 5 |
|---|---|---|---|---|---|
| 1 | 6 | 3 | 1 | 0 | 2 |
| 2 | 9 | 7 | 2 | 6 | 2 |
| 3 | 0 | 3 | 7 | 10 | 5 |

For example, in Shop 3 no hours have been lost on machine 1 while 3, 7, 10, and 5 hours have been lost respectively on machines 2, 3, 4, and 5.

It is desired to calculate the average hours lost on each type of machine. A program for this calculation is shown in Figure 8-1. Note how the data items are stored in the DATA statement (by rows) and how these items are processed by the two loops at statements 45 and 50 of Figure 8-1 to represent the preceding data table. In each reference to an element of the array A, the first subscript indicates the shop and the second subscript indicates the machine. In the program, a linear array S is created to store the sums, and later the averages of lost hours for the five machines.

```
10  REM AVERAGE HOURS LOST FOR WIDGET PRODUCTION FACILITY
20  DIM A(3, 5), S(5)
25  FOR I = 1 TO 5
30     PRINT TAB (13 * I - 7); "MACHINE"; I;        Print headers.
35  NEXT I
40  PRINT
45  FOR I = 1 TO 3
50     FOR J = 1 TO 5
55        READ A(I, J)                   Read (A(1,1), A(1,2), A(1,3), A(1,4), A(1,5),
                                            A(2,1), . . . A(2,5), A(3,1) . . . A(3,5).
60        PRINT TAB (13 * J - 4); A(I, J);      Print each value.
65     NEXT J
70     PRINT
75  NEXT I
80  PRINT
85  FOR J = 1 TO 5
90     LET S(J) = 0                      For each machine J, set S(J) = 0 and compute
95     FOR I = 1 TO 3                     the hours lost in each shop for machine J,
100       LET S(J) = S(J) + A(I, J)       i.e., S(J) = A(1,J) + A(2,J) + A(3,J).
105    NEXT I
110    LET S(J) = S(J)/3
115    PRINT TAB (12); "AVERAGE HOURS LOST ON MACHINE" ;J; "IS"; S(J)
120  NEXT J
125  STOP
130  DATA 6,3,1,0,2                       Data will be read by rows.
131  DATA 9,7,2,6,2
132  DATA 0,3,7,10,5


RUN
```

| MACHINE 1 | MACHINE 2 | MACHINE 3 | MACHINE 4 | MACHINE 5 |
|-----------|-----------|-----------|-----------|-----------|
| 6 | 3 | 1 | 0 | 2 |
| 9 | 7 | 2 | 6 | 2 |
| 0 | 3 | 7 | 10 | 5 |

```
AVERAGE HOURS LOST ON MACHINE 1 IS 5
AVERAGE HOURS LOST ON MACHINE 2 IS 4.33333
AVERAGE HOURS LOST ON MACHINE 3 IS 3.33333
AVERAGE HOURS LOST ON MACHINE 4 IS 5.33333
AVERAGE HOURS LOST ON MACHINE 5 IS 3
```

**Figure 8-1**  Calculations of column averages.

# 8-2    BASIC Statements

### 8-2-1    Two-Dimensional Arrays

Thus far, all the arrays we have considered have been one-dimensional or linear arrays; only one subscript is used in addressing elements of the array. When writing programs, it is often necessary to work with data arranged in table form (rows and columns of information). Two-dimensional arrays can be used in BASIC to represent such data structures. These arrays can be manipulated very conveniently for processing and for input/output purposes through the use of indices or subscripts.

For example, the table of numbers shown in Figure 8-2 could be stored in a two-dimensional array A containing three rows and five columns.[1] The conventional method of addressing elements of a two-dimensional array is to write the row number first, followed by the column number. Thus the element in the second row and third column of array A would be addressed A(2,3). In general, A(I,J) is the element found in the Ith row and Jth column. Note that the two subscripts are separated by a comma and enclosed in parentheses.

|  | Column 1 | Column 2 | Column 3 | Column 4 | Column 5 |
|---|---|---|---|---|---|
| Row 1 | 6. | 3. | ⁻1. | 0. | 2. |
|  | A(1, 1) | A(1, 2) | A(1, 3) | A(1, 4) | A(1, 5) |
| Row 2 | ⁻123. | 32.67 | ⁻.527 | .05 | 3345. |
|  | A(2, 1) | A(2, 2) | A(2, 3) | A(2, 4) | A(2, 5) |
| Row 3 | 3.1 | ⁻456. | 2.12 | 11111. | 0. |
|  | A(3, 1) | A(3, 2) | A(3, 3) | A(3, 4) | A(3, 5) |

Figure 8-2    A two-dimensional array.

---

[1] Most BASIC systems will allow a row 0 and a column 0.

## 8-2-2   The DIM Statement for Two-Dimensional Arrays

The general form of the DIM statement is

*Statement-number DIM variable (row-limit, column-limit) [, . . .]*

where *variable* is the name of the array

*row-limit* is a positive integer constant specifying the maximum number of rows

*column-limit* is a positive integer constant specifying the maximum number of columns

Any number of two- or one-dimensional arrays may be specified in a DIM statement. For example, the statement DIM B(6,8), C(10), I(10,25) reserves 48 memory locations for the array B, 10 memory locations for array C, and 250 locations for array I. Any reference to the variable name B or I must include two subscripts. For example, the statement LET B(I) = 0 is invalid, since only one subscript is included.

The row subscript value used in a reference to a two-dimensional array must be in the range 1 to the row limit specified in the DIM statement. A similar restriction applies to the column subscript. For example, given the size of the array A defined by DIM A(3,5), the references A(1,1), A(2,4), and A(3,5) are valid, whereas A(4,1) and A(3,6) are invalid, since one or more of the subscripts are outside the allowable subscript range.

Subscript expressions for two-dimensional arrays behave the same way as for one-dimensional arrays. The following references to a two-dimensional array are valid:

$$T(3 * K, I + 2) \; ; \; B(10/L - 7, J * 2)$$

## 8-2-3   Processing Two-Dimensional Arrays

Two-dimensional arrays can be processed in essentially the same way as one-dimensional arrays. For example, suppose that we wish to determine the number of elements with values less than 50 in an array of size 4 by 3. The search for values less than 50 can be accomplished by successively examining the first, second, third, and fourth rows of the array as shown in Figure 8-3.

```
10 DIM A(4,3)
30 LET K = 0            K is used to count array elements with value < 50.
35 FOR I = 1 TO 4       For a fixed value of I, J spans the column index of
40 FOR J = 1 TO 3       A, hence the search in the inner loop scans the
45 IF A(I,J) > = 50 THEN 55   rows of A starting with A_11,A_12,A_13, then A_21,
50 LET K = K + 1        A_22,A_23, etc.
55 NEXT J
60 NEXT I
```

**Figure 8-3**   Processing a two-dimensional array.

In general, if all elements of a two-dimensional array are to be processed, two loops with two indices controlling the row and column of the array are required. The ordering of these loops (which comes first) does not matter. In Figure 8-3, statements 35 and 40 could have been interchanged (with the NEXT statements, too). This would have meant that the array was searched by columns instead of by rows.

Another example will help clarify the index mechanism of a two-dimensional array. Suppose it is desired to

1.  Add all the entries of the Nth row of array A size 10 by 17, where N is accepted from input.

2.  Interchange column 3 with column 17.

The row sum to be calculated is SUM = A(N,1) + A(N,2) + A(N,3) + . . . + A(N,16) + A(N,17). The row index is fixed to N, while the column index varies from 1 to 17 (see Figure 8-4).

The interchange procedure can be accomplished by moving successively each element of column 3. into a temporary location T, then moving the corresponding element of column 17 into the vacated column 3 position and finally moving the saved value in T into the appropriate position in column 17 (see Figure 8-4). If no temporary location T were used, the elements of column 3 would be destroyed by the statement LET A(I,3) = A(I,17) as I ranges from 1 to 10.

```
10  DIM A (10, 17)
40  INPUT N
45  LET S = 0
50  FOR J = 1 TO 17
55      LET S = S + A(N, J)
60  NEXT J
65  FOR I = 1 TO 10
70      LET T = A(I, 3)
75      LET A(I, 3) = A(I, 17)
80      LET A(I, 17) = T
85  NEXT I
```

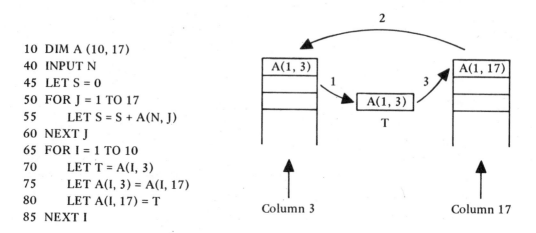

Figure 8-4    Column interchange.

## 8-2-4    Input/Output of Two-Dimensional Arrays

Another necessary manipulation of two-dimensional arrays involves input/output. Suppose the following table of numbers is to be loaded into array A while preserving the same geometrical arrangement (three rows and five columns) in A. The data can be typed on DATA statements in either row or column fashion.

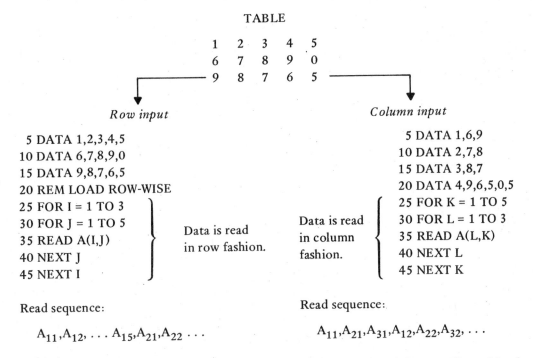

TABLE

```
1   2   3   4   5
6   7   8   9   0
9   8   7   6   5
```

*Row input*                                        *Column input*

| | |
|---|---|
| 5 DATA 1,2,3,4,5 | 5 DATA 1,6,9 |
| 10 DATA 6,7,8,9,0 | 10 DATA 2,7,8 |
| 15 DATA 9,8,7,6,5 | 15 DATA 3,8,7 |
| 20 REM LOAD ROW-WISE | 20 DATA 4,9,6,5,0,5 |
| 25 FOR I = 1 TO 3 | 25 FOR K = 1 TO 5 |
| 30 FOR J = 1 TO 5 | 30 FOR L = 1 TO 3 |
| 35 READ A(I,J) | 35 READ A(L,K) |
| 40 NEXT J | 40 NEXT L |
| 45 NEXT I | 45 NEXT K |

Data is read in row fashion.

Data is read in column fashion.

Read sequence:

$A_{11}, A_{12}, \ldots A_{15}, A_{21}, A_{22} \ldots$

Read sequence:

$A_{11}, A_{21}, A_{31}, A_{12}, A_{22}, A_{32}, \ldots$

To print the array A while preserving the geometrical configuration of the preceding table, the following code could be used:

```
10  REM ROW FASHION PRINT
15  FOR I = 1 TO 3
20      FOR J = 1 TO 5
25          PRINT A(I,J);          Print one row per line.
30      NEXT J
35      PRINT                      Advance to the next line before printing the next row.
40  NEXT I
```

# 8-3   You Might Want To Know

1.   Can I store character strings in two-dimensional arrays?

*Answer:*  Most systems will not allow it, i.e., A$(1,2) is invalid.

2.   What is the maximum row and column size for a two-dimensional array?

*Answer:*  Depends on your BASIC system. Check your reference manual.

3.   Can I reference row or column 0 of an array? That is, are A(0,4) and A(5,0) valid?

*Answer:*  Most systems will allow you to reference row 0 and column 0. For example, DIM A(4,8) reserves 5 rows and 9 columns for the array A.

4. Do I have to DIMension a two-dimensional array?

   *Answer:* Many systems do not require it if no more than 10 rows or 10 columns are needed.

# 8-4 Program Examples

### 8-4-1 A Frequency Distribution

Data regarding the smoking habits of students at a university have been gathered. The student's class (1 = freshman, 2 = sophomore, 3 = junior, 4 = senior, 5 = graduate) and a code representing the student's smoking habits (1 = don't smoke, 2 = one pack or less a day, 3 = more than one pack a day) have been recorded on records. Each record contains a student's class and smoking habit. It is desired to write a program to generate a frequency table displaying the frequency of the student's smoking habits by class; for example, how many seniors smoke one pack or less a day.

To better understand the problem, assume we have the data records shown below. We could manually record or check off each response in a table of five rows (for the five classes) and three columns (for the smoking habits) as shown in Figure 8-5. This suggests that we can use a two-dimensional array K(5,3) as a set of counters.

The first subscript indicates the class; the second represents the response code. For instance, the count in K(3,2) indicates the number of juniors (3) smoking one pack a day or less

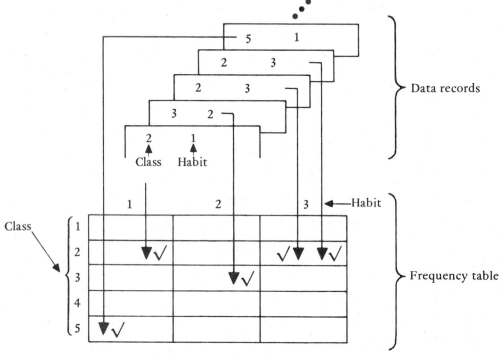

**Figure 8-5** Manual frequency count.

(2). Note that both class and smoking codes are used as subscripts of the array K to directly update the frequency count (see statement 80). The following output is produced by the program shown in Figure 8-6.

WHAT CLASS? 5 SMOKING HABITS? 1
WHAT CLASS? 5 SMOKING HABITS? 2
WHAT CLASS? 4 SMOKING HABITS? 3
WHAT CLASS? 4 SMOKING HABITS? 2
WHAT CLASS? 4 SMOKING HABITS? 2
WHAT CLASS? 3 SMOKING HABITS? 1
WHAT CLASS? 2 SMOKING HABITS? 1
WHAT CLASS? 0

| CLASS | DONT SMOKE | 1 PACK OR LESS | MORE THAN 1 |
|---|---|---|---|
| 1 | 0 | 0 | 0 |
| 2 | 1 | 0 | 0 |
| 3 | 1 | 0 | 0 |
| 4 | 0 | 2 | 1 |
| 5 | 1 | 1 | 0 |

```
0010 REM TWO DIMENSIONAL FREQUENCY DISTRIBUTION
0015 DIM K(5, 3)
0020 FOR I = 1 TO 5
0025 FOR J = 1 TO 3          Zero out array K.
0030 LET K(I, J) = 0
0035 NEXT J
0040 NEXT I
0050 REM ENTER STUDENT RESPONSES
0055 PRINT TAB (11); "WHAT CLASS";
0060 INPUT C
0065 IF C = 0 THEN 94                A code of 0 terminates input list.
0070 PRINT TAB (25); "SMOKING HABITS";
0075 INPUT S
0080 LET K(C, S) = K(C, S) + 1       Update the counters.
0087 PRINT                           For example, K(3,2) = K(3,2) + 1.
0090 GO TO 55
0094 PRINT
0095 PRINT
0096 PRINT TAB(0); "CLASS" ;TAB(11); "DONT SMOKE";
0098 PRINT TAB(23); "1 PACK OR LESS" ;TAB(39);
0099 PRINT "MORE THAN 1"
0100 FOR I = 1 TO 5
0105 PRINT I, K(I, 1), K(I, 2), K(I, 3)    Print frequency table.
0110 NEXT I
0999 END
```

Figure 8-6  Two-dimensional frequency distribution.

## 8-4-2    A Flagging Example

Tickets have been sold for a play in a small theater. There are 10 rows and six seats per row. Recorded on DATA statements, you have the row number and seat number for tickets already sold. You are now filling requests. Requests for row and seat numbers are made through the INPUT statement in that order. If the seat requested is empty, sell the seat. If the seat requested is already taken, sell the person the first empty seat in the requested row. If there are no available seats on that row, print out an appropriate message. Finally, print the complete theater seating arrangement. A typical communication with the terminal might be as follows:

```
?1,6
SEAT AT ROW 1 COLUMN 6 AVAILABLE
?1,4
SORRY NO SEATS AVAILABLE IN ROW 1
?2,1
REQUESTED SEAT NOT AVAILABLE, RESERVED SEAT AT ROW 2 COLUMN 2
?2,2
REQUESTED SEAT NOT AVAILABLE, RESERVED SEAT AT ROW 2 COLUMN 3
?10,4
REQUESTED SEAT NOT AVAILABLE, RESERVED SEAT AT ROW 10 COLUMN 1
?-1,0
```

The program then prints the following seating arrangement:

| | | | | | | |
|---|---|---|---|---|---|---|
| ROW 10 | 1 | 0 | 0 | ① | 0 | 0 |
| ROW 9 | 0 | 0 | 0 | 0 | 0 | 0 |
| ROW 8 | 0 | 0 | 0 | 0 | 0 | 0 |
| ROW 7 | 0 | 0 | 0 | 0 | 0 | 0 |
| ROW 6 | 0 | 0 | 0 | 0 | 0 | 0 |
| ROW 5 | 0 | 0 | 0 | 0 | 0 | 0 |
| ROW 4 | 0 | 0 | 0 | 0 | 0 | 0 |
| ROW 3 | 0 | 0 | 0 | 0 | 0 | 0 |
| ROW 2 | ① | 1 | 1 | 0 | 0 | 0 |
| ROW 1 | ① | ① | ① | ① | ① | 1 |

A ① indicates prepaid seats (statement 205 Figure 8-7). A 1 indicates seats reserved at run time.

Row 1 is closest to the stage.

The idea behind this program is to create 60 memory locations (a two-dimensional array SEAT(10,6)) representing the 60 seats and initially set all these locations to 0 to indicate an empty seat. Thus, when SEAT(4,5) = 0, this means that seat 5, at row 4 is empty. When a particular seat is sold, the appropriate memory location is set to 1; thus if row 6, seat 2 has been sold, SEAT (6,2) is set to 1. The program to solve this problem is shown in Figure 8-7.

```
  5 REM SEAT RESERVATION PROGRAM
 10 REM SET ALL 60 SEATS TO 0'S
 15 DIM S1 (10, 6)
 20 FOR R = 1 TO 10
 25    FOR S = 1 TO 6
 30       LET S1(R,S) = 0
 35    NEXT S
 40 NEXT R
 45 REM THE TICKETS SOLD ARE READ IN AND THE APPROPRIATE SEATS
 50 REM ARE RESERVED I.E., SET TO 1'S. NO SEATING CONFLICTS HERE
 55 READ R, S
 60 IF R = -1 THEN 80
 65 LET S1 (R, S) = 1
 70 GO TO 55
 75 REM INPUT REQUESTS AND DETERMINE IF SEAT IS EMPTY
 80 INPUT R, S
 85 IF R = -1 THEN 165
 90 IF S1 (R, S) = 1 THEN 120
 95 REM SEAT REQUESTED WAS EMPTY, SELL TICKET, AND PRINT MESSAGE
100 LET S1 (R, S) = 1
105 PRINT "SEAT AT ROW";R; "COLUMN" ;S;"AVAILABLE"
110 GO TO 80
115 REM REQUESTED SEAT FILLED, LOOK FOR EMPTY SEAT IN REQUESTED ROW
120 FOR J = 1 TO 6
125    IF S1 (R,J) = 1 THEN 150
130    LET S1 (R,J) = 1
135    PRINT "REQUESTED SEAT NOT AVAILABLE, RESERVED SEAT AT ROW";R;
140    PRINT "COLUMN"; J
145    GO TO 80
150 NEXT J
155 PRINT "SORRY NO SEATS AVAILABLE IN ROW"; R
160 GO TO 80
165 REM THE THEATRE SEATS ARE NOW PRINTED SHOWING EMPTY SEATS
170 FOR I = 1 TO 10
175    LET R = 11 - I
178    PRINT TAB (10) ;"ROW";R;TAB(20);
180    FOR S = 1 TO 6
185       PRINT S1 (R, S);
190    NEXT S
195    PRINT
200 NEXT I
205 DATA 1, 1, 1, 2, 1, 3, 1, 4, 1, 5, 2, 1, 2, 1, 10, 4, -1, -1
210 STOP
215 END
```

Figure 8-7    Seat reservation program.

### 8-4-3   A Bar Graph

The daily volume (vol.) in millions of shares of a major stock exchange for the three weeks starting July 8 is given as follows:

| JULY 8 | | JULY 15 | | JULY 22 | |
|---|---|---|---|---|---|
| VOL. TRANSACTION | WORKDAY | VOL. TRANSACTION | WORKDAY | VOL. TRANSACTION | WORKDAY |
| 5 | 1 | 5 | 1 | 3 | 1 |
| 7 | 2 | 3 | 2 | 2 | 2 |
| 8 | 3 | 5 | 3 | 1 | 3 |
| 9 | 4 | 4 | 4 | 2 | 4 |
| 7 | 5 | 2 | 5 | 4 | 5 |

Write a program to produce a bar graph as shown in Figure 8-8 for the first 15 days, starting July 8.

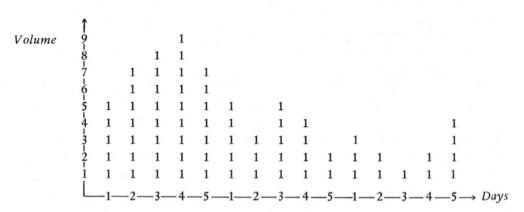

**Figure 8-8**   Transaction graph in millions of shares.

The basic technique is to use an array G of size 10 by 15 (9 for the highest daily volume and 15 for the number of days) initially set to 0's or blanks if the system permits it. In the first column of the array, we then insert five graphic symbols (1's, in this case, or an asterisk if the system permits) to represent the volume for the first day. In the second column, we insert seven graphic symbols to represent the volume of the second day, etc. In the last column (column 15), we insert four graphic symbols to represent the volume on day 15. We then obtain an array G, which looks like this:

Five 1's are inserted in the first column to represent volume for July 15.

Seven 1's are inserted in column 2 to represent volume for July 16.

Four 1's are inserted in the fifteenth column to represent the volume for the fifteenth day.

The grid must then be turned upside down so that the bar graph "peaks" up rather than down. This is achieved by printing the "bottom" of the array first, i.e., printing row 10 on the first line, row 9 on the second line, etc., as shown in statement 65 of Figure 8-9.

```
10  REM TWO DIMENSIONAL BAR GRAPH
15  DIM G(10, 15)                  Use G$ if system permits.
20  FOR I = 1 TO 10
25      FOR J = 1 TO 15            Initialize array with blanks if
30          LET G(I,J) = 0         system permits; otherwise
32      NEXT J                     with 0's.
34  NEXT I
35  FOR J = 1 TO 15
40      READ V                     Read a transaction volume.
45      FOR I = 1 TO V             Insert graphic symbols in each
50          LET G(I,J) = 1         column to represent daily volume.
55      NEXT I                     (Use * instead of 1 if system permits.)
57  NEXT J
60  LET R = 10
65  LET R = R - 1                  Print array starting with the
70  PRINT R; TAB (4);             bottom row of array G.
75  FOR J = 1 TO 15
80      PRINT G(R,J);
85  NEXT J
90  PRINT
100 IF R > 1 GO TO 65
101 PRINT
102 PRINT TAB (4);
105 FOR I = 1 TO 3
110     FOR J = 1 TO 5
115         PRINT J;               Identify each column by the
120     NEXT J                     corresponding business day.
125 NEXT I
130 DATA 5, 7, 8, 9, 7, 5, 3, 5, 4, 2, 3, 2, 1, 2, 4
135 STOP
140 END
```

Figure 8-9    Two-dimensional bar graph.

# 8-5    Matrices

## 8-5-1    Definition

A matrix is a rectangular arrangement of objects in row and column fashion. A chessboard is an example of a matrix; a plane from the core memory of a computer is a matrix. In this chapter, we will define a matrix as a rectangular array of numbers. Matrices play an important role in nearly all areas of science and as such are subject to various types of operations and manipulation.

## 8-5-2    A Matrix Case Study

Mr. Fish is a minicomputer salesman and the entire Fish family (10 children) have access to a minicomputer installed in the Fishes' living room. Mrs. Fish has just recently completed an introductory course in principles of management and as a result of her brief exposure to computers in that course, she has decided to "computer" watch her food expenditures. Mrs. Fish feeds her family store-bought sandwiches: hamburgers, hot dogs, and tacos. At the end of the week, Mrs. Fish has tabulated daily family consumption of delicacies as follows:

|             | MON | TUES | WED | THURS | FRI | SAT | SUN |
|-------------|-----|------|-----|-------|-----|-----|-----|
| Hamburgers  | 32  | 30   | 28  | 25    | 23  | 24  | 28  |
| Hot dogs    | 12  | 14   | 16  | 17    | 20  | 25  | 20  |
| Tacos       | 18  | 20   | 22  | 24    | 22  | 25  | 30  |

She has now kept track of her food expenses for two weeks in like fashion and would like a computer printout sheet of the two corresponding "consumption" tables. Initially, she writes a program with and without matrices, as shown in Figure 8-10.

ARRAY INPUT/OUTPUT WITHOUT MAT STATEMENT

```
100  REM WITHOUT MATRICES
150  DIM F1 (3, 7)
200  DIM F2 (3, 7)
250  FOR I = 1 TO 3
300  FOR J = 1 TO 7
350  READ F1 (I, J)
400  PRINT F1 (I, J);
450  NEXT J
500  PRINT
550  NEXT I
600  PRINT
650  FOR I = 1 TO 3
700  FOR J = 1 TO 7
750  READ F2 (I, J)
800  PRINT F2 (I, J);
850  NEXT J
900  PRINT
950  NEXT I
1000 REM FIRST WEEK DATA
1050 DATA 32, 30, 28, 25, 23, 24, 28
1100 DATA 12, 14, 16, 17, 20, 25, 20
1150 DATA 18, 20, 22, 24, 22, 25, 30
1200 REM SECOND WEEK DATA
1250 DATA 30, 28, 33, 27, 25, 26, 23
1300 DATA 15, 17, 14, 20, 21, 27, 25
1350 DATA 20, 21, 25, 19, 18, 27, 33
1400 STOP
1450 END
```

ARRAY INPUT/OUTPUT WITH MAT STATEMENTS

```
100  REM WITH MATRICES
150  DIM F1(3, 7)         Consumption table first week.
200  DIM F2(3, 7)         Consumption table second week.



350  MAT READ F1          Read first weekly table.
400  MAT PRINT F1         Print second weekly table.








750  MAT READ F2          Read second weekly table.
800  MAT PRINT F2         Print second weekly table.




1000 REM FIRST WEEK DATA
1050 DATA 32, 30, 28, 25, 23, 24, 28
1100 DATA 12, 14, 16, 17, 20, 25, 20
1150 DATA 18, 20, 22, 24, 22, 25, 30
1200 REM SECOND WEEK DATA
1250 DATA 30, 28, 33, 27, 25, 26, 23
1300 DATA 15, 17, 14, 20, 21, 27, 25
1350 DATA 20, 21, 25, 19, 18, 27, 33
1400 STOP
1450 END
```

**Figure 8-10**    Matrix input/output.

*Output: Weekly consumption tables*

| | | | | | | | |
|---|---|---|---|---|---|---|---|
| | 32 | 30 | 28 | 25 | 23 | 24 | 28 |
| Table F1 | 12 | 14 | 16 | 17 | 20 | 25 | 20 |
| | 18 | 20 | 22 | 24 | 22 | 25 | 30 |
| | | | | | | | |
| | 30 | 28 | 33 | 27 | 25 | 26 | 23 |
| Table F2 | 15 | 17 | 14 | 20 | 21 | 27 | 25 |
| | 20 | 21 | 25 | 19 | 18 | 27 | 33 |

**Figure 8-10**    Matrix input/output. (continued)

Mrs. Fish would now like to print an up-to-date table reflecting the accumulated daily consumption (sum of both tables) and an average consumption table for the last two weeks (each entry in the accumulated table is divided by 2). She adds to the existing program the code shown in Figure 8-11.

| ARRAY OPERATIONS WITHOUT MAT STATEMENTS | ARRAY OPERATIONS WITH MAT STATEMENTS | |
|---|---|---|
| 210  REM F IS THE SUM OF F1 + F2 | 210  REM F IS THE SUM OF F1 + F2 | |
| 220  DIM F(3,7) | 220  DIM F(3,7) | |
| 952  FOR I = 1 TO 3 | | |
| 954  FOR J = 1 TO 7 | | |
| 956  LET F(I,J) = F1(I,J) + F2(I,J) | 956  MAT F = F1 + F2 | Add both arrays. |
| 958  PRINT F(I,J); | 958  MAT PRINT F | Print result sum array. |
| | | |
| 960  NEXT J | | |
| 962  PRINT | | |
| 964  NEXT I | | |
| 966  FOR I = 1 TO 3 | | |
| 968  FOR J = 1 TO 7 | | |
| 970  LET F(I,J) = F(I,J)/2 | 970  MAT F = (.5) * F | Multiply each entry by .5. |
| | | |
| 972  REM F IS THE AVERAGE TABLE | | |
| 974  PRINT F(I,J); | 974  MAT PRINT F | Print resulting array. |
| | | |
| 976  NEXT J | | |
| 978  PRINT | | |
| 980  NEXT I | | |

*Output*

| Sum of two tables F = F1 + F2 | 62 58 61 52 48 50 51<br>27 31 30 37 41 52 45<br>38 41 47 43 40 52 63 |
|---|---|
| Average of two tables F = (F1 + F2)/2 | 31 29 30.5 26 24 25 25.5<br>13.5 15.5 15 18.5 20.5 26 22.5<br>19 20.5 23.5 21.5 20 26 31.5 |

**Figure 8-11**    Matrix addition and scalar multiplication.

Analyzing her new "average" table consumption, Mrs. Fish becomes concerned about excessive calorie intake. She decides to cut each entry in the "average table" by 10 percent. She adds to the existing program the code to print the resulting "calorie-adjusted" table shown in Figure 8-12.

ARRAY OPERATIONS
WITHOUT MAT STATEMENTS

ARRAY OPERATIONS
WITH MAT STATEMENTS

| ARRAY OPERATIONS WITHOUT MAT STATEMENTS | ARRAY OPERATIONS WITH MAT STATEMENTS |
|---|---|
| 225  REM L IS THE CALORIE ADJUSTED TABLE | 225  REM L IS THE CALORIE |
|  | 226  REM ADJUSTED TABLE |
| 230  DIM L(3,7) | 230  DIM L(3,7) |
| 982  FOR I = 1 TO 3 |  |
| 984  FOR J = 1 TO 7 |  |
| 986  LET L(I,I) = F(I,J) − .1 * F(I,J) | 986  MAT L = (.1) * F |
| 988  PRINT L(I,J); | 988  MAT L = F − L |
| 990  NEXT J | 990  MAT PRINT L |
| 992  PRINT |  |
| 994  NEXT I |  |

*Output*

| Adusted table L | 27.9 26.1 27.45 23.4 21.6 22.5 22.95 |
|---|---|
|  | 12.15 13.95 13.5 16.65 18.45 23.4 20.25 |
|  | 17.1 18.45 21.15 19.35 18 23.4 28.35 |

**Figure 8-12**    Matrix subtraction and scalar multiplication.

Mrs. Fish now becomes concerned about costs. She seems to recall that hamburgers cost 50 cents, hot dogs 35 cents and tacos 55 cents. She decides to compute the daily cost associated with last week's food purchases. To simplify her calculations, she rearranges the weekly consumption table in column form as follows:

| DAYS | HAM-BURGERS | HOT DOGS | TACOS | |
|---|---|---|---|---|
| 1 | 30 | 15 | 20 | daily cost = 30 X .5 + 15 X .35 + 20 X .55 = 31.25 |
| 2 | 28 | 17 | 21 | daily cost = 28 X .5 + 17 X .35 + 21 X .55 = 31.5 |
| 3 | 33 | 14 | 25 | . |
| 4 | 27 | 20 | 19 | .        Cost of        Cost of        Cost of |
| 5 | 25 | 21 | 18 | .        hamburgers    hot dogs       tacos |
| 6 | 26 | 27 | 27 | |
| 7 | 23 | 25 | 33 | |

She has computed the first two days' cost by hand and decides to add the code to her existing program to complete the problem. She first tries with multiplying arrays but soon can't extricate herself from the many loops. She then recalls how matrices can be used to do the job: multiply the preceding 7 row and 3 column consumption table by the cost matrix (.50, .35, .55). She writes the code shown in Figure 8-13.

| | | |
|---|---|---|
| 234 REM FINDING OUT DAILY COSTS | | |
| 235 DIM T(7,3) | Mrs. Fish's second weekly consumption table rearranged. | |
| 240 DIM C(3,1) | Cost array of sandwiches according to Mrs. Fish's recollections. | |
| 245 DIM Z(7,1) | Array to show daily costs of sandwich purchases. | |
| 1355 MAT T = TRN(F2) | Make rows of array F2 become columns of T. | |
| 1360 MAT PRINT T | Print rearranged array. | |
| 1365 MAT READ C | Read in the cost array. | |
| 1370 MAT Z = T * C | Find out the daily costs for the seven days. | |
| 1375 MAT PRINT Z | Print the costs. | |
| 1380 DATA .50, .35, .55 | Cost of sandwiches as Mrs. Fish seems to recall. | |

*Output*

```
30      15      20
28      17      21
33      14      25
27      20      19
25      21      18
26      27      27
23      25      33
```

This array T is the second week's daily consumption table F2, rearranged (transposed). The columns of T are just the rows of F2.

```
31.25
31.5
35.15
30.95
29.75
37.3
38.4
```

Sandwich costs for first day of second week.
Sandwich costs for second day of second week.

.

.

Array Z

**Figure 8-13** Matrix transpose and matrix multiplication.

The daily costs for the second week as shown in Figure 8-13 seem a little high to Mrs. Fish. As a meticulous housewife and manager, she has kept her daily food bills for the last week. The daily store receipts don't quite match the computerized list of daily costs shown in Figure 8-13. Her store receipts show the amounts given in Figure 8-14 (taxes excluded).

| DAY | STORE RECEIPTS |
|---|---|
| 1 | 31.00 |
| 2 | 31.00 |
| 3 | 34.85 |
| 4 | 30.35 |
| 5 | 29.05 |
| 6 | 35.90 |
| 7 | 36.65 |

**Figure 8-14** Store receipts for second week.

Mrs. Fish attributes the difference in costs to the fact that she wasn't one hundred percent sure about the cost of each sandwich when she wrote the program shown in Figure 8-13. She could call up the store and inquire about the cost of each sandwich, but she decides to do some double checking by calculating herself the cost per sandwich. She knows the number of sandwiches bought each day, and she knows what the store charged for the sandwiches each day. So she writes the following sets of equations:

$$30 \text{ hamburgers} + 15 \text{ hot dogs} + 20 \text{ tacos} = 31.00$$
$$28 \text{ hamburgers} + 17 \text{ hot dogs} + 21 \text{ tacos} = 31.00$$
$$33 \text{ hamburgers} + 14 \text{ hot dogs} + 25 \text{ tacos} = 34.85$$

.

.

.

$$23 \text{ hamburgers} + 25 \text{ hot dogs} + 33 \text{ tacos} = 36.65$$

Mrs. Fish tries to write a program without matrices to solve this problem, but simply can't do it. From her course in management, she recalls how to solve a system of equations using matrices. Mrs. Fish figures she needs only any three of these equations to determine the cost per sandwich. She arbitrarily selects the first three equations and rewrites them in a less cumbersome way:

$$30X + 15Y + 20Z = 31.00$$
$$28X + 17Y + 21Z = 31.00$$
$$33X + 14Y + 25Z = 34.85$$

X, Y, and Z represent the unit cost of hamburgers, hot dogs, and tacos to be computed.

She gives a name to the matrix of coefficients of the variables (unknowns).

$$T = \begin{pmatrix} 30 & 15 & 20 \\ 28 & 17 & 21 \\ 33 & 14 & 25 \end{pmatrix} \qquad R = \begin{pmatrix} X \\ Y \\ Z \end{pmatrix} \qquad Z = \begin{pmatrix} 31 \\ 31 \\ 35 \end{pmatrix}$$

Matrix of coefficients        Result array        Purchases for first three days

She is now ready to solve the system of equations shown in Figure 8-15.

```
246  REM DETERMINING COST PER ITEM
247  DIM I1 (3,3)          Array I1 is used to compute the inverse of the coefficient matrix.
249  DIM R (3,1)           Result array will show costs of the three sandwiches.
1385 MAT READ T(3,3)       Read the first three rows of the matrix of coefficients.
1387 MAT READ Z(3,1)       Read the first three daily costs.
1389 MAT I1 = INV(T)       Compute the inverse of part of the matrix of coefficients.
1391 MAT R = I1 * Z        Compute cost of each of the three items.
1393 MAT PRINT R           Print out results.
1395 DATA 30, 15, 20 ⎤
1396 DATA 28, 17, 21 ⎬    Matrix of coefficients.
1397 DATA 33, 14, 25 ⎦
1398 DATA 31, 31, 34.85
```

$$\text{Matrix R} = \begin{matrix} .54999999993 & \text{Cost of hamburgers} \\ .3000000003 & \text{Cost of hot dogs} \\ 0.5 & \text{Cost of tacos} \end{matrix}$$

**Figure 8-15**   Determining cost of each sandwich.

Mrs. Fish calls the store and finds out that hamburgers cost 55 cents, hot dogs 30 cents, and tacos 50 cents. She is satisfied that these figures match her figures as shown in Figure 8-15.

### 8-5-3 Matrix Statements

Figure 8-16 displays the thirteen matrix statements that are available on any BASIC system with the matrix features.

| OPERATION | BASIC STATEMENTS | COMMENTS |
|---|---|---|
| Dimension | DIM A(3,3),B(3,3),C(3,3) | Establish matrix sizes |

**Input/Output** — MAT READ A,B / MAT INPUT A,B / MAT PRINT A,B

$$A = \begin{pmatrix} 1 & 2 & -3 \\ -4 & 5 & 6 \\ 7 & 8 & 9 \end{pmatrix} \qquad B = \begin{pmatrix} 14 & -1 & 3 \\ 4 & -1 & 2 \\ 1 & 2 & -3 \end{pmatrix}$$

**Replacement** — MAT C = A

$$C = \begin{pmatrix} 1 & 2 & -3 \\ -4 & 5 & 6 \\ 7 & 8 & 9 \end{pmatrix}$$

**Addition** — MAT C = A + B

$$C = \begin{pmatrix} 1 & 2 & -3 \\ -4 & 5 & 6 \\ 7 & 8 & 9 \end{pmatrix} + \begin{pmatrix} 14 & -1 & 3 \\ 4 & -1 & 2 \\ 1 & 2 & -3 \end{pmatrix} = \begin{pmatrix} 15 & 1 & 0 \\ 0 & 4 & 8 \\ 8 & 10 & 6 \end{pmatrix}$$

**Subtraction** — MAT C = A - B

$$C = \begin{pmatrix} 1 & 2 & -3 \\ -4 & 5 & 6 \\ 7 & 8 & 9 \end{pmatrix} - \begin{pmatrix} 14 & -1 & 3 \\ 4 & -1 & 2 \\ 1 & 2 & -3 \end{pmatrix} = \begin{pmatrix} -13 & 3 & -6 \\ -8 & 6 & 4 \\ 6 & 6 & 12 \end{pmatrix}$$

**Scalar multiplication** — MAT C = (3)*A

$$C = 3 \begin{pmatrix} 1 & 2 & -3 \\ -4 & 5 & 6 \\ 7 & 8 & 9 \end{pmatrix} = \begin{pmatrix} 3 & 6 & -9 \\ -12 & 15 & 18 \\ 21 & 24 & 27 \end{pmatrix}$$

**Multiplication** — MAT C = A * B

$$C = \begin{pmatrix} 1 & 2 & -3 \\ -4 & 5 & 6 \\ 7 & 8 & 9 \end{pmatrix} * \begin{pmatrix} 14 & -1 & 3 \\ 4 & -1 & 2 \\ 1 & 2 & -3 \end{pmatrix} = \begin{pmatrix} 19 & -9 & 16 \\ -30 & 11 & 20 \\ 139 & 3 & 10 \end{pmatrix}$$

**Replace by constant 0** — MAT C = ZER

$$C = \begin{pmatrix} 0 & 0 & 0 \\ 0 & 0 & 0 \\ 0 & 0 & 0 \end{pmatrix}$$

All entries of the matrix are set to zero.

**Replace by constant 1** — MAT C = CON

$$C = \begin{pmatrix} 1 & 1 & 1 \\ 1 & 1 & 1 \\ 1 & 1 & 1 \end{pmatrix}$$

All entries are set to one (1).

**Identity** — MAT C = IDN

$$C = \begin{pmatrix} 1 & 0 & 0 \\ 0 & 1 & 0 \\ 0 & 0 & 1 \end{pmatrix}$$

C is set to the identity matrix. 1's down the main diagonal and 0's elsewhere.

**Transpose** — MAT C = TRN(A)

$$C = \begin{pmatrix} 1 & -4 & 7 \\ 2 & 5 & 8 \\ -3 & 6 & 9 \end{pmatrix}$$

C is the transpose of matrix A: the rows of C are equal to the columns of A.

**Inverse** — MAT C = INV(B)

$$C = \begin{pmatrix} 1 & -3 & -1 \\ -14 & 45 & 16 \\ -9 & 29 & 10 \end{pmatrix}$$

C is the inverse of B; that is, C * B = B * C = I, where I is the identity matrix.

**Figure 8-16** BASIC operations on matrices.

## 8-5-4 Matrix Input/Output

The general form for matrix input/output statements is

$$statement\text{-}number\ \mathrm{MAT} \begin{Bmatrix} \mathrm{READ} \\ \mathrm{PRINT} \\ \mathrm{INPUT} \end{Bmatrix} list\text{-}of\text{-}matrices$$

where MAT is a required key word and the operation to be performed is specified by choosing one of the key words READ, PRINT, or INPUT. A *list-of-matrices* is a list of variable names separated by commas. Each variable *must* be dimensioned. No literals, undimensioned variable names, or constants may appear in a *list-of-matrices*.

**Examples**

| | |
|---|---|
| 5 MAT READ X,Y,Z1 | Valid if X,Y,Z1 appear in DIM statement. |
| 10 MAT PRINT X1,Y1 | Valid if X1,Y1 appear in DIM statement. |
| 15 MAT PRINT "MATRIX A";A | Invalid literal string in output list. |

The matrix input/output statements allow the programmer to load or print one- or two-dimensional arrays without indexing the array.

Matrices are read into memory or printed out in row order. The number of elements (entries) to be read/printed per row and the number of rows to be read/printed are taken from the size declaration of the matrix in the DIM statement. Figure 8-17 displays the code to read and print two matrices of unequal sizes. X has two rows and two columns, and Y has two rows and three columns.

```
05 DIM X(2,2),Y(2,3)
10 MAT READ X,Y
15 MAT PRINT X,Y
20 DATA 11,22,33,44
25 DATA 15,17,13
30 DATA 12,20,40
35 END

RUN
```

Note: All X and Y matrix elements could have been typed on just one DATA statement.

| | | | |
|---|---|---|---|
| 11 | 22 | | } Matrix X |
| 33 | 44 | | |

| | | | |
|---|---|---|---|
| 15 | 17 | 13 | } Matrix Y |
| 12 | 20 | 40 | |

**Figure 8-17** Example of matrix input/output.

In the case of the MAT PRINT statement, each new matrix will be printed on a new line starting in the leftmost zone. Each entry will occupy one zone. If there are more row entries than there are zones on the line, two or more lines of output may be required to account for one matrix row. See Figure 8-18. Automatic single spacing is provided for each matrix row, and double spacing is used to separate matrices.

A blank PRINT statement following a MAT PRINT statement is generally recommended, as subsequent lines of nonmatrix output will be continued on the last row of the matrix output.

05 DIM X(1,7)  The seven entries will not fit on one line
10 MAT READ X  of output.
15 MAT PRINT X
20 DATA 1,2,3,4,5,6,7

RUN

| 1 | 2 | 3 | 4 | 5 |
| 6 | 7 | | | |

Figure 8-18  Example of MAT PRINT statement.

To provide for more compact matrix output, a semicolon (;) should follow the matrix for which compact output is desired. See Figure 8-19.

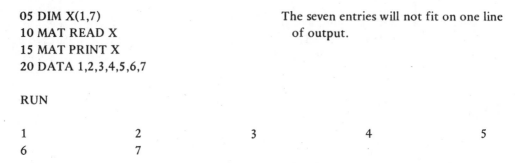

05 DIM X(2,2),Y(2,3)
10 MAT READ X,Y
15 MAT PRINT X;Y;   Note the semicolons.
20 DATA 11,22,33,44
25 DATA 15,17,13
30 DATA 12,20,40
35 END

RUN

11 22
33 44        } Matrix X written in compact form.

15 17 13
12 20 40     } Matrix Y written in compact form.

Figure 8-19  Compact matrix output.

In the case of the MAT INPUT statement, the system will generally respond with a ?. The user should then enter an entire matrix row at one time before pressing the RETURN key. Entries should be separated by commas. On some systems, if fewer or more entries than there are in a matrix row are entered (as specified in the DIM statement), the system will respond with an error message. The user then needs to retype the exact number of entries for that row.

See Figure 8-20. On some other systems, it is possible to enter the entire matrix data on just one line.

```
05 DIM X(2,2),Y(2,3)
10 MAT INPUT X,Y
15 MAT PRINT X;Y
35 END

RUN

? 11,22
? 33,44
? 2E14,1.98,−7.6E − 3
? 1E − 3,25,32.4
11      22
33      44

2E + 14 1.98 −7.6E−03
1E − 03 25 32.4
```

} Matrix X entered.

} Matrix Y entered.

**Figure 8-20**   MAT INPUT example.

## 8-5-5   Matrix Operations

The following are the elementary matrix operations that can be handled by BASIC:

| | | |
|---|---|---|
| Replacement | MAT C = X | Set matrix C equal to matrix X. |
| Addition/subtraction | MAT C = X±Y | Set C to sum or difference of X and Y. |
| Scalar multiplication | MAT C = (expression)∗X | Note the use of the parentheses around the expression. |
| Multiplication | MAT C = X ∗ Y | C is set to the product of X and Y. |

All of these matrix operations require that the matrix operands be "conformable," that is, matrices must be equal in size for addition and subtraction. In the case of multiplication X ∗ Y, the number of columns of X must equal the number of rows of Y (see Section 8-6, item 5).

Only *one* matrix operation is allowed on the right-hand side of the equal sign.

**Examples**

| | |
|---|---|
| 5 MAT C = (2)X + Y | Two matrix operations—invalid. |
| 6 MAT C = X − Y + Z | Two matrix operations—invalid. |
| 7 MAT C = − X | Invalid use of scalar multiplication. |

In the case of matrix multiplication, the same matrix is not allowed on both sides of the matrix statement.

**Examples**

| | |
|---|---|
| 5 MAT X=X*X | X is on both sides—invalid for multiplication. |
| 6 MAT C=C+X | C is on both sides—valid for addition/subtraction. |

### 8-5-6  Matrix Functions

In addition to the aforementioned matrix operations, BASIC conveniently allows the user to initialize matrices to elementary matrix configurations and to determine the transpose and the inverse of a given matrix. The following functions are provided:

MAT C = ZER — All entries of C are set to 0's. The size of C is defined in the DIM statement. C need not be square.

MAT C = CON — All entries of C are set to 1's. The size of C is defined in the DIM statement.

MAT C = IDN — C is set to the identity matrix: 1's down the main diagonal and 0's elsewhere. If C is not square, the main diagonal of 1's will start at the right-hand bottom corner of the matrix.

*Example:*

$$\begin{pmatrix} 0 & 1 & 0 & 0 \\ 0 & 0 & 1 & 0 \\ 0 & 0 & 0 & 1 \end{pmatrix}$$

MAT C = TRN(X) — The matrix C becomes the matrix X where all symmetric entries across the main diagonal have been interchanged (each row has been replaced by its corresponding column).

*Example:*

If $X = \begin{pmatrix} 1 & 2 \\ 4 & 5 \\ 7 & 8 \end{pmatrix}$

then $TRN(X) = \begin{pmatrix} 1 & 4 & 7 \\ 2 & 5 & 8 \end{pmatrix}$

MAT C = INV(X) — C becomes the inverse matrix of X. The inverse of X is that matrix C is such that C * X = X * C = I, where I is the identity matrix.

*Example:*

If $X = \begin{pmatrix} 1 & 2 & -3 \\ 4 & -1 & 2 \\ 14 & -1 & 3 \end{pmatrix}$

then $INV(X) = \begin{pmatrix} -1 & -3 & 1 \\ 16 & 45 & -14 \\ 10 & 29 & -9 \end{pmatrix}$

In the case of the INV function, the matrix must be square. The inverse of a matrix is only defined for square matrices; yet not all square matrices have inverses. The INV routine will print an appropriate message if no matrix inverse exists.

# 8-6  You Might Want To Know

1.  Once I have processed an array with a MAT statement, can I still process that array without using MAT statements?

    *Answer:* Yes. Suppose M is a 3 by 4 matrix containing scores and we wish to determine the highest score in row 3 and print all scores in the second column. The code in Figure 8-21 could be used:

```
 5 DIM M(3,4)
10 DATA 1,2,3,4,5,9,7,6,5,4,1,3
15 MAT READ M                      Read matrix.
20 LET L = M(3,1)                  Initialize L to first score in row 3.
25 FOR J = 2 TO 4
30    IF L > = M(3,J) THEN 40
35    LET L = M(3,J)               L is largest score in row 3.
40 NEXT J
45 FOR I = 1 TO 3
50    PRINT M(I,2);                Print elements of second column.
60 NEXT I
```

**Figure 8-21**   Use of FOR/NEXT with MAT statements.

2.  In the *list-of-matrices* in a MAT PRINT statement, can I make use of both the comma and the semicolon, as follows?

```
 5 DIM A(2,3), B(2,2), C(2,2)
10 MAT READ A,B,C
15 MAT PRINT A;B,C                 Note semicolon and comma.
20 DATA 1,2,3,4,5,6
25 DATA 11,22,33,44
30 DATA 99,88,77,66
```

*Answer:* Yes. This code would yield

```
1 2 3                              Matrix A in compact form.
4 5 6
```

$$\left.\begin{array}{ll} 11 & 22 \\ 33 & 44 \\ \\ 99 & 88 \\ 77 & 66 \end{array}\right\}$$ Matrices B and C in zone form.

3. Can I use MAT statements on arrays that have only one index in the DIM statement?

   *Answer:* On most systems, you can. The following, for example, is valid:

   | | |
   |---|---|
   | 5 DIM A(5) | Only one index in the DIM statement. |
   | 10 MAT A = ZER | Zero out matrix and print it. |
   | 15 MAT PRINT A | |

4. Once a matrix has been dimensioned to a certain size, is it possible to change its size at run time?

   *Answer:* Matrices must be dimensioned before MAT statements can be used. Since the MAT statements make use of the stated sizes of the matrices in the DIM statement, one might think that once a matrix has been dimensioned one can no longer use that same matrix to store matrices of different sizes. Sometimes it may be more efficient or convenient to reuse the same matrix X to read or process matrices of varying sizes. This can be accomplished by redimensioning the matrix at execution time. Redimensioning is valid as long as the dimensions of the new matrices *do not* exceed the dimension of the original matrix stated in the DIM statement. Figure 8-22 shows how the two matrices X and Y can be redimensioned by stating the new dimensions in the MAT READ statement.

   | | |
   |---|---|
   | 05 DIM X(2,2), Y(2,3) | |
   | 10 MAT READ X(1,2),Y(2,2) | Both matrices X and Y have been redimensioned. |
   | 15 MAT PRINT X,Y | Note the absence of dimensions in the PRINT statement. |
   | 20 DATA 11,22,33,44,55,65,75,84,90,95 | |
   | 35 END | |
   | | |
   | RUN | |

   $$\left. \begin{array}{ll} 11 & 22 \end{array} \right\}$$  Matrix X

   $$\left. \begin{array}{ll} 33 & 44 \\ 55 & 65 \end{array} \right\}$$  Matrix Y

   **Figure 8-22**    Input of redimensioned matrix.

   Figure 8-23 shows how matrices can be redimensioned using variable subscripts. The same matrices X and Y will be used to compute C = X + Y with X and Y varying from 3 X 3 to 1 X 1. Note the use of the RESTORE statement, which forces any READ statement to start at the beginning of the DATA statement. Once a matrix A has been redimensioned, any reference to that matrix A, such as in MAT READ A, implies the most recently redimensioned size.

```
05 DIM X(3,3),Y(3,3),C(3,3)
10 MAT C = ZER                          Zero out matrix C.
15 FOR I = 3 TO 1 STEP -1
20      MAT READ X(I,I),Y(I,I)
25      RESTORE                         The next READ will start at the beginning of
                                           the DATA list.
30      MAT C = X + Y                   Note how C is automatically redimensioned
                                           to the successive sizes of matrices X and Y
                                           by the statement MAT C = X + Y. In some
35      MAT PRINT X;Y;C                 systems, it may be necessary to redimension
40 NEXT I                              C before calculating the sum. A statement
50 DATA 1,2,3,4,5,6,7,8,9              such as 29 MAT C = ZER(I,I) could be used.
60 DATA 11,22,33,44,55,66
70 DATA 77,88,99
RUN
```

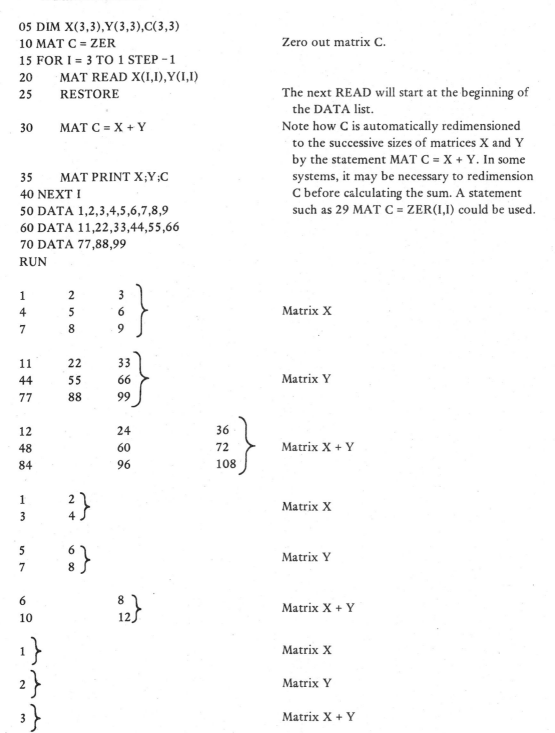

Figure 8-23    Redimensioning matrices using variable subscripts.

5. How is matrix multiplication performed?

*Answer:* To multiply two matrices $A \times B$ together, $A$ and $B$ must be conformable; that is, the number of columns of $A$ must equal the number of rows of $B$. For example,

$$\begin{pmatrix} a_{11} & a_{12} & a_{13} \\ a_{21} & a_{22} & a_{23} \end{pmatrix} \cdot \begin{pmatrix} b_{11} & b_{12} \\ b_{21} & b_{22} \\ b_{31} & b_{32} \end{pmatrix} = \begin{pmatrix} a_{11}b_{11} + a_{12}b_{21} + a_{13}b_{31} & a_{11}b_{12} + a_{12}b_{22} + a_{13}b_{32} \\ a_{21}b_{11} + a_{22}b_{21} + a_{23}b_{31} & a_{21}b_{12} + a_{22}b_{22} + a_{23}b_{32} \end{pmatrix}$$

If $A$ is $m \times n$ ($m$ rows, $n$ columns) and $B$ is $n \times q$ then the product matrix $C = A \times B$ is of size $m \times q$.

6. Which matrix statements can be used to redimension matrices?

*Answer:* Only the following matrix statements can redimension matrices:

$$\text{MAT} \begin{Bmatrix} \text{READ} \\ \text{INPUT} \end{Bmatrix} dimensioned\text{-}variable \ (expression_1, \ expression_2) \ [, \ldots]$$

$$\text{MAT } dimensioned\text{-}variable = \begin{Bmatrix} \text{ZER} \\ \text{IDN} \\ \text{CON} \end{Bmatrix} (expression_1, \ expression_2)$$

where $expression_1$ and $expression_2$ become, respectively, the number of rows and the number of columns of the redimensioned matrix.

*Examples:*

MAT C = CON(A+B, 4 *3)          Initializes matrix C with A + B rows and 12 columns to 1's.

MAT C = ZER(3,5)                Zero out a 3 × 5 matrix.

MAT PRINT X(3,3)                Invalid—PRINT cannot redimension matrices.

MAT READ X(3,3),Y(2,2)          More than one matrix can be redimensioned in a MAT READ statement.

# 8-7    Solving a System of Equations

Solve the following systems of equations using matrix operations:

$$\begin{aligned}
x + \ \ y + \ \ 2z + \ \ 3w &= 2 \\
12x + 23y + 45z + \ \ 5w &= 3 \\
-9x + 67y + 56z + 23w &= 4 \\
2x + \ \ 3y + \ \ 5z - 34w &= 5
\end{aligned}$$

The system of equations can be written in matrix form as

$$
\begin{pmatrix}
1 & 1 & 2 & 3 \\
12 & 23 & 45 & 5 \\
-9 & 67 & 56 & 23 \\
2 & 3 & 5 & -34
\end{pmatrix}
\cdot
\begin{pmatrix}
x \\ y \\ z \\ w
\end{pmatrix}
=
\begin{pmatrix}
2 \\ 3 \\ 4 \\ 5
\end{pmatrix}
$$

Let A be the 4 × 4 matrix consisting of the coefficients of the variables (unknowns). Let X be the 4 × 1 matrix of variables $x, y, z, w$. Let B be the 4 × 1 matrix of constants. Then the preceding matrix equation becomes A · X = B. By multiplying both sides of the equation by the inverse $A^{-1}$, if it exists, we obtain

$$
A^{-1} \cdot A \cdot X = A^{-1} \cdot B \quad \text{or} \quad I \cdot X = A^{-1} \cdot B \quad \text{or} \quad X = A^{-1} \cdot B
$$

B is known; $A^{-1}$ may be calculated since A is given; hence the column matrix X can be easily computed. Figure 8-24 displays the program to solve any square system of equations up to size 10. Note the redimensioning of the matrix A at statement-number 35 to allow the user to enter his specific system of equations.

```
05 DIM A(10,10),B(10,1)
10 DIM C(10,10),X(10,1)
15 PRINT "WHAT IS THE SIZE OF THE SYSTEM OF EQUATIONS . ."
20 PRINT "SIZE SHOULD BE LESS THAN 11"
25 INPUT N
26 REM THE PROGRAM MAY SOLVE SYSTEMS OF VARIOUS SIZES (UP TO 10)
27 PRINT
30 PRINT "ENTER MATRIX OF COEFFICIENTS ROW-WISE"
35 MAT INPUT A(N,N)
36 REM THE MATRICES ARE NOW REDIMENSIONED TO USER SPECIFICATION
37 PRINT
40 PRINT "ENTER MATRIX OF CONSTANTS"
45 MAT INPUT B(N,1)
46 MAT C = ZER(N,N)          May be required to redimension matrix C.
50 MAT C = INV(A)
51 MAT X = ZER (N,1)         May be required to redimension matrix X.
55 MAT X = C * B
57 PRINT
60 PRINT "THE MATRIX OF COEFFICIENTS IS"
65 MAT PRINT A;
```

**Figure 8-24**    Solution to system of linear equations using matrix inverse.

```
70 PRINT "THE MATRIX OF CONSTANTS IS"
75 MAT PRINT B
80 PRINT "THE SOLUTIONS TO THE EQUATIONS ARE IN COLUMN FORM"
85 MAT PRINT X
99 END
RUN
```

WHAT IS THE SIZE OF THE SYSTEM OF EQUATIONS . .
SIZE SHOULD BE LESS THAN 11
? 4
ENTER MATRIX OF COEFFICIENTS ROW-WISE

? 1,1,2,3
? 12,23,45,5
? -9,67,56,23
? 2,3,5,-34
ENTER MATRIX OF CONSTANTS
? 2
? 3
? 4
? 5

THE MATRIX OF COEFFICIENTS IS

| 1 | 1 | 2 | 3 |
|-----|-----|-----|------|
| 12 | 23 | 45 | 5 |
| -9 | 67 | 56 | 23 |
| 2 | 3 | 5 | -34 |

THE MATRIX OF CONSTANTS IS

2
3
4
5

THE SOLUTIONS TO THE EQUATIONS ARE IN COLUMN FORM

| 4.23996 | result for x |
|-----------------|--------------|
| 2.65938 | result for y |
| -2.42111 | result for z |
| -1.90416E - 02 | result for w |

**Figure 8-24**   Solution to system of linear equations using matrix inverse. (continued)

# 8-8   Assignments

## 8-8-1   Self Test

1.   Assume arrays A, B, and C contain the following data:

A

| 1 | 2 | 3 | 4 |
|---|---|---|---|
| 5 | 6 | 7 | 8 |
| 9 | 10 | 11 | 12 |

B

| 10 | 20 | 30 | 40 |
|----|----|----|----|
| 50 | 60 | 70 | 80 |
| 90 | 100 | 110 | 120 |

C

| 500 |
|-----|

Write the code to print the following arrangements (no computations are to be performed):

a.   1    2    3    4    ...   11  12    10    20    30    40    ... 110 120    500

b.   1    2    3    4          10    20    30    40                500
     5    6    7    8          50    60    70    80                500
     9    10   11   12         90   100   110   120               500

c.   1    5    9         500        10    50    90
     2    6    10        500        20    60    100
     3    7    11        500        30    70    110

d.   1    10   2    20   3    30   4    40
     5    50   6    60   7    70   8    80
     9    90   10   100  11   110  12   120

e.   1    10   5    50   9    90   2    20   6    60   10   100
     3    30   7    70   11   110  4    40   8    80   12   120

2.   Data is recorded on records (DATA statement) as follows. Generate the input statements to process these records in the order shown:

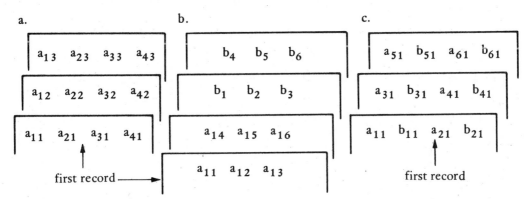

d.                                    e.                                    f.

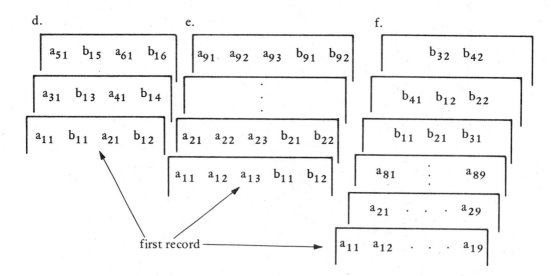

first record ────────────────────▶

3.  If A is an array of size 16 × 6, initialize the first column of A with 1's, the second column with 2's, the third column with 3's, etc., up to column 6 with 6's.

4.  An array A of size 5 × 5 is to be read from five DATA statements (five entries per DATA statement for each row).

    a.  Read in the array and write it out in row form (one row per line). Print each column on one line.

    b.  Calculate the sum of the elements in the third row.

    c.  Find the largest value in the first column.

    d.  Create a linear array B consisting of five elements initialized to zero. Calculate the sum of each column A storing the result in the corresponding column position of B.

    e.  Add corresponding elements of rows 2 and 3 of the array A, storing results in row 3; that is, $A(3,1) = A(3,1) + A(2,1)$, etc.

    f.  Interchange column 3 and column 4.

    g.  Compute the sum of the entries of the first diagonal.

    h.  Compute the sum of the entries of the second diagonal and determine the largest entry of that diagonal.

    i.  Input values for I and J such that $1 \leqslant I, J \leqslant 5$ and interchange row I with column J.

    j.  Print the smallest element of the array A and its position in the array (column, row).

5.  Read in two arrays C and D of size 3 × 3 given the following input description:

    DATA        1,2,3,        1,2,3,        4,5,6,        4,5,6,  . . .
                └──┬──┘      └──┬──┘      └──┬──┘      └──┬──┘
              Row 1 of C    Row 1 of D    Row 2 of C    Row 2 of D

## 8-8-2    Exercises

1.  Using the random number generator routine, write the code to store random numbers in an array F of size 40 × 17 (use the statement LET J = INT(RND(1) * 100 + 1) to generate random numbers J between 1 and 100). Then store the rows of the array F sequentially into a one-dimensional array G of size 680 (40 × 17) as follows:

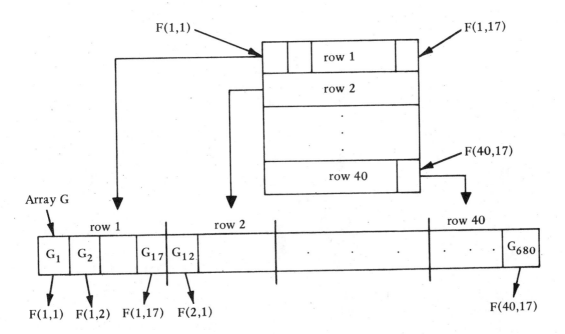

2.  An array A has size 4 × 9. Write the code to interchange the first column with the ninth column, the second column with the eighth column, etc.

3.  Write a program using two-dimensional arrays to draw the checkerboard illustrated in exercise 10, Section 5-6-2.

4.  Write a program using two-dimensional arrays to generate the illustrations of exercise 9, Section 7-6-1.

5.  The personnel department of a small insurance company (seven employees) maintains a payroll file for its insurance representatives who work in different states. Each employee's record contains among other information the following data:

| EMPLOYEE NUMBER | HOURS WORKED | RATE OF PAY | STATE TAX |
|---|---|---|---|
| 111222333 | 45 | 10.00 | .05 |

Generate seven DATA statements using the same format (one for each representative) and initialize an array A(7,4) with your data base. Write a program to

a.  Compute and print each employee's pay before and after tax.

b.  Compute the total payroll for the firm (not including state tax withholdings).

c. Give a $1,000 bonus to the employee with lowest hourly rate who has worked the most hours.

The output should be similar to

| EMPLOYEE NUMBER | HOURS WORKED | RATE OF PAY | GROSS PAY | STATE TAX | NET PAY |
|---|---|---|---|---|---|
| 111222333 | 45 | 10.00 | 475.00 | .05 | 451.25 |
| . | . | . | . | . | . |
| . | . | . | . | . | . |
| . | . | . | . | . | . |

COMPANY PAYROLL = XXXX.XX
BONUS OF $1,000 GOES TO NUMBER XXXXXXXXX WHO WORKED XX HOURS AT XX.XX PER HOUR.

6. You own four warehouses across the country, each of which can stock five particular items (see arrangement below). The data is recorded on one record, for example: 14, 15, 25, 5, 15, 20, 25, 3, . . . , 16, 5, 20, 10. Write a program to read the data into a two-dimensional array to produce the following output. Identify any item that has zero stock in three or more warehouses (one item number per line):

ITEMS

|  | 1 | 2 | 3 | 4 | 5 | TOTAL/WAREHOUSE |
|---|---|---|---|---|---|---|
| Warehouse 1 | 14 | 15 | 5 | 0 | 16 | 50 |
| Warehouse 2 | 15 | 20 | 25 | 0 | 5 | 65 |
| Warehouse 3 | 25 | 25 | 40 | 30 | 20 | 140 |
| Warehouse 4 | 5 | 3 | 10 | 0 | 10 | 28 |
| Totals | 59 | 63 | 80 | 30 | 51 | |

(Zero stock in three or more warehouses: item no. 4.)

7. Complete exercise 6 by printing those warehouses and item numbers where the stock is below 10. Given the data of exercise 10, the output should be similar to:

| WAREHOUSE | ITEM NUMBER |
|---|---|
| 1 | 3,4 |
| 2 | 4,5 |
| 4 | 1,2,4 |

8. You are calculating returns from a primary election where five candidates were running. Each vote is recorded using a DATA statement with two entries per DATA statement. The first entry is a number identifying the party of the voter (1 = Democrat, 2 = Republican, 3 = Independent). The second entry identifies the candidate (1, 2, 3, 4, or 5). Write a program to determine

a. How many votes each candidate received from the Democrats, Republicans, and Independents (and print the results).

b.  In the event a candidate obtains more than 10 votes from any party, print out the candidate's number and the number of votes given to him by that party as well as his total vote. For example:

| CANDIDATE | PARTY | NUMBER OF VOTES | TOTAL VOTES |
|-----------|-------|-----------------|-------------|
| 1 | 2 | 15 | |
| 1 | 3 | 20 | 43 |
| 2 | 1 | 14 | 14 |
| 3 | 1 | 15 | |
| 3 | 2 | 15 | |
| 3 | 3 | 10 | 40 |
| 4 | | | 10 |

(Note the total votes received by candidates 1 and 4.)

9. A small airplane has a seating capacity of five rows with three seats per row. Seat reservations are handled by a computer. Seat preferences for each passenger are entered on DATA statements with the name of the passenger, the row, and seat number on the DATA statement. If a requested seat is vacant, reserve the seat for the passenger and print his name and seat number. If the requested seat is already taken, assign seats in row fashion, starting with leftmost seat in row 1 and moving to the end of the row before starting with the second row, etc. Print the passenger's name and his assigned seat and row. Print a message if the plane is fully loaded. For example, given the following data the output should be as follows:

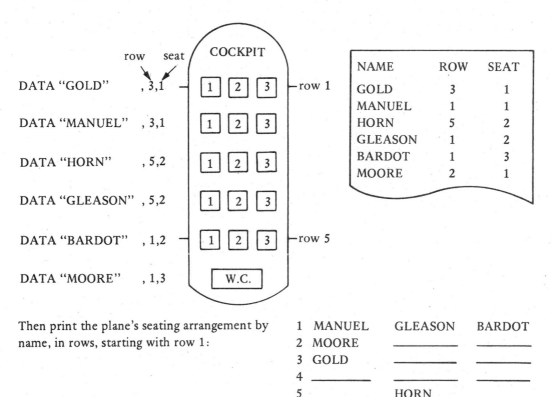

Then print the plane's seating arrangement by name, in rows, starting with row 1:

```
1  MANUEL    GLEASON   BARDOT
2  MOORE     _____   _____
3  GOLD      _____   _____
4  _____   _____   _____
5  _____   HORN      _____
```

10.  You work at a federal penitentiary as a social worker and are asked to provide certain information about the prisoners. Each prisoner record consists of the following:

   a.   The prisoner's last name

   b.   Month entered prison

   c.   Year entered prison

   d.   Type offense: Murder 1, Murder 2, Rape, Arson, Forgery, etc.

   e.   Age of prisoner at the time of incarceration

   f.   Sentence length in months (999 means life imprisonment)

   Write a program to:

   a.   List all prisoner names and their date of release. If the sentence has 999 months, print the message LIFE SENTENCE. (Date of release implies month and year.)

   b.   Determine the number and average age of the murder 1 perpetrators.

   c.   Determine the number of prisoners having a sentence between 24 and 120 months.

   d.   Sort names of prisoners by descending time sentence.

11.  A directory of students at a small college has been compiled to include the following description about each student: first and last name, sex code, age, hair color code, telephone number, marital status code. The following codes are used:

|                |                       |                         |
| -------------- | --------------------- | ----------------------- |
| Sex:  1 = male | Hair color:  1 = brown | Marital status:  1 = single |
|       2 = female |             2 = blond |                 2 = divorced |
|                |             3 = black |                 3 = married |

   A sorority is attempting to produce a listing of males who are less than 25 years of age and who have blond hair. The list must be in alphabetical order and must include telephone numbers. In case a selected male is married, add the word MARRIED to his description. Could you write a program to oblige the sorority?

12.  Grid analysis is a marketing strategy technique used to examine product-related needs of customers. The following market grid for apartments was developed in Dallas to help builders better understand needs (dotted squares) of customers:

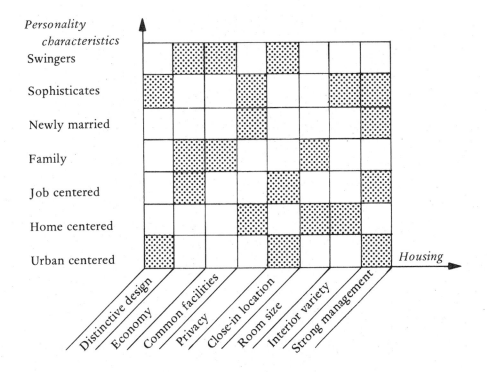

Write a program to read the data shown (using any code you wish) into an array to perform the following functions:

a.  Accept one personality characteristic from input and list corresponding housing needs. For instance, for INPUT PERSONALITY CHARACTERISTIC? FAMILY, the output should be FOR FAMILY CHARACTERISTIC THE FOLLOWING NEEDS ARE

1 ECONOMY<br>
2 COMMON FACILITIES<br>
3 ROOM SIZE

b.  Accept one housing need from input and list personality characteristics sharing that need. For input/output considerations, use the same format as in part a above.

c.  Accept one housing need from input and list the personality characteristics that do *not* require that need.

d.  Accept a pair of personality characteristics and list its corresponding needs. For example, newly wed, urban centered: distinctive design, privacy, close-in location, strong management.

13.    At the end of every semester, Dr. Landrum, department head of Business Data Systems, likes to check grade reports of his freshman class (100 students at most). Each student's final grades in three subject areas are entered on DATA statements, one DATA statement per student; for example:

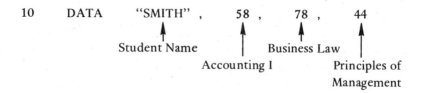

10    DATA    "SMITH" ,    58 ,    78 ,    44

Student Name         Business Law

Accounting I       Principles of Management

Enter in an array N$ all student names and enter each student's grades into a corresponding two-dimensional array G. For example, G(3,2) represents the third student's score in Business Law.

Write a program for Dr. Landrum to

a.    Compute the average score of each student across all disciplines.

b.    Compute the freshman average score for all Accounting I tests, the average score for Business Law, and average score for Principles of Management.

c.    Provide a list of all students whose three final scores are each above the freshman average test scores for each of the three subject areas.

d.    Award a prize to student(s) with highest scores in Principles of Management. Print name(s) of recipient(s).

e.    Award a scholarship to any student who might have obtained the three highest scores in the three subject areas.

The output should be similar to the following report:

SEMESTER END REPORT

| | ACCT. I | BUSINESS LAW | MANAGEMENT | AVERAGE |
|---|---|---|---|---|
| HORNET | 40 | 50 | 60 | 50 |
| BOILLOT | 50 | 90 | 40 | 60 |
| SMITHEN | 20 | 60 | 10 | 30 |
| | | | | |
| CLASS AVERAGE | 36.7 | 66.7 | 36.7 | |

NAMES OF STUDENTS WHOSE 3 TESTS ARE ABOVE THE 3 CLASS AVERAGES
BOILLOT

AWARD GOES TO HORNET
SCHOLARSHIP IS AWARDED TO NO ONE

**Exercises Requiring Matrix Operations**

14. Write a program to verify that for any conformable matrices X, Y, Z of your choice the following is true:

    a. $(X+Y)Z = X \cdot Z + Y \cdot Z$

    b. $(X \cdot Y)Z = X \cdot (Y \cdot Z)$

    c. $X \cdot X^{-1} = X^{-1} \cdot X = I$     (assuming X has an inverse)

15. Let us refer to $A'$ (read as A prime) as the transpose of matrix A. Write a program to demonstrate that

    $$(A')^{-1} = (A^{-1})'$$

    for a square matrix of five rows (assuming that matrix has an inverse).

16. An $n \times n$ matrix A is said to be *symmetric* if and only if $A = A'$. Write a program to demonstrate that

    a. $A \cdot A'$ is symmetric and

    b. $A + A'$ is symmetric.

17. A strictly triangular matrix can be defined as a square matrix with all entries on and below the main diagonal equal to zero. Write a program to demonstrate that if A is such a 4 x 4 matrix, then $A^4 = A \cdot A \cdot A \cdot A$ is the zero matrix (in general $A^n$ = zero matrix if A is an $n \times n$ strictly triangular matrix).

18. Write a program to verify that $DET(A \cdot B) = DET(A) \cdot DET(B)$ where A and B are square matrices and DET refers to the determinant of the matrix.

19. The XYZ Company manufactures four products: $P_1$, $P_2$, $P_3$, $P_4$. Each of these products must undergo some type of operation on five different machines: A, B, C, D, E. The time (in units of hours) required for each of these products on each of the five machines is shown as follows:

|       | A   | B   | C   | D   | E   |
|-------|-----|-----|-----|-----|-----|
| $P_1$ | .2  | .2  | .1  | .58 | .15 |
| $P_2$ | .26 | .1  | .13 | .61 | .3  |
| $P_3$ | .5  | .21 | .56 | .45 | .27 |
| $P_4$ | .6  | .17 | 1.3 | .25 | .31 |

For example, product $P_1$ requires .2 hour on machine A, .2 hour on machine B, .1 hour on machine C, etc.

a. The XYZ Company has been requested to fill an order for 356 products $P_1$, 257 products $P_2$, 1,058 products $P_3$, and 756 products $P_4$. Write a program to determine the total number of hours that *each* machine will be used. (*Hint:* Express the above table as a 4 X 5 matrix and the order as a 1 X 4 matrix and multiply both matrices.)

b.   The XYZ Company is renting the five machines A, B, C, D, E from a tooling company. The hourly rental cost for each machine is as follows:

| MACHINES | A | B | C | D | E |
|---|---|---|---|---|---|
| RENTAL COST/HOUR | $10.00 | $5.75 | $3.50 | $10.00 | $5.76 |

Write a program to compute total rental expense for all machines. (*Hint:* Express rental costs as a 1 × 5 matrix and multiply by matrix result of part a.)

20.   Write a program to verify that the determinant of a triangular matrix is equal to the product of its diagonal elements; choose a square matrix of size 4.

21.   An iterative method[1] for computing the inverse of a matrix A is given by

$$A^{-1} = I + B + B^2 + B^3 + B^4 + \cdots,$$

where $B = I - A$ (I is the identity matrix). Compute the inverse of

$$A = \begin{pmatrix} 1/2 & 1 & 0 \\ 0 & 2/3 & 0 \\ -1/2 & -1 & 2/3 \end{pmatrix}$$

Stop at $B^{10}$ in the expansion for $A^{-1}$. Check result by computing $A^{-1}*A$.

22.   The trace of a matrix is defined as the sum of its diagonal elements. Let A be a 5 x 5 matrix and B be a 5 x 5 matrix. Write a program to demonstrate that $tr(A \cdot B) = tr(B \cdot A)$ and $tr(A+B) = tr(A)+tr(B)$.

23.   A method for computing the inverse of any matrix on a computer is as follows: Let A be an $n$ x $n$ matrix ($n \geqslant 1$). Then

$$A^{-1} = -\frac{1}{c_n}\left(A^{n-1} + c_1 A^{n-2} + c_2 A^{n-3} + \cdots + c_{n-1}I\right)$$

where the $c$'s are all constants defined as

$c_1 = -tr(A)$ (See exercise 9 for the definition of the trace.)
$c_2 = -1/2\,(c_1\ tr(A) + tr(A^2))$
$c_3 = -1/3\,(c_2\ tr(A) + c_1\ tr(A^2) + tr(A^3))$
.
.
.
$c_n = -1/n\left(c_{n-1}\ tr(A) + c_{n-2}\ tr(A^2) + \cdots + c_1\ tr(A^{n-1}) + tr(A^n)\right)$

Write a program to compute the inverse of a 5 x 5 matrix A and check that it is indeed the inverse by verifying that $A \cdot A^{-1} = I$.

For example, the inverse of a 2 x 2 matrix X is $X^{-1} = -\frac{1}{c_2}(X + c_1 I)$

where $c_2 = -1/2\left(c_1\ tr(X) + tr(X^2)\right)$ and $c_1 = -tr(X)$.

---

[1] This method will work only when the eigenvalues of A are less than 1 in absolute value.

## 8-8-3  Projects

1.  The following questionnaire is used in a survey to determine people's attitudes toward abortion:

### ABORTION ATTITUDE SURVEY

Male ☐   Female ☐   Married ☐   Single ☐

Children ☐   No children ☐   Widowed ☐   Divorced ☐

Age group: Below 20 ☐   20–30 ☐   31–40 ☐   41–above ☐

If you are opposed to abortion, answer part A below. If you are not opposed to abortion, answer part B below. If in part A or part B there are questions about which you feel undecided, leave both boxes blank.

PART A          If you are opposed to abortion, is it

| YES | NO | |
|-----|-----|---|
| ☐ | ☐ | On religious grounds? |
| ☐ | ☐ | Because you believe the fetus has an absolute right to life? |
| ☐ | ☐ | Because you believe physical pain is inflicted on the fetus in the abortion process? |
| ☐ | ☐ | Do you feel abortion would be justified in specific instances (such as rape, malformed fetus, danger to mother's life, etc.)? |

PART B          If you are not opposed to abortion, is it because you feel:

| YES | NO | |
|-----|-----|---|
| ☐ | ☐ | A woman has a right to control her own body? |
| ☐ | ☐ | Abortion is a private decision for the parents alone to make? |
| ☐ | ☐ | Abortion can be a valid means to control population growth? |
| ☐ | ☐ | No physical pain is inflicted on the fetus in the abortion process? |
| ☐ | ☐ | Unwanted children should not be born? |
| ☐ | ☐ | A fetus is an incomplete human being and as such no moral or legal laws are applicable to it? |
| ☐ | ☐ | Laws against abortion would increase criminal abortions? |

The number of respondents should be at least 10. Either simulate responses or hand out questionnaires to friends to be completed. Before you start writing the program, think of the most efficient way to handle input and special code considerations. Try to use just one two-dimensional array to store the responses of all 10 candidates.

Determine how many yes, no, and undecided responses there were for the four questions to be completed by those opposed to abortion. The printout should be as follows:

OPPOSED TO ABORTION

|  | YES | NO | UNDECIDED |
|---|---|---|---|
| Question 1 | X | X | X |
| Question 2 | X | X | X |
| Question 3 | X | X | X |
| Question 4 | X | X | X |

2.  A *graph* is a structure made up of a set of vertices and edges connecting the vertices. A common means of representing a graph is with points and line segments as shown in the example of Figure 8-25. In the example the vertices are labeled 1, 2, 3, . . . , 8; the line segments connecting the numbered points represent edges. For example, there is an edge connecting vertices 1 and 3. A way of representing a graph in a computer is by means of an *adjacency matrix*. An adjacency matrix has a row and a column for each vertex in the graph. The graph of Figure 8-25 could be represented by the matrix A shown in Figure 8-26. In an adjacency matrix A, the value of $a_{ij}$ is 1 if there is an edge connecting vertices $i$ and $j$; otherwise the value of $a_{ij}$ is 0. For example, $a_{13} = 1$ represents an edge connecting vertices 1 and 3.

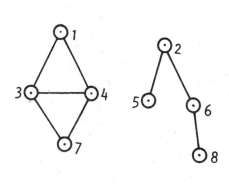

|  | 1 | 2 | 3 | 4 | 5 | 6 | 7 | 8 |
|---|---|---|---|---|---|---|---|---|
| 1 | 0 | 0 | 1 | 1 | 0 | 0 | 0 | 0 |
| 2 | 0 | 0 | 0 | 0 | 1 | 1 | 0 | 0 |
| 3 | 1 | 0 | 0 | 1 | 0 | 0 | 1 | 0 |
| 4 | 1 | 0 | 1 | 0 | 0 | 0 | 1 | 0 |
| 5 | 0 | 1 | 0 | 0 | 0 | 0 | 0 | 0 |
| 6 | 0 | 1 | 0 | 0 | 0 | 0 | 0 | 1 |
| 7 | 0 | 0 | 1 | 1 | 0 | 0 | 0 | 0 |
| 8 | 0 | 0 | 0 | 0 | 0 | 1 | 0 | 0 |

Figure 8-25   Geometric representation of a graph.

Figure 8-26   An adjacency matrix for the graph of Figure 8-25.

A *walk* in a graph is defined as a series of vertices connected by edges. In the example of Figure 8-25, 134 would represent a walk, since edges exist connecting vertices 1 and 3, and 3 and 4. The sequence 12 would not represent a walk, since no edge connects these two vertices. The *length* of a walk is defined as the number of edges traversed in the walk. For example, the walk 134 is of length 2, since the edges 13 and 34 are traversed. The walk 14 is of length 1; the walk 13741 is of length 4. The matrix of Figure 8-26 may be thought of as representing the number of walks of length 1 connecting any two vertices of the graph.

We wish to solve the problem of counting the number of walks of a specific length connecting any two vertices on a graph. For example, consider vertices 3 and 4. The walks 314 and 374 both connect the vertices and are of length 2. An interesting connection exists between this problem and matrix multiplication. Suppose we multiply row 3 and column 4 of A. The value is calculated as

$$a_{31}a_{14} + a_{32}a_{24} + a_{33}a_{34} + a_{34}a_{44} + a_{35}a_{54} + a_{36}a_{64} + a_{37}a_{74} + a_{38}a_{84} =$$

$$1 \cdot 1 \;+\; 0 \cdot 0 \;+\; 0 \cdot 1 \;+\; 1 \cdot 0 \;+\; 0 \cdot 0 \;+\; 0 \cdot 0 \;+\; 1 \cdot 1 \;+\; 0 \cdot 0 = 2$$

the walk 314                                                                    the walk 374

The result of the multiplication represents the number of walks of length 2 connecting vertices 3 and 4. In general, if we multiply $A \cdot A = A^2$, the element in the position $i, j$ represents the number of walks of length 2 connecting vertex $i$ and vertex $j$. By extension, entries in $A \cdot A \cdot A = A^3$ represent the number of walks of length 3 connecting specified vertices; $A^n$ represents the number of walks of length $n$.

a.   Write a BASIC program to accept adjacency matrices of any desired size and output the number of walks of length 2, 3, . . . , connecting vertices on the graph. Test your program using the graphs shown in Figure 8-28.

b.   Note that a valid adjacency matrix must be symmetric. Add to the program of part a above a procedure to verify the validity of an adjacency matrix.

It is not always possible to proceed from one vertex to another of a graph by walks of any length, because connecting edges do not exist. A set of vertices which are connected to one another by at least one walk of some length is called a *connected segment.* In the example of Figure 8-25, vertices 1, 3, 4, 6 and vertices 1, 5, 6, 8 represent connected segments. It is usually easy to recognize connected segments from the geometric representation of a graph, but it is not easy when the adjacency matrix is used. Consider the matrix $B = A^2 + A^3$. The element $b_{ij}$ represents the number of walks of length 2 or 3 connecting vertices $i$ and $j$. If we compute the matrix $C = A + A^2 + A^3 + \cdots + A^{n-1}$ the element $c_{ij}$ would represent the number of walks of length 1, 2, 3, . . . , $n-1$ connecting vertices $i$ and $j$. If $n$ represents the number of vertices in the graph, we can calculate the matrix C and examine the elements $c_{ij}$ to find connected segments. If the element $c_{ij} = 0$, there is no path connecting vertices $i$ and $j$; if $c_{ij} \neq 0$, there exists at least one walk connecting vertices $i$ and $j$. (It can be shown that if two vertices are connected by a walk of length greater than or equal to $n$, then they are connected by a walk of length less than $n$. Hence it is necessary only to compute powers of A up to $A^{n-1}$.) For the example of Figure 8-26 the matrix C would be as shown in Figure 8-27. Examination of row 1, for example, shows non-zero entries in columns 1, 3, 4, and 7 indicating a connected segment composed of those vertices.

|   | 1 | 2 | 3 | 4 | 5 | 6 | 7 | 8 |
|---|---|---|---|---|---|---|---|---|
| 1 | 220 | 0 | 291 | 291 | 0 | 0 | 220 | 0 |
| 2 | 0 | 20 | 0 | 0 | 21 | 33 | 0 | 12 |
| 3 | 291 | 0 | 365 | 366 | 0 | 0 | 291 | 0 |
| 4 | 291 | 0 | 366 | 365 | 0 | 0 | 291 | 0 |
| 5 | 0 | 21 | 0 | 0 | 8 | 12 | 0 | 12 |
| 6 | 0 | 33 | 0 | 0 | 12 | 20 | 0 | 21 |
| 7 | 220 | 0 | 291 | 291 | 0 | 0 | 220 | 0 |
| 8 | 0 | 12 | 0 | 0 | 12 | 21 | 0 | 8 |

**Figure 8-27**   The matrix $C = A + A^2 + A^3 + A^4 + A^5 + A^6 + A^7$.

c.   Write a BASIC program to analyze an adjacency matrix of size $n$ and output all connected segments. (Handle as a special case segments of size one, that is, vertices not connected to any other vertex.) Test your program using the graphs shown in Figure 8-28.

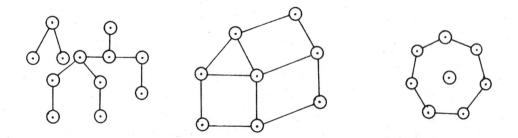

**Figure 8-28**   Sample graphs.

Games

3.   The following diagram depicts a former prisoner-of-war camp where the point S identifies the prisoners' living quarters. The points marked R identify 15-foot walls that cannot be climbed. The points marked E are escape points; any prisoner reaching such a point is considered to have escaped. The points marked A identify secret traps which the prisoner falls into and is subsequently captured.

Escape attempts are made every night where darkness is so total that prisoners wander randomly, hoping to stumble on the escape markers. Escape attempts originate at point S; prisoners are free to travel one mesh step at a time in any of the four cardinal directions (1 = north, 2 = west, 3 = south, 4 = east) with equal probability. On hitting a wall, the prisoner steps back to the location he was in prior to bumping into the wall, taking two steps in the process. The point S is considered to be an ordinary mesh point.

```
        E  E  E  E  E  E
   E  .  .  .  .  .  .  .  A  A  A
      A  .  .  .  A  .  .  .  .  .  A
   R  .  .  .  .  .  .  .  .  .  .  A
   R  .  .  .  A  .  .  .  A  .  .  .  A  E  E  A  A
   R  .  .  .  .  .  .  .  .  .  .  .  .  .  .  .  A
   R  .  .  .  .  .  .  .  .  .  .  .  .  .  A  A  A
   R  .  .  .  .  .  .  .  .  .  .  .  .  .  .  .  .  E
   R  .  .  .  .  .  .  .  .  .  .  .  .  .  .  .  .  E
   R  .  .  .  .  .  .  .  .  .  .  .  .  .  .  .  .  E
   R  .  S  .  .  .  A  .  .  .  A  .  .  .  .  .  .  .  E
   R  .  .  .  .  .  .  .  .  .  .  .  .  .  .  .  .  E
   R  .  .  .  .  .  .  .  .  .  .  .  .  .  .  .  .  E
   R  .  .  .  .  .  .  .  .  .  .  .  .  .  .  .  .  E
   R  .  .  .  .  .  .  .  .  .  .  .  .  .  .  .  .  E
   R  .  .  .  .  .  .  .  .  .  .  .  .  .  .  .  A  A  A
   R  .  .  .  .  .  .  A  A  A  .  .  .  .  .  .  E
   R  .  .  .  .  A  .  .  .  .  .  E  A  E  E  A
      E  E  A  A     E  A  E  E  E
```

Write a program that starts individual prisoners one at a time from point S and follows them one at a time to their escape or capture.

a.  Run 500 prisoners (one at a time). Keep track of each prisoner in an array that records the number of steps taken and whether the prisoner was captured or escaped.

b.  Print out the percentage of prisoners who escaped.

c.  Print out the number of prisoners who escaped versus the number of steps taken (so many escaped on the fifth step, so many escaped on the sixth step, etc.)

d.  Print how many prisoners escaped through the rightmost points (last column).

e.  Print the number of prisoners captured versus the number of steps as in question c.

Use the BASIC statement LET J = INT(RND(1) * 4 + 1), which will return for J a random number 1, 2, 3, or 4. J can then be used to determine whether the prisoner will move one position to the north, one position to the west, one position to the south, or one position to the east.

## 8-8-4    Answers to Self Test

1.  a.

```
10  DIM A(3,4),B(3,4)
15  LET K=1
20  FOR I=1 TO 3
30  FOR J=1 TO 4
40  LET A(I,J)=K
50  LET B(I,J)=10*A(I,J)
55  LET K=K+1
60  NEXT J
70  NEXT I
80  LET C=500
100  FOR I=1 TO 3
200  FOR J=1 TO 4
300  PRINT A(I,J);
400  NEXT J
500  NEXT I
600  FOR I=1 TO 3
700  FOR J=1 TO 4
800  PRINT B(I,J);
900  NEXT J
1000  NEXT I
1100  PRINT C
```

*Output*

```
1  2  3  4  5  6  7  8  9  10  11  12  10  20  30  40  50  60  70  80  90
100  110  120  500
```

b.

```
1200  FOR I=1 TO 3
1300  FOR J=1 TO 4
1400  PRINT A(I,J);
1500  NEXT J
1600  FORJ=1 TO 4
1700  PRINT B(I,J);
1800  NEXT J
1900  PRINT C
2000  NEXT I
```

*Output*

```
1 2 3 4 10 20 30 40 500
5 6 7 8 50 60 70 80 500
9 10 11 12 90 100 110 120 500
```

c.

```
2100  FOR J=1 TO 3
2200  FOR I = 1 TO 3
2300  PRINT A(I,J);
2400  NEXT I
2500  PRINT C;
2600  FOR I=1 TO 3
2700  PRINT B(I,J);
2800  NEXT I
2900  PRINT
3000  NEXT J
```

*Output*

```
1 5 9 500 10 50 90
2 6 10 500 20 60 100
3 7 11 500 30 70 110
```

d.
```
3100  FOR I=1 TO 3
3200  FOR J=1 TO 4
3300  PRINT A(I,J);B(I,J);
3400  NEXT J
3450  PRINT
3500  NEXT I
```

*Output*

```
1 10 2 20 3 30 4 40
5 50 6 60 7 70 8 80
9 90 10 100 11 110 12 120
```

e.
```
3600  FOR K=2 TO 4 STEP 2
3700  FOR J=K-1 TO K
3800  FOR I=1 TO 3
3900  PRINT A(I,J);B(I,J);
4000  NEXT I
4100  NEXT J
4200  PRINT
4300  NEXT K
4400  END
```

*Output*

```
1 10 5 50 9 90 2 20 6 60 10 100
3 30 7 70 11 110 4 40 8 80 12 120
```

2. a.
```
10  DIM A(4,3)
50  DATA 1,2,3,4,5,6,7,8,9,10,11,12
100  FOR J=1 TO 3
200  FOR I=1 TO 4
300  READ A(I,J)
400  NEXT I
500  NEXT J
550  MAT PRINT A
600  END
```

*Output*

```
1   5   9
2   6   10
3   7   11
4   8   12
```

b.
```
100   DIM A(1,6),B(6)
200   DATA 1,2,3,4,5,6,1,2,3,4,5,6
300   FOR J=1 TO 6
400   READ A(1,J)
500   NEXT J
600   FOR I=1 TO 6
700   READ B(I)
800   NEXT I
900   MAT PRINT A;B
1000  END
```

*Output*

```
1 2 3 4 5 6
1       2       3       4       5
6
```

c.
```
100 DIM A(6,1),B(6,1)
200 DATA 1,1,2,2,3,3,4,4,5,5,6,6
300 FOR I=1 TO 6
400 READ A(I,1),B(I,1)
500 NEXT I
600 MAT PRINT A;B;
700 END
```

*Output*

```
1
2
3
4
5
6

1
2
3
4
5
6
```

d.
```
100 DIM A(6,1),B(1,6)
200 DATA 1,1,2,2,3,3,4,4,5,5,6,6
300 FOR I = 1 TO 6
400 READ A(I,1),B(1,I)
500 NEXT I
600 MAT PRINT A;B;
700 END
```

*Output*

```
1
2
3
4
5
6

1 2 3 4 5 6
```

e.
```
 100 DIM A(9,3),B(9,2)
 200 DATA 1,1,1,1,1,2,2,2,2,2,3,3,3,3,3,4,4,4,4,4
 300 DATA 5,5,5,5,5,6,6,6,6,6,7,7,7,7,7,8,8,8,8,8,9,9,9,9,9
 400 FOR I=1 TO 9
 500 FOR J=1 TO 3
 600 READ A(I,J)
 700 NEXT J
 800 FOR J=1 TO 2
 900 READ B(I,J)
1000 NEXT J
1100 NEXT I
1200 MAT PRINT A;B;
1300 END
```

*Output*

```
1   1   1
2   2   2
3   3   3
4   4   4
5   5   5
6   6   6
7   7   7
8   8   8
9   9   9

1   1
2   2
3   3
4   4
5   5
6   6
7   7
8   8
9   9
```

f.     100  DIM A(8,9),B(4,2)
       200  DATA 1,1,1,1,1,1,1,1,1,2,2,2,2,2,2,2,2,2,3,3,3,3,3,3,3,3,3
       300  DATA 4,4,4,4,4,4,4,4,4,5,5,5,5,5,5,5,5,5,6,6,6,6,6,6,6,6,6
       350  DATA 7,7,7,7,7,7,7,7,7,8,8,8,8,8,8,8,8,8
       400  DATA 1,2,3,4,5,6,7,8
       500  FOR I=1 TO 8
       600  FOR J=1 TO 9
       700  READ A(I,J)                    *Output*
       800  NEXT J
       900  NEXT I                         1  1  1  1  1  1  1  1  1
      1000  FOR J=1 TO 2                    2  2  2  2  2  2  2  2  2
      1100  FOR I=1 TO 4                    3  3  3  3  3  3  3  3  3
      1200  READ B(I,J)                     4  4  4  4  4  4  4  4  4
      1300  NEXT I                          5  5  5  5  5  5  5  5  5
      1400  NEXT J                          6  6  6  6  6  6  6  6  6
      1500  MAT PRINT A;B;                  7  7  7  7  7  7  7  7  7
      1600  END                            8  8  8  8  8  8  8  8  8

                                           1  5
                                           2  6
                                           3  7
                                           4  8

3.     100  DIM A(16,6)                    *Output*
       200  FOR I=1 TO 16
       300  FOR J=1 TO 6                 1   2   3   4   5   6
       400  LET A(I,J) = J               1   2   3   4   5   6
       500  NEXT J                       1   2   3   4   5   6
       600  NEXT I                       1   2   3   4   5   6
       700  MAT PRINT A;                 1   2   3   4   5   6
       800  END                         1   2   3   4   5   6
                                        1   2   3   4   5   6
                                        1   2   3   4   5   6
                                        1   2   3   4   5   6
                                        1   2   3   4   5   6
                                        1   2   3   4   5   6
                                        1   2   3   4   5   6
                                        1   2   3   4   5   6
                                        1   2   3   4   5   6
                                        1   2   3   4   5   6
                                        1   2   3   4   5   6

4.  a.
```
10  REM EXERCISE 4A
20  DIM A(5,5)
30  DATA 1,2,3,4,5
40  DATA 6,7,8,9,10
50  DATA 11,12,13,14,15
60  DATA 16,17,18,19,20
70  DATA 21,22,23,24,25
80  FORI=1 TO 5
90  FOR J=1 TO 5
100 READ A(I,J)
110 NEXT J
120 NEXT I
130 FOR I=1 TO 5
140 FOR J=1 TO 5
150 PRINT A(I,J);
160 NEXT J
170 PRINT
180 NEXT I
185 PRINT "**************"
190 REM ALTERNATE SOLUTION TO 4A
200 RESTORE
210 MAT READ A
220 MAT PRINT A;
```

*Output*

```
1   2   3   4   5
6   7   8   9   10
11  12  13  14  15
16  17  18  19  20
21  22  23  24  25
**************
1   2   3   4   5
6   7   8   9   10
11  12  13  14  15
16  17  18  19  20
21  22  23  24  25
```

b.
```
230 REM EXERCISE 4B
240 LET S=0
250 FOR J=1 TO 5
260 LET S=S+A(3,J)
270 NEXT J
280 PRINT "SUM OF 3RD ROW =";S
290 PRINT
```

*Output*

SUM OF 3RD ROW = 65

c.
```
300 REM EXERCISE 4C
310 LET L=A(1,1)
320 FOR I=2 TO 5
330 IF A(I,1)>L THEN LET L=A(I,1)
340 NEXT I
350 PRINT "LARGEST VALUE IN FIRST COLUMN IS"; L
360 PRINT
```

*Output*

LARGEST VALUE IN FIRST COLUMN IS 21

d.
```
370 REM EXERCISE 4D
380 DIMB(5)
390 FORI=1 TO 5
400 LET B(I) = 0
410 NEXT I
420 FOR I=1 TO 5
430 FOR J=1 TO 5
440 LET B(J)=B(J)+A(I,J)
450 NEXT J
460 NEXT I
470 PRINT "SUM OF COLUMNS"
475 MAT PRINT B;
```

*Output*

SUM OF COLUMNS
55  60  65  70  75

e.
```
480 REM EXERCISE 4E
490 PRINT "OLD CONTENT OF A"
500 MAT PRINT A;
510 FOR I=1 TO 5
520 LET A(3,I)=A(3,I)+A(2,I)
530 NEXT I
540 PRINT "NEW CONTENT OF A"
550 MAT PRINT A;
```

*Output*

OLD CONTENT OF A
```
1   2   3   4   5
6   7   8   9   10
11  12  13  14  15
16  17  18  19  20
21  22  23  24  25
```

NEW CONTENT OF A
```
1   2   3   4   5
6   7   8   9   10
17  19  21  23  25
16  17  18  19  20
21  22  23  24  25
```

f.
```
560 REM EXERCISE 4F
570 PRINT "OLD CONTENT OF A"
580 MAT PRINT A;
590 FOR I=1 TO 5
600 LET H=A(I,3)
610 LET A(I,3)=A(I,4)
620 LET A(I,4)=H
630 NEXT I
640 PRINT "NEW CONTENT OF A"
650 MAT PRINT A;
```

*Output*

OLD CONTENT OF A
```
1   2   3   4   5
6   7   8   9   10
17  19  21  23  25
16  17  18  19  20
21  22  23  24  25
```

NEW CONTENT OF A
```
1   2   4   3   5
6   7   9   8   10
17  19  23  21  25
16  17  19  18  20
21  22  24  23  25
```

g.   660  REM EXERCISE 4G
     670  PRINT "ARRAY A"
     680  MAT PRINT A;
     690  LET S=0
     700  FOR I=1 TO 5
     710  LET S=S+A(I,I)
     720  NEXT I
     730  PRINT "SUM OF DIAGONAL ELEMENTS =";S

*Output*

```
1    2    4    3    5
6    7    9    8    10
17   19   23   21   25
16   17   19   18   20
21   22   24   23   25
```

SUM OF DIAGONAL
ELEMENTS = 74

h.   740  REM EXERCISE 4H
     750  LET S2=0
     760  FOR I=1 TO 5
     770  LET S2=S2+A(I,6−I)
     780  NEXT I
     790  PRINT "SUM OF SECOND DIAGONAL"; S2

*Output*

SUM OF SECOND DIAGONAL 74

i.   800  REM EXERCISE 4I
     810  PRINT "INPUT ROW AND COLUMN TO BE INTERCHANGED"
     820  INPUT I,J
     830  PRINT "OLD CONTENT OF ARRAY A"
     840  MAT PRINT A;
     850  FOR K=1 TO 5
     860  LET H=A(I,K)
     870  LET A(I,K)=A(K,J)
     880  LET A(K,J)=H
     890  NEXT K
     900  PRINT "RESULT AFTER INTERCHANGE OF ROW";I;" AND COLUMN";J
     910  MAT PRINT A;

*Input/Output*

INPUT ROW AND COLUMN TO BE INTERCHANGED
?2,3
OLD CONTENT OF ARRAY A
```
1    2    4    3    5
6    7    9    8    10
17   19   23   21   25
16   17   19   18   20
21   22   24   23   25
```

RESULT AFTER INTERCHANGE OF ROW 2 AND COLUMN 3
```
1    2    6    3    5
4    9    23   19   24
17   19   7    21   25
16   17   8    18   20
21   22   10   23   25
```

j.  920  REM EXERCISE 4J
    930  REM C REPRESENTS ROW POSITION OF LARGEST ELEMENT
    940  REM R REPRESENTS COLUMN POSITION OF LARGEST ELEMENT
    950  LET R=1
    960  LET C=1
    970  FOR I=1 TO 5
    980  FOR J=1 TO 5
    990  IF A(I,J)<=A(R,C) THEN 1020
    1000 LET R=I
    1010 LET C=J
    1020 NEXT J
    1030 NEXT I
    1040 PRINT "LOCATION OF LARGEST ELEMENT IS ROW"; R;" COLUMN";C
    1050 END

*Output*

LOCATION OF LARGEST ELEMENT IS ROW 3 COLUMN 5

# SUBROUTINES
# AND FUNCTIONS

## 9-1    Problem Example

Final grades have been computed for students enrolled in Business Management, sections 58 and 59. The grade file consists of two sets of DATA statements. In each set, the first DATA statement identifies the class section number and the number of students in that class. The following DATA statements in the set contain the grades for the particular section number (see Figure 9-1).

Write a program to compute the grade average for each section and the average for the combined sections. Print the number of grades over the average for each section and for the combined group. Given a sample input shown in Figure 9-1, the output should be similar to the listing in Figure 9-1. The program to solve this problem is shown in Figure 9-2.

In the program of Figure 9-2, note the use of the GOSUB statements in statements 150, 160, 270, and 280. The complete program in Figure 9-2 can be thought of as consisting of three independent program segments:

1.  The main program (statement numbers 10–290), which reads the grades, computes the average A, and coordinates the use of the two subroutines.

2.  One subroutine at statement 300, which processes N grades and stores the number of grades above the average in the variable K.

3.  Another subroutine at statement 360, which prints out the results (statements 360–400).

Note that the subroutine to determine the number of grades above the average always processes N grades in an array always called G1 and always refers to the variable A as the grade average. These three variables G1, N, and A are referred to as the *dummy-arguments* of the subroutine. It is very important that the program wishing to make use of this subroutine initialize these

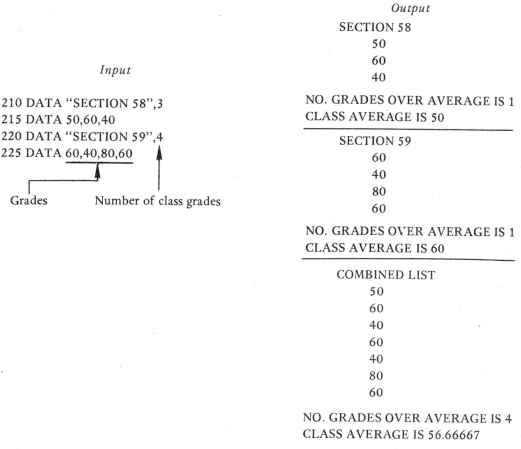

*Output*

SECTION 58
50
60
40

NO. GRADES OVER AVERAGE IS 1
CLASS AVERAGE IS 50

SECTION 59
60
40
80
60

NO. GRADES OVER AVERAGE IS 1
CLASS AVERAGE IS 60

COMBINED LIST
50
60
40
60
40
80
60

NO. GRADES OVER AVERAGE IS 4
CLASS AVERAGE IS 56.66667

**Figure 9-1**    Sample input/output for subroutine problem.

arguments to their desired values before transferring to the subroutine. This is done in the program of Figure 9-2, as follows:

1.  Just before the first call to the subroutine at 300, G1 is used to store the grades of section 58, N is 3, and A is 50. Return from the subroutine is made to statement 160.

2.  Just before the second call to the subroutine, G1 is used to store the grades of section 59, N is 4, and A is 60.

3.  Just before the third call to the subroutine (statement 270), G1 is used to store the combined grades of both sections and N is set to $J - 1 = 7$ in statement 200. Return is made to statement 280.

4.  In the case of the second subroutine at 360, the dummy arguments are K and A, which are initialized at three different times to their respective values by the calling program. A is computed twice at statement 140 and once at 260, while K is computed three times in the subroutine starting at 300 (three calls to the subroutine).

Note that through the use of subroutines it is possible to avoid duplication of code as shown on the right-hand side of Figure 9-2. Whenever a procedure or task is to be performed, a transfer to that procedure is made through the GOSUB statement.

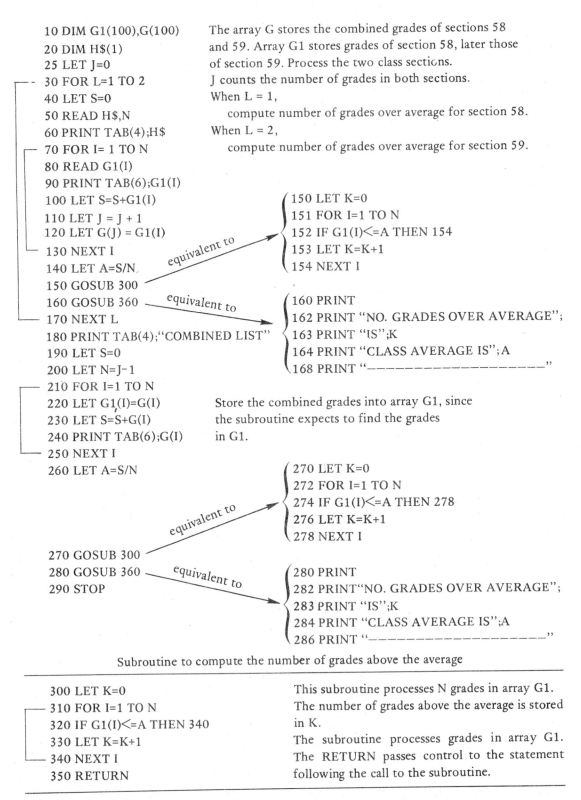

```
10 DIM G1(100),G(100)        The array G stores the combined grades of sections 58
20 DIM H$(1)                 and 59. Array G1 stores grades of section 58, later those
25 LET J=0                   of section 59. Process the two class sections.
30 FOR L=1 TO 2              J counts the number of grades in both sections.
40 LET S=0                   When L = 1,
50 READ H$,N                     compute number of grades over average for section 58.
60 PRINT TAB(4);H$           When L = 2,
70 FOR I= 1 TO N                 compute number of grades over average for section 59.
80 READ G1(I)
90 PRINT TAB(6);G1(I)
100 LET S=S+G1(I)                              150 LET K=0
110 LET J = J + 1                              151 FOR I=1 TO N
120 LET G(J) = G1(I)                           152 IF G1(I)<=A THEN 154
130 NEXT I            equivalent to           153 LET K=K+1
140 LET A=S/N                                  154 NEXT I
150 GOSUB 300
160 GOSUB 360   equivalent to                 160 PRINT
170 NEXT L                                     162 PRINT "NO. GRADES OVER AVERAGE";
180 PRINT TAB(4);"COMBINED LIST"              163 PRINT "IS";K
190 LET S=0                                    164 PRINT "CLASS AVERAGE IS";A
200 LET N=J-1                                  168 PRINT "——————————————————————"
210 FOR I=1 TO N
220 LET G1(I)=G(I)           Store the combined grades into array G1, since
230 LET S=S+G(I)            the subroutine expects to find the grades
240 PRINT TAB(6);G(I)        in G1.
250 NEXT I
260 LET A=S/N                                  270 LET K=0
                                               272 FOR I=1 TO N
                                               274 IF G1(I)<=A THEN 278
                             equivalent to     276 LET K=K+1
                                               278 NEXT I

270 GOSUB 300
280 GOSUB 360   equivalent to                 280 PRINT
290 STOP                                       282 PRINT"NO. GRADES OVER AVERAGE";
                                               283 PRINT "IS";K
                                               284 PRINT "CLASS AVERAGE IS";A
                                               286 PRINT "————————————————————"
```

Subroutine to compute the number of grades above the average

```
300 LET K=0                  This subroutine processes N grades in array G1.
310 FOR I=1 TO N             The number of grades above the average is stored
320 IF G1(I)<=A THEN 340     in K.
330 LET K=K+1                The subroutine processes grades in array G1.
340 NEXT I                   The RETURN passes control to the statement
350 RETURN                   following the call to the subroutine.
```

**Figure 9-2**   Subroutine example.

Subroutine to perform the output functions.

---

```
360 PRINT
370 PRINT"NO. GRADES OVER AVERAGE IS";K
380 PRINT "CLASS AVERAGE IS";A
390 PRINT "————————————————————"
400 RETURN                          Return is made to 170 and later to 290.
```

---

```
410 DATA "SECTION 58",3            Grades for section 58.
420 DATA 50,60,40
430 DATA "SECTION 59",4            Grades for section 59.
440 DATA 60,40,80,60
450 END
```

**Figure 9-2**   Subroutine example. (continued)

# 9-2   BASIC Statements

### 9-2-1   Subroutines

Subroutines are written for three basic purposes:

1.  To carry out generalized procedures that are data-independent; for example, sorting or merging arrays, calculating averages for different sets of grades, etc. Parameters or arguments (sometimes called *dummy-arguments*) are used in the subroutine to illustrate the way in which the task or procedure is to be carried out. These arguments must be initialized by the program segment wishing to make use of the subroutine.

2.  To facilitate program documentation (readability), program development, and program modification and debugging. Each subroutine is an independent module that performs a specific task. The logic of the entire program is modularized and clarified.

3.  To avoid code duplication, thus avoiding loss of programmer time.

### 9-2-2   GOSUB

The general form of the GOSUB statement is

$$\textit{statement-number}_1 \text{ GOSUB } \textit{statement-number}_2$$

where  $\textit{statement-number}_1$  is required

   GOSUB is a keyword

   $\textit{statement-number}_2$  is the statement-number identifying the beginning of the subroutine.

The distinguishing feature of the subroutine is that at its conclusion the point to which the subroutine returns is variable.

**Example**

| | |
|---|---|
| 10 GOSUB 40 | Transfer to statement 40 and, on return |
| 60 GOSUB 900 | from the subroutine, transfer to |
| | subroutine 900. |

The GOSUB statement causes the *statement-number*$_2$ to be the next statement executed and (unlike the GO TO statement) sets up the necessary internal code for transfer to be made to the statement immediately following the GOSUB on completion of the subroutine.

## 9-2-3   RETURN

The general form of the RETURN statement is

*statement-number* RETURN

where RETURN is a key word. The RETURN statement causes transfer to the statement immediately following a GOSUB statement. Any number of RETURN statements may be used in a subroutine. For example, consider the following code:

| | |
|---|---|
| 50 LET X = 1 | |
| 60 GOSUB 200 | Return is made to statement 70. |
| 70 | |

| | |
|---|---|
| 90 LET X = 5 | |
| 100 GOSUB 200 | Return is made to statement 110. |
| 110 | |

| | |
|---|---|
| 190 GO TO 250 | Bypass the subroutine. |
| 200 LET X = X + 1 | This subroutine consists of statements 200 through |
| 210 IF X > 4 THEN 230 |     statement 240. |
| 220 RETURN | |
| 230 PRINT X | Note the two RETURN statements in the |
| 240 RETURN |     subroutine. |
| 250 ------- | |

The subroutine beginning at statement 200 has two RETURN statements. If the subroutine is called from statement 60, the RETURN statement would return control to statement 70; if the subroutine is called from statement 100, the return would be made to statement 110.

It is important that a subroutine not be executed except by a GOSUB statement. If transfer is made into a subroutine by a means other than a GOSUB statement, the transfer that will be made by the RETURN statement is unpredictable.

# 9-3    You Might Want To Know

1.  Must all references to a subroutine be made to the same initial statement?

    *Answer:* No. A subroutine can be entered at any point. For example, consider the following code:

        10 GOSUB 200
        .
        .
        .
        40 GOSUB 220
        .
        .
        .
        200 LET X=X+1 ◄──────── Note the two entry points to the
        210 GO TO 230              subroutine.
        220 LET X=X-1 ◄
        230 PRINT X
        240 RETURN
        .
        .

2.  Does it matter where in the program a subroutine is placed?

    *Answer:* No, but it is important that the routine not be executed except by a GOSUB statement.

3.  What statements may be used in a subroutine?

    *Answer:* Any BASIC statement may be used in a subroutine.

4.  Can a subroutine call another subroutine?

    *Answer:* Yes.

5.  Can a subroutine call itself?

    *Answer:* Yes in some versions of BASIC, but this programming technique (called *recursion*) is outside the scope of this text.

6.  Can a subroutine return to another GOSUB statement?

    *Answer:* Yes.

# 9-4   Programming Examples

### 9-4-1   An Investment Decision

Mr. X must decide whether to buy a house now at a relatively high interest rate or wait 1 year and buy at what is anticipated to be a lower interest rate. He is looking at a $30,000 house that he can purchase with 10 percent down and a 30-year mortgage at 8.5 percent. The current rate of inflation for housing is 10 percent per year; thus in 1 year the house is expected to be worth $33,000. However, the interest rate may decline to 7.5 percent in the next year. Should Mr. X buy the house now or wait? The program in Figure 9-3 could be used to help make the decision. Note the use of a subroutine to calculate the total amount of interest due on each loan, one at 8.5 percent and the other at 7.5 percent. The dummy-arguments are I (interest rate), P1 the mortgage amount. The result is transmitted through the variable T. Another subroutine performs all output functions.

```
10 DATA .085, 30000, .075, 33000
20 READ I,P                           Read $30,000 mortgage at 8.5 percent.
30 REM P1 REPRESENTS AMOUNT OF MORTGAGE
40 LET P1 = P - .1 * P
50 GOSUB 200                          Calculate monthly payment.
60 LET X1 = P + T                     Compute total cost.
70 GOSUB 290                          Print results.
75 PRINT "TOTAL COST IS";X1
90 READ I,P                           Read $33,000 mortgage at 7.5 percent.
100 LET P1 = P - .1 * P
110 GOSUB 200                         Calculate monthly payment.
112 GOSUB 290                         Print results.
114 LET X2 = P + T                    Compute total cost.
115 PRINT "TOTAL COST IS";X2
135 PRINT
150 PRINT "DIFFERENCE IN COST IS"; ABS (X1 - X2)
160 GO TO 999
200 REM CALCULATE AMOUNT OF MONTHLY PAYMENT R
210 LET R = P1 * (I/12/(1 - (1 + I/12)↑(-360)))
220 REM CALCULATE TOTAL INTEREST DUE ON LOAN
230 LET T = R * 360 - P1
240 RETURN
290 PRINT
300 PRINT "INTEREST RATE",I
310 PRINT "COST OF HOUSE",P
320 PRINT "DOWN PAYMENT",.1 * P
330 PRINT "TOTAL INTEREST",T;
350 RETURN
999 END
```

Figure 9-3   Investment decision program.

RUN
INTEREST RATE .085
COST OF HOUSE 30000
DOWN PAYMENT 3000
TOTAL INTEREST 47739.1 TOTAL COST IS 77739.1

INTEREST RATE .075
COST OF HOUSE 33000
DOWN PAYMENT 3300
TOTAL INTEREST 45059.5 TOTAL COST IS 78059.5

DIFFERENCE IN COST IS 320.328

**Figure 9-3**    Investment decision program. (continued)

## 9-4-2    A Sort Example

Mr. X has calculated the final grades for two Management Science classes. He wishes to sort the grades for each class into ascending sequence and also to produce one list with the grades for the two classes merged and sorted into ascending sequence. Since the code for sorting is fairly long and the program needs the sorting procedure performed several times, utilization of a subroutine for sorting is an efficient way to construct the program. Also, since the output of an array is performed several times, the code to produce the output can also be placed in a subroutine. A BASIC program using a subroutine to perform the sorting and a subroutine to perform output is shown in Figure 9-4.

```
001 DIM G1(50),G2(50),T(100)
002 REM INPUT GRADES FOR CLASS 1
003 REM N1 REPRESENTS THE NUMBER OF GRADES FOR CLASS 1
004 READ N1
005 FOR I = 1 TO N1
006    READ G1(I)                    Read first set of grades.
007 NEXT I
010 LET N = N1                       N represents the number of grades
011 FOR I = 1 TO N1                    to be sorted.
012    LET T(I) = G1(I)              T stores the grades to be sorted.
013 NEXT I
020 REM CALL SUBROUTINE FOR SORT
021 GOSUB 300                        Both N and T are used by the
022 PRINT "CLASS 1 GRADES"            subroutines.
023 REM CALL OUTPUT SUBROUTINE
024 GOSUB 400
030 REM INPUT GRADES FOR CLASS 2
031 REM N2 REPRESENTS NUMBER OF GRADES IN CLASS 2
```

**Figure 9-4**    Sorting with subroutines.

```
032 READ N2
033 FOR I = 1 TO N2
034     READ G2(I)                          Read second set of grades.
035 NEXT I
040 LET N = N2
041 FOR I = 1 TO N2
042     LET T(I) = G2(I)
043 NEXT I
050 GOSUB 300                               Go and sort grades for class 2.
060 PRINT "CLASS 2 GRADES"                  Print sorted grades.
070 GOSUB 400

081 FOR I = 1 TO N1
082     LET T(I) = G1(I)
083 NEXT I
084 LET N = N1 + N2                         Merge the two arrays.
085 FOR I = N1 + 1 TO N
087     LET T(I) = G2(I - N1)
088 NEXT I
091 GOSUB 300                               Go and sort the merged list.
100 PRINT "ALL GRADES"
111 GOSUB 400                               Go and print the sorted merged
120 GO TO 999                               list.
```

```
300 REM THE FOLLOWING SUBROUTINE SORTS N ELEMENTS
301 REM OF ARRAY T INTO ASCENDING SEQUENCE
310 FOR I = 1 TO N - 1
311     FOR J = 1 TO N - I
312         IF T(J) <= T(J + 1) THEN 316
313         LET Q = T(J)
314         LET T(J) = T(J+1)
315         LET T(J + 1) = Q
316     NEXT J
317 NEXT I
318 RETURN
```

```
400 REM THE FOLLOWING SUBROUTINE OUTPUTS
401 REM N ELEMENTS OF ARRAY T
402 FOR I = 1 TO N
403     PRINT T(I);
404 NEXT I
405 PRINT
406 RETURN
```

```
501 DATA 6,46,92,70,80,48,82              The first number in each DATA statement
602 DATA 7,20,48,100,26,40,78,82         specifies the number of grades.
999 END
```

**Figure 9-4**    Sorting with subroutines. (continued)

RUN
CLASS 1 GRADES
46 48 70 80 82 92
CLASS 2 GRADES
20 26 40 48 78 82 100
ALL GRADES
20 26 40 46 48 48 70 78 80 82 82 92 100

**Figure 9-4**     Sorting with subroutines. (continued)

## 9-4-3   On-Line Inquiry System

The Furniture Company has stock in three different warehouses. The controller-dispatcher needs to know at any given time the number of particular furniture items at any of the three warehouses; he may also need to know the number of each particular item at a warehouse. Initially the stock of items in all warehouses is as follows:

|         | WAREHOUSE 1 | WAREHOUSE 2 | WAREHOUSE 3 |
|---------|-------------|-------------|-------------|
| Desks   | 123         | 44          | 76          |
| Chairs  | 789         | 234         | 12          |
| Beds    | 67          | 456         | 90          |

He has at his fingertips a terminal where he can inquire about a particular item. For example, when he types "BEDS" the system furnishes him with the number of beds at the three warehouses. He can also type a warehouse number to list all items at that warehouse. A program is to be written to allow the following communications between the dispatcher and the data base.

ENTER REQUEST
?BEDS

|           | WAREHOUSE1 | WAREHOUSE2 | WAREHOUSE3 |           |
|-----------|------------|------------|------------|-----------|
| BEDS      | 67         | 456        | 90         | TOTAL 613 |

ENTER REQUEST
?WAREHOUSE3

|            | DESKS | CHAIRS | BEDS |           |
|------------|-------|--------|------|-----------|
| WAREHOUSE3 | 76    | 12     | 90   | TOTAL 178 |

ENTER REQUEST
?CHAIRS

|        | WAREHOUSE1 | WAREHOUSE2 | WAREHOUSE3 |            |
|--------|------------|------------|------------|------------|
| CHAIRS | 789        | 234        | 12         | TOTAL 1035 |

ENTER REQUEST
?

The program to solve such a problem is shown in Figure 9-5.

```
10 DIM F$(3),G$(3),A$(3),P(3),V(3,3)
15 FOR I= 1 TO 3              Initialize the inventory at the three warehouses
20    FOR J=1 TO 3              in array V.
25       READ V(I,J)          Array F$ contains the words DESKS,CHAIRS,BEDS.
30    NEXT J                  Array G$ contains the words WAREHOUSE 1,
35 NEXT I                       WAREHOUSE 2, etc.
40 FOR I=1 TO 3              Array A$ is a dummy array used by subroutine to
45    READ F$(I),G$(I)         print either the items or the warehouses.
50 NEXT I                    Array P is a dummy array used by subroutine to
55 PRINT                       manipulate either row or column elements of V.
60 PRINT "ENTER REQUEST"
65 INPUT R$                  Enter warehouse or furniture request.
70 GOSUB 165                 Determine numerical index corresponding to the request.
75 IF F=0 GO TO 120          Go to 120 for warehouse information.
80 FOR I=1 TO 3              Report on the stock at each warehouse.
85    LET A$(I)=G$(I)        Initialize A$ with the words WAREHOUSE 1, . . . ,
90    LET P(I)=V(K,I)          WAREHOUSE 3.
95 NEXT I                    Initialize P with the elements of row K of V.
100 GOSUB 220               Subroutine to print headings and data.
105 GOSUB 275               Subroutine to add all elements of a row or column.
110 GOSUB 305               Subroutine to print total of a row or column sum.
115 GO TO 55                Wait for another request.
120 FOR I=1 TO 3            Report on the inventory of furniture at warehouses.
125    LET A$(I)=F$(I)      Initialize A$ with the words DESKS,CHAIRS,BEDS.
130    LET P(I)=V(I,K)      Set P to the elements of column K of V.
135 NEXT I
140 GOSUB 275               Compute total elements in column K.
145 GOSUB 220               Print headings and data.
150 GOSUB 305               Print total.
155 GO TO 55                Wait for another request.
```

```
165 FOR I=1 TO 3                        GOSUB 165
170    IF F$(I)=R$ GO TO 195
175    IF G$(I)=R$ GO TO 185   GOSUB 165 returns in K the row or column index of
180 NEXT I                       V associated with the request entered. For example,
185 LET F=0                      if BEDS is entered, K = 3; if WAREHOUSE 2 is
190 GO TO 200                    entered, K = 2.
195 LET F=1                    F is a flag set to 0 if warehouse information is
200 LET K=I                      requested and set to 0 if furniture item is requested.
210 RETURN
```

```
220 PRINT TAB(12);                      GOSUB 220
225 FOR I= 1 TO 3
230    PRINT A$(I).           GOSUB 220 prints the headings and underneath the
235 NEXT I                      headings prints the number of a specific furniture
240 PRINT                       item at all 3 warehouses or the inventory of all
245 PRINT R$,                   furniture items at a particular warehouse.
250 FOR I= 1 TO 3
255    PRINT P(I),
260 NEXT I
265 RETURN
```

**Figure 9-5**    On-line inquiry system.

```
275 LET S=0                           GOSUB 275
280 FOR J= 1 TO 3
285     LET S=S+P(J)        GOSUB 275 computes a total of furniture items
290 NEXT J                      across rows or columns.
295 RETURN
```

```
305 PRINT "TOTAL";S                   GOSUB 305
310 RETURN                  GOSUB 305 prints the total of furniture items.
```
315 DATA 123,44,76,789,234,12,67,456,90
320 DATA "DESKS","WAREHOUSE1","CHAIRS","WAREHOUSE2"
323 DATA "BEDS", "WAREHOUSE 3"
325 END

**Figure 9-5**    On-line inquiry system. (continued)

# 9-5    Functions

## 9-5-1    Definition

The reader is probably familiar with many mathematical functions, such as square root, the exponential, and the trigonometric functions. These functions, as well as others, are available in BASIC through the use of libraries that are provided by the computer system. BASIC also allows the programmer to define and code his or her own functions through the DEF statement. In BASIC, a function reference may be included as a part of any arithmetic expression. The general form for referencing a function is

*function-name (argument-expression)*

All BASIC functions require an *argument-expression* enclosed in parentheses after the function-name. The *argument-expression* may take the form of a constant, a variable, another function reference, or an expression containing constants, variables, arithmetic operations, and function references. The expression is evaluated to a single value, which is then passed to the function as an argument. Logically, we may think of the function as being evaluated at the point of invocation. Internally, a function consists of a series of statements that calculate the value of the function based on the value of the argument. A function (like a subroutine) returns control to the point at which it is called.

## 9-5-2    Mathematical Functions

Common mathematical functions supplied with BASIC are shown in Figure 9-6. Note that there are restrictions on the range of values acceptable as arguments for some functions. For example, the square root (SQR) and natural logarithm (LOG) functions require arguments greater than zero. If an invalid argument is detected by a function, an error message will be printed.

| FUNCTION | ARGUMENT[1] | VALUE |
|----------|-------------|-------|
| SIN($x$) | Must be expressed in radians | The sine of $x$ |
| COS($x$) | Must be expressed in radians | The cosine of $x$ |
| TAN($x$) | Must be expressed in radians | The tangent of $x$ |
| ATN($x$) | Must be expressed in radians | Arctangent of $x$ ($-\pi/2 \leqslant \text{ATN}(x) \leqslant \pi/2$) |
| EXP($x$) | A real number | The value of $e^x$ ($e = 2.718\ldots$) |
| LOG($x$) | A positive real number | The natural logarithm of $x$ |
| ABS($x$) | A real number | The absolute value of $x$ ($\lvert x \rvert = x$ if $x \geqslant 0$, $\lvert x \rvert = -x$ if $x < 0$) |
| SQR($x$) | A positive real number | The square root of $x$ |

[1]Argument may be any arithmetic expression containing one or more functions.

Figure 9-6    BASIC-supplied mathematical functions.

## 9-5-3   Other BASIC-Supplied Functions

Certain other functions shown in Figure 9-7 are also included in BASIC.

| FUNCTION | ARGUMENT | VALUE |
|----------|----------|-------|
| INT(X) | A real number | Greatest integer less than or equal to X |
| SGN(X) | A real number | $-1$ if $x < 0$<br>$0$ if $x = 0$<br>$1$ if $x > 0$ |
| RND(X) | May or may not be required | A random number between 0 and 1 $0 < \text{RND}(X) < 1$ |

Figure 9-7    Miscellaneous BASIC-supplied functions.

Example 1

In the case of the INT function, note that by adding .5 to the argument we are able to round to the nearest integer (see Figure 9-8).

The INT function can be very useful to truncate or round off numbers to a specified number of fractional digits (decimal positions). The reader should realize that numerical computations are carried out internally to at least six digits on most computer systems, yet often no more than two or three decimal places (fractional digits) are needed for the computed

```
1 PRINT
2 PRINT" X","INT(X)","INT(X + .5)","SGN(X)"
10 INPUT X
20 PRINT, INT(X),INT(X + .5),SGN(X)
30 GO TO 10
40 END
RUN
```

| X | INT(X) | INT(X + .5) | SGN(X) |
|---|---|---|---|
| ? 3 | 3 | 3 | 1 |
| ? 3.4 | 3 | 3 | 1 |
| ? 3.5 | 3 | 4 | 1 |
| ? 3.99 | 3 | 4 | 1 |
| ? 0 | 0 | 0 | 0 |
| ? − 3 | − 3 | − 3 | − 1 |
| ? − 3.4 | − 4 | − 3 | − 1 |
| ? − 3.5 | − 4 | − 3 | − 1 |
| ? − 3.99 | − 4 | − 4 | − 1 |

**Figure 9-8**    Sample values of INT and SGN.

result. For example, suppose that internally $X = 32.4562$ and we wished to truncate the last two digits (retain two fractional digits). We could use the following method:

1.  Multiply X by 100 to obtain 3245.62.        (LET X = 100 * X)

2.  Take the integer part to obtain 3245.00.      (LET X = INT(X))

3.  Divide by 100 to obtain 32.45.                (LET X = X/100)

To be even more precise, we could round off the second fractional digit by adding .005 to X to get

$$\begin{array}{r} 32.4562 \\ \underline{.005} \\ 32.4612 \end{array}$$

We then follow the same steps described in the preceding list. The entire round-off procedure can be carried out in one step, as follows:

$$10 \ \ \text{LET X} = \text{INT}((X + .005) * 100)/100$$

**Example 2**

The random number function RND usually requires an argument but may or may not evaluate its argument. The function RND returns a random number in the range 0 to 1. The output from

RND is uniformly distributed in the interval 0 to 1; any value in that range is equally likely to be produced. Sample values for RND are shown in Figure 9-9.

```
10 FOR I = 1 TO 10
20 PRINT RND (0)
30 NEXT I
40 END

RUN

.263884
.708429
.197174
.79064
2.5235E - 3
.674609
.851822
.657218
.166961
.285339
```

**Figure 9-9**    Sample values of RND.

Strictly speaking, the RND function produces not random numbers but pseudo random numbers. The output of the RND function is deterministic in the sense that the same program will always generate the same series of values.

To generate real or integer random numbers between 1 and 10, the following statements could be used:

LET X = RND(1) * 10          Real numbers between 0 and 10.          $(0 < X < 10)$
LET I = INT(RND(1) * 10 + 1)          Integers between 1 and 10.          $(1 \leqslant 1 \leqslant 10)$

In general, to generate real or integer random numbers between L (low) and H (high), the following formulas can be used:

LET X = RND(1) * (H - L) + L          Real numbers between L and H.
LET I = INT(RND(1) * (H - L + 1) + L)          Integers between L and H.

The function RND may differ from one system to another. In some systems, RND does not require an argument; that is, the statement Y = RND will generate different random values for Y each time the statement is encountered. However, this will result in generating the same string of random numbers each time the program is reexecuted. To generate different strings of random numbers for the same program, some systems permit the use of the RANDOM or RANDOMIZE statement, which tells BASIC to start at a random point in the list of random numbers. The RANDOMIZE statement would then be used once in the program before generating any random numbers. In this way, the outcome of the program would not be the same every time the program is run.

The RND function can be used conveniently to play games and to simulate events. Figure 9-10 illustrates a drill and practice multiplication program. The program drills a student on his multiplication tables (0 through 12). The learner is allowed three tries, after which the program asks a different question.

```
1 LET X = 0
10 LET M1 = INT(RND(0) * 13)
20 LET M2 = INT(RND(0) * 13)
30 PRINT M1;"*";M2;"=";
40 INPUT P
50 IF M1 * M2 = P THEN 140
60 LET X = X + 1
70 IF X = 3 THEN 100
80 PRINT "INCORRECT TRY AGAIN"
90 GO TO 30
100 PRINT "INCORRECT ANSWER";M1;"*";M2;"=";M1 * M2;
110 PRINT "LETS TRY ANOTHER PROBLEM"
120 GO TO 1
140 PRINT "CORRECT"
150 GO TO 1
999 END

RUN

11 * 7=?77 CORRECT
4 * 5=?34 INCORRECT TRY AGAIN
4 * 5=?20 CORRECT
10 * 4=?68 INCORRECT TRY AGAIN
10 * 4=?12 INCORRECT TRY AGAIN
10 * 4=?79 INCORRECT ANSWER 10 * 4 = 40 LETS TRY ANOTHER PROBLEM
10 * 3=?30 CORRECT
5 * 2=?10 CORRECT
9 * 4=?
STOP @ 40
```

Select two random numbers between 0 and 13.

Enter answer.

If the response is incorrect the third time around, BASIC types the correct answer.

This program is terminated by pressing the ESCape key.

**Figure 9-10**   Drill program.

## 9-5-4   User-Defined Functions

The DEF (*def*inition) statement is used to define a programmer-written function. It allows the user to define a function just once in a program and to make use of that same function with different arguments anywhere in the program whenever needed. The DEF statement is non-executable and hence (like the DATA statement) may be placed anywhere in the program. However, it should be placed before the first statement which calls it. The general form of the DEF statement is

*statement-number* DEF *name (dummy-argument) = expression*

where  DEF is a BASIC key word

*name* is the function name

*dummy-argument* is a nonsubscripted variable that will assume the value of the actual argument when the function is referenced (only one argument may be used)

*expression* is any arithmetic expression

The *name* that can be given to a programmer-defined function is restricted to FNA, FNB, . . . , FNZ. The *dummy-argument* should always appear in the expression (see example 1). Note that the *dummy-argument* in the DEF statement takes on no real value; its only purpose is to illustrate the way in which it is used to produce a functional value. Hence, it is possible to have a *dummy-argument* with the same name as another variable in the program (see example 2) or, for that matter, to have all user functions defined with the same dummy-argument name (see example 5).

In addition to the *dummy-argument*, the *expression* may contain other variables used in the program (see example 3) or function names other than the one being defined (see example 5). Recursive definitions of functions are not permissible as in example 4.

Functions may also be nested; most BASIC systems will allow a depth of four (see example 6).

When referencing user-defined functions, the *argument* can consist of subscripted variables or expressions (see example 7).

Function definitions must be limited to one line of code and one argument only. If more than one argument or if longer definitions are necessary, subroutines must be used.

**Examples**

**1.** 10 DEF FNB(X) = (X + 2)/(X − 2) + X↑2      $F(x) = \dfrac{x+2}{x-2} + x^2$
20 LET A = 4
30 PRINT FNB(A)                    Result printed would be 19.

**2.** 10 LET A = 3          The value of A is not changed by its use as a
20 DEF FNA(A) = A↑2          dummy-argument.
The value printed for A is still 3, as defined by
30 PRINT A          statement 10.

**3.** 10 LET A = 2
20 LET B = 3
30 LET C = 4
40 DEF FNC(X) = A * X↑2 + B * X + C      $F(x) = ax^2 + bx + c$
50 LET Z = FNC(2)      $Z = 2 \cdot 4 + 3 \cdot 2 + 4 = 18$

**4.** 5 DEF FNA(X) = FNA(X) + C     Invalid definition. A function cannot be used to define itself.

**5.** 10 DEF FNS(X) = (3.14 * X)/180   FNS(X) converts $x$ degrees into radians.

20 DEF FNR(X) = SIN(FNS(X))    FNR(X) computes sin $(x)$ with $x$ in degrees.
FNR(90) = sin(FNS(90)) = sin $(\pi/2)$ = 1

30 LET Y = 90                   Y = 90
40 PRINT Y,FNS(Y),FNR(Y)        FNS(90) = $\pi/2$
FNR(90) = sin $(\pi/2)$ = 1

**6.** 10 DEF FNA(X) = ABS(X)        $F_1(x) = |x|$
20 DEF FNB(Y) = (FNA(Y))↑2      $F_2(y) = |y|^2$

30 DEF FNC(Z) = LOG(FNB(Z))/10   $F_3(z) = \dfrac{\log z^2}{10}$

**7.** 10 DEF FNA(Z) = (Z + 2)/(Z − 2)   $F(z) = \dfrac{z+2}{z-2}$

15 LET B(3) = 4
20 LET Z = 2
30 LET X = FNA(B(3) + Z)        $x = \dfrac{B(3)+z+2}{B(3)+z-2} = \dfrac{8}{4} = 2$

To illustrate the simplicity and convenience of the DEF statement, we shall consider the following two problems:

**Problem 1: Determining Easter Sunday Date**

The date for any Easter Sunday can be computed as follows. Let X be the year for which it is desired to compute Easter Sunday.

Let A be the remainder of the division of X by 19.
Let B be the remainder of the division of X by 4.
Let C be the remainder of the division of X by 7.
Let D be the remainder of the division of (19A + 24) by 30.
Let E be the remainder of the division of (2B + 4C + 6D + 5) by 7.

The date for Easter Sunday is then March (22 + D + E). Note that this can give a date in April. To compute the remainder R of the division of I by J use the BASIC statement LET R = I − J * INT(I/J). Write a program to assign a year for the variable X and compute the date for Easter Sunday for that year using the formula 22 + D + E.

Without user-defined functions, this problem would be very tedious to code. Note the simplicity of the code in Figure 9-11.

```
10 DEF FNE(X) = Y - X * INT (Y/X)     Define the remainder function.
20 INPUT Y                            Y is the year.
30 LET A = FNE(19)
40 LET B = FNE(4)
50 LET C = FNE(7)
60 LET Y = 19 * A + 24                Reset the value of Y to compute D.
70 LET D = FNE(30)
80 LET Y = 2 * B + 4 * C + 6 * D + 5  Reset value of Y to compute E.
90 LET E = FNE(7)
100 LET R = 22 + D + E
110 IF R<= 31 THEN 140                Is Easter in March or April?
120 PRINT "EASTER SUNDAY IS APRIL"; R - 31
130 GO TO 20
140 PRINT "EASTER SUNDAY IS MARCH";R
150 GO TO 20
160 END
RUN
? 1979 EASTER SUNDAY IS APRIL 15
? 1980 EASTER SUNDAY IS APRIL 6
? 2000 EASTER SUNDAY IS APRIL 23
? 2050 EASTER SUNDAY IS APRIL 10
? 10000 EASTER SUNDAY IS APRIL 12
? 1 EASTER SUNDAY IS APRIL 9
? 1978 EASTER SUNDAY IS MARCH 26
?
```

**Figure 9-11**    Easter Sunday date.

### Problem 2: Plotting a Graph

The TAB function lends itself conveniently to graph plotting, since the expression in the TAB function allows the programmer to position a character in a variable position on the line (see Figure 9-12). Note how a horizontal line of stars (*) is obtained in Figure 9-13. This can be

```
0010 FOR I = 1 TO 5
0015 PRINT TAB(I);"*"
0020 NEXT I

RUN

 *
  *
   *
    *
     *
```

```
0010 FOR I = 1 TO 20
0015 PRINT TAB (I);"*";
0020 NEXT I

RUN
*******************
```

**Figure 9-12**    Use of TAB function.        **Figure 9-13**    Printing a line of characters.

useful to print a line of special characters. Note that TAB(0) identifies the first print position, TAB(10) the 11th, etc.

More complicated graphs can be plotted. For example, consider the following break-even analysis problem. Systems analysts at the XYZ Company computed the revenue function associated with the manufacture and marketing of a new company product. A cost function was also projected for that product. Both functions are given as follows:

Revenue function $\qquad y = 15xe^{-x/3}$

Cost function $\qquad y = \dfrac{x^3}{16} - \dfrac{x^2}{2} + \dfrac{7x}{4} + 4$

Determine graphically the break-even point(s). A solution to the problem is shown in Figure 9-14. Note that

$$y = \frac{x^3}{16} - \frac{x^2}{2} + \frac{7x}{4} + 4 = \frac{x^3 - 8x^2 + 28x + 64}{16}$$

The numerator is then factored to yield $((x - 8)x + 28)x + 64$ as in statement 15 in Figure 9-14. The latter expression of the cost function is more efficient in terms of computations, since it contains only two multiplications and one division, as opposed to four and three, respectively, in the original cost function.

```
 5 REM BREAK EVEN ANALYSIS
10 PRINT "REVENUE"; TAB (9); "COST"
15 DEF FNA(X) = INT ((((X – 8) * X + 28) * X + 64)/16)      Define cost function.
20 DEF FNB(Z) = INT (15 * Z * EXP (–Z/3))                   Define revenue function.
25 FOR X = 0 TO 12
30      LET C = FNA(X)
35      LET R = FNB(X)
36      PRINT R; TAB (9);C;
40      LET K = 22 + R + .5                 If the cost C is less than the revenue R,
45      LET L = 22 + C + .5                 plot first the cost and then the revenue;
50      IF C < R GO TO 65                    otherwise, plot the revenue first and
55      PRINT TAB (K);"R"; TAB (L);"C"       then the cost. In any event, both points
60      GO TO 70                             must be on same line.
65      PRINT TAB (L);"C"; TAB (K);"R"
70 NEXT X
99 END
RUN
```

**Figure 9-14**    Break-even analysis.

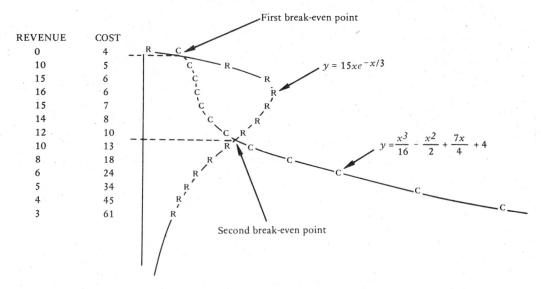

| REVENUE | COST |
|---------|------|
| 0 | 4 |
| 10 | 5 |
| 15 | 6 |
| 16 | 6 |
| 15 | 7 |
| 14 | 8 |
| 12 | 10 |
| 10 | 13 |
| 8 | 18 |
| 6 | 24 |
| 5 | 34 |
| 4 | 45 |
| 3 | 61 |

First break-even point

$y = 15xe^{-x/3}$

$y = \dfrac{x^3}{16} - \dfrac{x^2}{2} + \dfrac{7x}{4} + 4$

Second break-even point

**Figure 9-14**    Break-even analysis. (continued)

Another technique for plotting a graph is to use an array to print a horizontal line one at a time. The line array is initially set to blanks. For a given value of X the corresponding value of the function Y is computed and a graphic symbol such as "*" is inserted at position Y in the line array. The array (line) is then printed, and the same process is repeated for the different values of X. (Care must be exercised if Y is negative. In this case, an appropriate constant should be added to all values of Y; this causes the graph to be shifted to the right on the output line, but the angles [shape] of the graph are preserved. Also, if the changes in the magnitude of Y are fractional, Y should be scaled [multiplied by a constant].)

In the break-even analysis problem, for example, we initialize the array N$ to blanks, compute a value for R and C and insert the graphic symbols "R" and "C" in position R and C of the array N$, and print the array N$ (line). The process is repeated as X varies from 0 to 12. The program code displayed below yields a graph identical to the one shown in Figure 9-14.

```
10 DIM N$(50)
15 PRINT "REVENUE";TAB(9);"COST"
20 FOR X=0 TO 12
25     LET C=INT(((((X-8)*X+28)*X+64)/16)
30     LET R=INT(15*X*EXP(-X/3))
35     FOR J=0 TO 50
40         LET N$(J)=" "              Blank out line.
45     NEXT J
50     LET N$(C)="C"                  Insert graphic symbols.
55     LET N$(R)="R"
60     PRINT TAB(2);R;TAB(9);C;TAB(16)
65     FOR J=0 TO 50
70         PRINT N$(J);               Print the line.
75     NEXT J
80     PRINT
85 NEXT X
90 END
```

# 9-6   Assignments

## 9-6-1   Self Test

**True or False**

1.   Functions make use of dummy-arguments; subroutines do not.

2.   Functions and subroutines can help avoid duplication of programming effort.

3.   The RETURN statement is used in functions but not in subroutines.

4.   Names for subroutines follow the same convention as other variable names.

5.   ABC is a valid programmer-defined function name.

6.   Subroutines may have only one entry point.

7.   The RETURN statement causes control to return to a statement in the program which follows a GOSUB statement.

8.   If a program enters a subroutine other than by a GOSUB statement, the results are unpredictable.

9.   Modularization within a program is to be avoided, since it has an adverse effect on program readability.

10.   Certain BASIC statements cannot be used in a subroutine.

## 9-6-2   Exercises and Problems

1.   Each DATA statement consists of an employee name, a number of hours worked and a rate of pay. Write a main program to read the DATA statements and write a subroutine to compute each employee's pay. Hours over 40 are paid at time and a half the regular rate. The printout should list the employee name, number of hours, rate of pay and pay.

2.   A salesman is assigned a commission on the following basis:

| SALE | COMMISSION |
|------|------------|
| $ 00–$ 500 | 1% |
| 500– 5000 | 5% |
| over   5000 | 8% |

Write a main program to read sales and use a subroutine to compute the commission.

3.   A class consists of five students. There are five DATA statements. Each DATA statement contains a student's name and 10 test scores. The student is allowed to drop his lowest score to figure his average. Use a subroutine to find the sum of his scores and another subroutine to find his minimum score. Print the student's name and his average.

4.  a.  Write a subroutine to accept a number between 1 and 10 and return the correspond-
        ing word. For example, 3 would yield THREE.

    b.  Accept a number between 20 and 99 and return the corresponding words. For
        example, 25 would yield TWENTY FIVE.

5.  The coordinates of three ships are accepted as input. Write a program to print the
    distances between each ship. If $x_1$ and $y_1$, and $x_2$ and $y_2$ are the coordinates of any two
    ships, the formula to compute the distance separating them is

$$d = \sqrt{|x_1 - x_2|^2 + |y_1 - y_2|^2}$$

    where the symbol $|x_1 - x_2|$ means the absolute value. Use GOSUB to compute $d$.

6.  You are the personnel director of a large company, and for every person you place in a
    job you enter the following two entries on a DATA statement:

    Sex code (2 = male, 1 = female)

    First year's starting salary

    Write a program using different subroutines to determine each of the following:

    a.  Total number of persons placed in a job.

    b.  Total amount of salaries paid the first year.

    c.  Average salary per person.

    d.  Maximum salary paid to males.

    e.  Average salary paid to females.

7.  On the first DATA statement, we have entered the answers (1, 2, 3, 4) to a multiple
    choice test of 10 questions. On the second DATA statement, we have entered the number
    of students taking the test. Each following DATA statements consists of a student's name
    and 10 answers to the 10 questions. Write a main program to determine the percentage of
    correct answers for each student and write another subroutine to determine the grade
    (90–100 = A, 80–89 = B, 60–79 = C, below 60 = D). The output should be performed by
    a subroutine to print the student name, the letter grade, and percentage. Given the
    following input, the output should be as follows:

Correct answers to the 10 questions

```
DATA 1,1,2,3,1,4,2,4,3,3
DATA 3      ← number of students
DATA "JONES", 1, 1, 2, 3, 1, 4, 2, 4, 3, 3
DATA "SATO", 1, 1, 2, 3, 1, 1, 1, 3, 2, 4
DATA "LAKY", 4, 1, 2, 3, 1, 4, 2, 4, 3, 2
```

| NAME  | GRADE | PERCENTAGE |
|-------|-------|------------|
| JONES | A     | 100        |
| SATO  | D     | 50         |
| LAKY  | B     | 80         |

8.  Write a program to generalize the on-line inquiry system of Section 9-4-3 to allow the manager to keep track of supply and exit shipments. He should be able to type in commands similar to the following to mean:

| | |
|---|---|
| Chairs, −36, 1 | Ship out 36 chairs from warehouse 1. |
| Beds, 57, 2 | Supply warehouse 2 with an additional 57 beds. |

The inventory should be updated automatically and a warning message printed whenever any furniture stock item falls below 20.

9.  The Stayfirm Company accounting system keeps sales records for each salesman on a day-to-day basis. This data is transcribed on DATA statements as follows:

| | SALESMAN NAME | | DATE OF SALE | | AMOUNT OF SALE |
|---|---|---|---|---|---|
| DATA | "SMITH JOHN" | , | 011576 | , | 100.00 |
| DATA | "SMITH JOHN' | , | 011376 | , | 50.00 |
| DATA | "GRANT CARY" | , | 012776 | , | 10.00 |
| DATA | "SMITH JOHN" | , | 012776 | , | 150.00 |
| DATA | "GRANT CARY" | , | 012676 | , | 190.00 |
| DATA | "HOLBERT LOU" | , | 011376 | , | 100.00 |

Note that the transactions are not arranged alphabetically by salesman name. Also note that the dates are not sorted in ascending order. (Assume the dates cover only a 30-day period starting with the first day of the month to the thirtieth day of that month.)

  Write a program using a sort subroutine to produce a monthly sales report summarizing total sales and total sales for each salesman. Entries in the report must be listed by salesman name in alphabetical order, and these in turn must be sorted by date of sales. For example, given the preceding data the output should be as follows:

| SALESMAN | DATE OF SALE | SALE AMOUNT | TOTAL AMOUNT |
|---|---|---|---|
| GRANT CARY | 012676 | 190.00 | |
| GRANT CARY | 012776 | 10.00 | |
| | | | 200.00 |
| HOLBERT LOU | 011376 | 100.00 | |
| | | | 100.00 |
| SMITH JOHN | 011376 | 50.00 | |
| SMITH JOHN | 011576 | 100.00 | |
| SMITH JOHN | 012776 | 150.00 | |
| | | | 300.00 |
| | TOTAL SALES | | 600.00 |

10. The following table illustrates the dimensions of U.S. companies (1977 in thousands of dollars):

| COMPANY | ASSETS | SALES | MARKET VALUE | NET PROFIT |
|---|---|---|---|---|
| Citicorp | 64,281,504 | 4,843,838 | 4,085,923 | 401,352 |
| Celanese | 1,910,000 | 2,123,000 | 685,511 | 69,000 |
| Bendix | 1,653,600 | 2,965,500 | 941,945 | 104,700 |
| American Motors | 991,586 | 2,315,470 | 116,641 | −46,340 |
| Borden | 1,808,479 | 3,381,075 | 1,045,840 | 112,807 |

Write a program to read the company names in array N$ and the other associated data in a two-dimensional array A(4,5). Entries should be read by rows. For example, N$(3) and A(3,1), A(3,2), A(3,3), A(3,4) describe the financial characteristics of the Bendix Corporation. The program should sort and print the names of the various companies by ascending asset value, then by sales, then by market value, and then by net profit. Additionally, names of companies with highest assets, sales, market value, and net profit should be listed. Use subroutines for sorting and for determining highest values.

11. Dr. X. has unusual grading practices. He assigns random grades (1–100) to his class of N students (where N is accepted from input). Each student gets three random test scores for three tests. Write a program to compute the average grade of each student and the average of the entire class. The results should be tabulated in page form as follows:

PAGE 1

| STUDENT NUMBER | SCORE 1 | SCORE 2 | SCORE 3 | AVERAGE |
|---|---|---|---|---|
| 1 | 20 | 30 | 40 | 30 |
| 2 | 20 | 80 | 20 | 40 |
| . | . | . | . | . |
| . | . | . | . | . |
| . | . | . | . | . |
| 15 | 1 | 0 | 98 | 33 |

2 blank lines
1 dotted line      ------------------------------------------------------------------------

2 blank lines                                                              PAGE 2

| STUDENT NUMBER | SCORE 1 | SCORE 2 | SCORE 3 | AVERAGE |
|---|---|---|---|---|
| 16 | 50 | 60 | 70 | 60 |
| 17 | . | . | . | . |
| . | . | . | . | . |
| . | . | . | . | . |
| . | | | | |
| 30 | | | | |

1 blank line (before the second table header)

2 blank lines
1 dotted line      ------------------------------------------------------------------------

2 blank lines                                                              PAGE 3

| STUDENT NUMBER | SCORE 1 | SCORE 2 | SCORE 3 | AVERAGE |
|---|---|---|---|---|
| . | . | . | . | . |
| . | . | . | . | . |
| . | . | . | . | . |

A subroutine should be used to simulate automatic ejection to the top of a new page to provide for a page number, headings, and a demarcation line to be used by Dr. X. to cut each page and bind them in booklet form. The average class grade should be printed all by itself on a new numbered page. Would you expect the class average grade to be close to 50?

12. Modify the program of Figure 9-10 to give special aid to a student who misses a multiplication problem. For example, the program might reverse the order of the multiplicands and write the problem again. If the answer is still incorrect, the program might start with multiplication problems in which multiplicands range from 1 * M2 to M1 * M2 (handle M1 = 0 as a special case). If an incorrect answer is given at any point in this series, the program might rephrase the problem as a repeated addition. Print laudatory comments when the response is correct.

13. Modify the problem of Figure 9-10 to allow the student to enter his name initially and to terminate execution of the program after any correct answer. On termination, the program should print a personalized "homework" assignment consisting of all the problems to which an incorrect answer was given during that session.

14. There are five sections of a financial management course FI 550. For each of these sections, we have entered on separate DATA statements the section number and the number of students who enrolled in that section during pre-registration (two entries per DATA statement). Following these five DATA statements, we have other DATA statements for students wishing to add FI 550. These student DATA statements contain two entries: a name and the section number the student wants to add. The maximum number of students in sections 1 through 5 is 13, 15, 17, 9, 8 respectively (enter in an array). Write a program using subroutines to process these student DATA statements. If a request for a section cannot be filled, print out the student name and the section requested. At the conclusion of the program, print out each section number and the updated enrollment. For example, given the following input, the output should be as follows:

*Input*

|  | |
|---|---|
| | DATA 100, 13 |
| | DATA 110, 14 |
| Pre-registration | DATA 105, 10 |
| | DATA 121, 9 |
| | DATA 107, 3 |
| | |
| | DATA "JOE", 100 |
| Late | DATA "SUE", 110 |
| registration | DATA "CLO", 107 |
| | DATA "FLO", 100 |
| | DATA "MIK", 110 |

*Output*

```
          SECTIONS CLOSED

SECTION 100
     JOE
     FLO

SECTION 110
     MIK


       UPDATED FILE

SECTION        ENROLLMENT
   100             13
   110             15
   105             10
   121              9
   107              6
```

15.  Write a program to enter a number with five fractional digits using four user-defined functions to round the number to 0, 1, 2, and 3 fractional digits. Print the rounded values on one line.

16.  Write user-defined functions to compute the Julian date as described in exercise 1, Section 3-7-2. Also, define a function to convert temperature readings from Fahrenheit to centigrade.

17.  Mr. Mathis has taken out a loan for $18,750 at 16.5 percent. His payments are to be quarterly (every four months). He can manage quarterly payments anywhere between $900 to $1,500 but would prefer to keep them as close to $900 as possible. He would also like to stick to a 10-year repayment schedule. Write a program to determine his minimum quarterly payments. (*Hint:* Vary his quarterly payments from $900 to $1,500 and analyze the term $T$ (duration) of the loan, given by the formula

$$T = -\frac{\log\left(1 - \dfrac{P \cdot i}{N \cdot R}\right)}{\log\left(1 + \dfrac{i}{N}\right)} \cdot \frac{1}{N}$$

where    $T$ = duration of payments in years
$P$ = principal
$i$ = interest rate
$N$ = number payments per year
$R$ = amount of payments

Use the DEF function to compute $T$ as a function of $R$.)

18.  Systems of two equations in two unknowns, such as

$$a_1\, x + b_1\, y = c_1$$

$$a_2\, x + b_2\, y = c_2$$

can be solved by using Cramer's rule:

$$x = \frac{\begin{vmatrix} c_1 & b_1 \\ c_2 & b_2 \end{vmatrix}}{\begin{vmatrix} a_1 & b_1 \\ a_2 & b_2 \end{vmatrix}} \qquad\qquad y = \frac{\begin{vmatrix} a_1 & c_1 \\ a_2 & c_2 \end{vmatrix}}{\begin{vmatrix} a_1 & b_1 \\ a_2 & b_2 \end{vmatrix}}$$

where, in general,    $\begin{vmatrix} a & b \\ c & d \end{vmatrix} = a \cdot d - c \cdot b$

Write a program to enter sets of values for $a_1$, $b_1$, $c_1$, $a_2$, $b_2$, $c_2$ and determine the solution, using GOSUB to calculate each determinant $\left(\begin{vmatrix} a & b \\ c & d \end{vmatrix} \text{ is a determinant}\right)$.

19. The president of the XSTAR Company realizes that the company's present accounting procedures are too slow, too inefficient, and not sufficiently accurate to deal with the increasing annual volume of processing of the company. Plans have been made to replace manual accounting operations with a wholly computerized system. The current total manual operating costs in dollars in terms of annual processing volume is given by $y = x + .5$ (where $y$ is the dollar cost and $x$ the annual processing volume). Projected total computerized cost is given by the formula $y = .75x + 2$. The anticipated annual processing volume will be close to four units.

   Write a program to

   a. Determine graphically whether the president's decision to switch to a computerized system is economically sound (graph both lines).

   b. Determine graphically the break-even point (the annual volume of processing that would justify the president's plan for changing method of operation).

   Realizing that an annual volume of processing of four units is not sufficient to warrant such a change in operations, a compromise is effected. The new operational procedures will involve both manual and computer operations. The cost attached to such a new system is given by $y = .445x + 1.5$.

   Write a program to

   a. Determine graphically whether such a system would be economically beneficial to the company.

   b. Determine graphically the break-even point for the total computerized system versus the computer manual plan.

20. The Toystar Corporation is marketing a new toy. Expected revenues are approximated by the function $y = 3 \sqrt{x}$. Costs associated with the production and the sales of the toy are defined by the function $y = 2 + x^2/4$. Write a program to determine graphically the break-even point for the production of the new toy.

21. Write a program to graph the total profit function of the example in exercise 20. The total profit function is defined as the difference between the cost and revenue functions; that is, $T(x) = |R(x) - C(x)|$, where $R$, $C$, and $T$ are respectively the revenue, the cost, and the total profit functions. In the case of exercise 20, identify on the total profit graph the point at which profit is maximum.

22. Sometimes it is helpful to expand or contract a graph. Scale factors are used for this purpose. Rewrite the break-even analysis program of Figure 9-14 to change both graphs by using the functions

$$y = n \left(15xe^{-x/3}\right) \text{ and } y = n\left(\frac{x^3}{16} - \frac{x^2}{2} + \frac{7x}{4} + 4\right)$$

where $n$ is a scale factor accepted from input. If $n = 1$, the graph should be identical to the one depicted in Figure 9-14. If $n = 10$, the graph should be steeper and if $n = .5$ the graph should be wider (more elongated). Try various scale factors.

23. Write a program to plot a circle. (*Hint:* The equation of a circle of radius $r$ centered on the $y$ axis passing through the origin is

$$(y - r)^2 + x^2 = r^2 \quad \text{or} \quad y = \pm\sqrt{r^2 - x^2} + r$$

Plot both branches by adding .5 to the $y$ positive branch and −.5 to the $y$ negative branch. Use $r = 4.5$ initially.)

## 9-6-3   Projects

1. LUXURMART is an exclusive clothing store where Luxurmart members are required to maintain $1,000 in their accounts at all times. Members charge all purchases on Luxur credit cards. Write a main program to create a master member file consisting of member names with an initial $1,500 credit for all members.

   Some members frequently return merchandise that must be credited to their accounts; others may purchase items that cause their credit to fall below $1,000, in which case a message is to be printed requesting the member to write a check for an amount bringing his credit back to $1,000. In some cases, a member name may not be on the master file, and an appropriate message should be printed.

   Write a subroutine to update each customer's account. Transaction records contain member names and dollar amounts for credit or debit. The subroutine tells the main program whether a message is to be printed. The main program performs all output functions and should produce an updated member file after all transaction records have been processed. For example, input and output data are shown as follows:

MASTER FILE

| HOWARD | 1500 |
| NIARCO | 1500 |
| PELLON | 1500 |
| ROCKER | 1500 |

TRANSACTION FILE

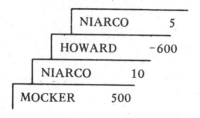

| NIARCO | 5 |
| HOWARD | −600 |
| NIARCO | 10 |
| MOCKER | 500 |

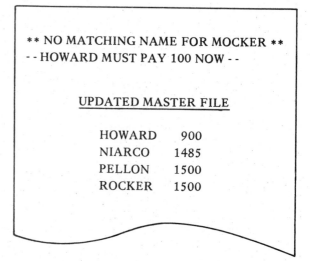

** NO MATCHING NAME FOR MOCKER **
- - HOWARD MUST PAY 100 NOW - -

UPDATED MASTER FILE

| HOWARD | 900 |
| NIARCO | 1485 |
| PELLON | 1500 |
| ROCKER | 1500 |

2.   Same as preceding exercise, with the following variation:

To simplify and minimize transcription errors, tag numbers, instead of dollar amounts, for items purchased or returned are recorded on transaction records. A "D" or a "C" signifies debit and credit, respectively. For example:

| | | |
|---|---|---|
| HOWARD | 9 D | means debit HOWARD's account by whatever item 9 costs. |
| NIARCO | 10 C | means credit NIARCO's account by the value of item 10. |

Create a table of costs for the different items. For example:

| ITEM TAG | COST |
|---|---|
| 1 | 44.50 |
| 2 | 100.75 |
| 3 | |
| . | |
| . | |
| . | |
| 10 | 46.00 |

3.   Write a check writer program to accept a name, a date and a dollar amount, and transcribe this information numerically and in words on a computer-produced check as follows:

NAME? ARIPE CAYENNO
DATE (MM,DD,YY)? 11,18,78
AMOUNT? 104.98

```
                                                                    2385

        ARIBA GIVEAWAY
        4206 GABRIELLA DR.
        PENSACOLA, FLORIDA  32503              NOVEMBER 18    19 78


PAY TO THE ORDER OF _____ ARIPE CAYENNO _____ $_____ 104.98 _____

  ONE HUNDRED FOUR AND 98/100                              DOLLARS
_____

        FIRST AMFED BANK
```

Assume dollar amounts will not exceed $999.99.

4.   Plot the graph of the sine function for values of $x$ ranging between 0 and 7 (see program in Figure 9-14).

## Games

5. As a promotional gimmick, every patron of the Circle K gas station gets a lucky card with three numbers on it ranging between 10 and 10,000. The station manager then draws at random a number between 1 and 10,000. If any of the customer numbers matches the one drawn by the manager, the customer gets a dollar amount equal to 1/10 of his lucky number. Write a program to read 10 customer lucky cards and determine the dollar amount of any lucky win. For example, if the lucky card contains the numbers 50, 100, and 200 and the manager draws the number 50, the customer wins 5 cents. Use a subroutine to determine lucky wins.

6. Verify that all 13 possible values of INT(RND(0) * 13) occur with approximately equal frequency. Generate several thousand values and construct a frequency distribution.

7. You are dealt 13 cards. These are entered on one DATA statement as follows: 2 of spades to the ace of spades are identified by the numbers 1 to 13; 2 to ace of hearts by the numbers 14–26; 2 to ace of diamonds by 27–39; and 2 to ace of clubs by 40–52.

   a. Use the RND function to deal your hand. Determine the number of kings you have and print their suit.

   b. Can you print your hand as follows?

      | Clubs    | 1, 10, 12      |                                 |
      |----------|----------------|---------------------------------|
      | Diamonds | 5, 7, 9, 13    |                                 |
      | Hearts   | 10, 11, 12, 13 | Not necessarily in ascending order. |
      | Spades   | 11, 9          |                                 |

   c. Print your hand with the words ACE, KING, QUEEN, JACK spelled out, rather than their corresponding numerical codes.

   d. Determine your best poker hand.

8. The number of different poker hands of five cards that could be dealt from a deck of 52 cards is

$$\frac{52!}{5!(52-5)!}$$

where $52! = 52 \cdot 51 \cdot 50 \cdot \cdots 2 \cdot 1$. Can your computer figure out the number of different poker hands if you apply the formula as it is shown?

9. Write a program to play tic-tac-toe. The program should allow the user to make the first move, then calculate its next move and so forth. Can you make the program always win? If not, can you design the program so that it can never lose?

10. Write a program to play blackjack. The program should deal cards from the deck in a randomized fashion (use INT(RND(1) * 52 + 1)). You may choose to start with a new deck for each hand or keep track of all cards dealt until the entire deck has been used. The program should act as the dealer and include routines to evaluate its own hand to determine whether to deal itself more cards or stand pat. It must also evaluate the player's hand to determine the winner of each hand.

**11.**   a.   Write separate subroutines to print each of the following geometric symbols:

   b.   Write a main program to generate primitive art artificially (through random generator routine) by vertical spacing of the preceding geometric symbols in random fashion. Assign numbers 1–5 to the five symbols. For example:

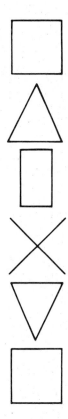

**12.**   Write a program to play the game of Chinese War. Assume that there are 25 sticks in a pile. Players take turns removing 1, 2, 3, or 4 sticks from the pile. The player who is forced to take the last stick loses.

## 9-6-4   Answers to Self Test

1. F    2. T    3. F    4. F    5. F    6. F    7. T    8. T    9. F    10. F

# INDEX

†